Social Science Research

Social Science Research
Theory and Practice

K. W. Taylor
University of Manitoba

Nelson Canada

to my students, my mother, Jane, Terese, and Audra

© Nelson Canada,
A Division of Thomson Canada Limited

Published in 1990 by
Nelson Canada
A Division of Thomson Canada Limited
1120 Birchmount Road
Scarborough, Ontario
M1K 5G4

Canada Cataloguing in Publication Data

Main entry under title:

Taylor, K.W. (Kenneth Wayne)
Social science research

ISBN 0-17-603457-9

1. Social sciences—Research.   I. Title.
H62.T39 1190   300′.7′2   C89-095442-9

Printed and bound in Canada

1   2   3   4   5   WB   94   93   92   91   90

CONTENTS

Preface and Acknowledgements

PREFACE AND ACKNOWLEDGEMENTS

The primary objective of this book is to provide a basic introduction to the "nuts and bolts" of social research methods. The intended audience is students who have already taken at least one introductory course in a social science discipline: sociology, political science, anthropology, history, psychology, social work, nursing, and so on.

This book is based on the following beliefs:

1. Social science is primarily about bettering the human condition.
2. Method is about how to do social science.
3. Social science methods are mostly simple common sense, a thoughtful use of universal human abilities to observe, argue, reason, compare, measure, count, and judge.
4. Successful social science research requires nothing more than native intuition and common sense, the confidence to use them, and a measure of patience and discipline.
5. Method is always about how to do things: it is primarily a subject matter of examples and exercises.
6. Method is about evidence: what it is, why it's needed, how to get it, and how to use it.

In the light of these beliefs I have tried to present the basic ideas involved in social research in simple language, profuse with examples and exercises.

The approach to social science research taken here is summarized in the following terms: theorizing, alternative theories, facts and artifacts, and a phase model of research design.

First, theorizing and its product, theory, is seen as central to social science research. I attempt to demystify social science theory as primarily a way of talking about observation. In contrast, everyday language is a way of talking about problems and the actions necessary to solve them. Everyday talk can always be translated into theory and vice versa. (In line with this, I use a terminology of "cause" and "effect" rather than the usual jargon of "independent" and "dependent" variables.)

The use of alternative theories is advocated as a tool for organizing research projects and for keeping the goals of research clear and useful. Useful information permits people to choose among practical options. Practical options in scientific research are stated in the form of alternative theories. Social science research attempts to show which is better.

The important matters of theory and alternative theories are discussed in Part I of this volume. Translating theoretical statements into research hypotheses are also discussed in Part I. Part II takes up the question of research design and execution. It is here that facts, artifacts, and research design phases are examined.

The idea of "fact" and its counterpart "artifact" are employed to make sense of research as work that produces evidence. Researchers desire facts and to avoid artifacts. While projects may differ enormously in the types of facts they investigate, they differ little in the types of artifacts they must avoid or attempt to control: variation, sampling, measurement, and data analysis. Consequently, the approach to research design taken here is a "phase" approach: one design phase for each type of possible artifact. The focus in this approach is on the problems that all research projects try to solve. Typical ways of solving the problems—the standard research designs such as surveys, experiments, and so on—appear as examples but not as the focus of the research design material.

Readers may be unfamiliar with the idea of a "variation design." While most researchers employ a variation design implicitly, it is less commonly recognized as a feature of research that can and should be planned. I advocate the use of a variation design phase as one that sets the boundaries for the sampling design but is separate from it. In addition, the idea is specially useful for showing the similarity of all types of research: it is something case studies, surveys, experiments, participant observation studies, historical studies, time series studies, and the like have in common. Without the notion of variation design, the similarities are less apparent.

Over the years, based on positive feedback from students, I have moved away from examinations toward a research project as the means of evaluating my students. The course runs for an entire academic year (8 months). The first half is taken up with planning, the second with applications.

I use four planning assignments. The first is a topic and policy relevence assignment where students are encouraged to select topics that are important and interesting to them personally. Up-to-date policy and practice relevent to their topics are researched in mostly non-academic sources: current magazines, newspapers, electronic media, and informants such as victims, workers, administrators, professionals, and so on.

In the second assignment—a bibliography and review of theoretical literature—students survey the academic literature on their topics and identify and analyse the major alternative theories employed in current work.

The third assignment reviews the data and methods in the research literature. The emphasis here is on finding several published project descriptions that can serve as models for the student's own projects. In each succeeding assignment, students attempt to specify in greater detail the hypotheses they intend to research.

In the final planning assignment, students prepare a detailed research proposal.

The target date for completing the data collection is the end of January. February is set aside for data analysis and writing the final report.

In March four follow-up assignments are used. One of these involves spelling out the policy/practice application of their project findings. Another is a critical analysis/correction of their project: problems that require small amounts of new data collection or re-analysis of data are corrected; for larger problems, project plans are revised in detail.

In the third follow-up assignment, students search for agencies or other sources of research funds for their particular topics and projects, and go through the initial stages of completing a research grant application, estimating various costs on the basis of their own experience. In the final follow-up assignment, students assume their findings are accurate and use the computer to estimate what sample size would be required to produce statistically significant results if the project were to be done again.

I would like to thank all my students who read and commented on earlier drafts of the manuscript. Their enthusiasm and ingenuity, and their remarkable (and often wonderful) research projects helped convince me that the approach taken in this book was a workable one.

I want to thank four people whose questions and comments were especially useful in clarifying my thinking about the ideas presented in this book. Two of them, Bob Stirling and Victor Thiessen, refereed the manuscript for Nelson. My close friends, Alfred Hunter, and Jane Ursel listened patiently to my endless talk about this book. Of course, none of these people are responsible for any remaining problems in the book.

Two editors at Nelson, Mary Lynn Mulroney and Freya Godard did a prodigious amount of work to improve my prose. Many thanks to both of them, and special thanks to Dave Ward of Nelson Canada for his unfailing enthusiasm and encouragement.

PART 1

THEORY AND METHODS IN SOCIAL RESEARCH

CHAPTER 1

What Are Social Science Research Methods?

CHAPTER CONTENTS

1.1 DEFINITIONS VS DEBATES

We can get a simple idea of what social science research methods are by looking at definitions; a less simple idea can be obtained by looking at the debates that produce the definitions.

Definitions

One simple way to determine what social research methods are is first to define social science and research. We could then examine examples of social science research and look for descriptions of the methods used. Another simple answer to the question could be obtained by looking at how social scientists define their work and examine the methods they use.

EXAMPLE: Durkheim's definition of sociology excludes psychological phenomena, but Weber's definition includes it.

Durkheim defined sociology as the investigation of "social facts": his methods were observation and measurement.

Weber defined social science as the study of actions with "subjective meaning." Subjective meanings are those that take account of the behaviour of other individuals. In keeping with this definition, Weber used the method of "empathetic understanding."

Definitions are rules for inclusion and exclusion. If we get the definition wrong, we include things that should be excluded or exclude things that should be included or both. But who is to say whether the definition is right or wrong? Obviously we can make up a definition that will include the things we want included and exclude those we want excluded. But this means that the goals of the definer determine the definition. Different ideas about what social science *is and ought to be* will lead to different definitions of what its methods are.

Debates

The question of what social science is and ought to be has been under debate since its inception, by both the producers and consumers of its products, and the debate continues today. Among other things, the debate produces definitions of social science that each represent merely one way among many of taking a position on the issues debated. It is the nature of definitions that debates and the issues debated don't appear in them. However, in the author's opinion, the debates and the issues debated are as important as the definitions (and probably more important).

The problem with looking at the debates and the issues debated is that we cannot get "simple" answers to the question "What are social science research methods?" On the other hand, consideration of the debates and issues can provide readers with some of the means to construct their own answers to the question—answers that are useful for their own goals.

It was decided to present an introduction to the debates—enough material for readers to begin critiqing the decisions to include some subjects in this book and exclude others. There is also enough material for some good arguments. Before we look at the debates, let's first look at the framework in which the debate takes place.

1.2 THE FRAMEWORK OF THE DEBATE OVER SCIENCE

The framework of the debate over social science methods is a set of issues that are not debated because there is very little disagreement about them. Three of these issues are worth briefly describing here: (1)the principle of demonstration or "proof," (2) the social nature of social science, and (3) "methods" as sets of prescriptions for doing social research.

1. The first issue not debated is what may be called the "principle of demonstration" or the "principle of proof." There is a commitment in social science to going beyond illustration to demonstration or proof. Any belief or statement (scientific, religious, astrological, proverbial, deluded, etc.) can be illustrated in the sense that the statement or belief can be used to interpret an event and make sense of it.

EXAMPLE: The proverb "You can lead a horse to water but you can't make it drink" can be used to make sense of things as diverse as contrary children, unpopular party leaders who won't step down, and aging professors who are reluctant to retire.

Only a small number of such beliefs or statements can be demonstrated. Demonstration requires that a statement or belief be shown to provide explanations of all similar events and to provide better explanations than other beliefs or statements.

Thorough demonstration requires two things:

1. that *all* relevant observations be employed to demonstrate the accuracy of a statement, and
2. that the accuracy of one statement be assessed in relation to the accuracy of *all* alternative statements that may provide interpretations.

In practice, of course, researchers have to decide how thorough their demonstrations will be. Some cases are selected for observation while others are ignored; some comparisons are made and some are not; some measurement and data analysis procedures are used, and some are not; some beliefs that provide interpretations are tested, while others are ignored.

EXAMPLE: In order to demonstrate thoroughly that the criminal justice system is biased against natives, for example, the relevant observations include the entire past and present records of the operation of the justice system, relevant comparisons to non-natives, non-European minorities, and groups of residents of the same age, sex, employment, and income and with similar charges, a similar history of plea bargaining, and similar defence counsel. All these comparisons are necessary because they state other ways that an appearance of bias could be produced. An apparent bias against natives might be a random event of a month or year, a bias against youth, males, the unemployed, or the poor, for example. Before we conclude that a bias has been demonstrated, alternative interpretations of the data must be shown to be wrong.

So, while there is debate about how thorough demonstrations have to be and about when a particular demonstration is thorough enough, there is none about the necessity of demonstration. We will see later that there are some kinds of beliefs or statements that cannot be demonstrated— such as those based on faith alone—which are naturally excluded by the principle.

2. A second issue not debated is that social science is itself a social activity (though there is much debate over what to make of this fact). The observation of human social activity is obviously social and cannot be otherwise. Any attempt to be scientific in this kind of work requires that the theories and methods used include the users themselves as part of what is investigated. The social nature of social science provides a kind of test: methods that are inapplicable or useless or unilluminating when turned to the examination of social science fail to qualify as social scientific methods. In other words, not only *can* the theories and methods of social research be turned on social science, but they *must* be so turned in order to determine if they "pass."

EXAMPLE: Methods suitable for researching sexism and racism in the hiring, paying, and promoting of employees in the banking industry ought to be appropriate for examining sexism and racism in hiring, paying and promoting employees in the social research industry as found in university social science faculties.

EXAMPLE: Methods and theories useful for investigating the origin and development of the *practice and policy* of discrimination ought also to illuminate the origin and development of the *theory* of sex discrimination used by social scientists to investigate it. If they do not, it may be argued that the methods employed are not social scientific, whatever their non-social scientific status.

Although non-social science is a social activity, the question of whether the methods have any value when turned to the examination of non-social science is unimportant. The methods of biochemistry, for example, that are used to investigate the processes of sex determination of fertilized eggs are unlikely to be much help in investigating the causes of the sex distribution of biochemists. Nor does it matter that they aren't.

3. A third issue not debated is the prescriptive nature of methods. Social science methods are prescriptions for observational practice. Given the goals of relevant and accurate information, the methods prescribe how

the goals can be met. We think the bases for methods prescriptions are theories of science. The situation here is analogous to medical prescriptions.

EXAMPLE: Suppose you go to a doctor with a health problem and obtain a prescription for drugs, diet, exercise, or surgery. If you then ask why the prescription should work, you will be given a theory about (1) what disease or diseases may be causing the problem, (2) how the diseases can be destroyed or controlled, and (3) how the various remedies have been tailored to your age, weight, sex, and so on. The bases for medical prescriptions are theories of disease. The goal is health and fitness. Health prescriptions are policy applications of theories of disease. In similar fashion, the basis for social science methods prescriptions are theories of social science.

EXAMPLE: If you believe, like Van Maanen (1983:9-12), that an important goal of social science is to understand the "unfolding of social processes rather than social structures" and that the meaning of behaviour can only be determined from the context in which it takes place, then your prescription for methods will be to get direct, first-hand, and more or less intimate knowledge; and to stay away from "formal interviews, paper-and-pencil surveys, the lab study, the use of official statistics, records, documents and the like."

Methods prescriptions are policy applications of theories of social science. The prescriptions and theories come more or less together: both are products of debates over what social science is and what its methods are. The final justification of method prescriptions are theories of science. But experience with the methods is the basis for the theory of science in the first place. Changes in one, then, require changes in the other.

1.3 DEBATES ABOUT SOCIAL SCIENCE METHODS

Some of the important issues under debate are how and why social science changes and develops; how effective searches should be carried out; what constitutes error and how it can be controlled; and what is and should be the relationship between social science, its sponsors, and its objects of study. These debates revolve around the most fundamental issue: what are the goals of social science and what ought they to be?

Rather than recount the debates or discuss them in detail at this point we will only examine summaries of two competing positions in these debates. These positions will be referred to as the "explanation" theory and the "control" theory of science. The theories are presented as parallel polar opposites, even though the positions are not strictly parallel in every regard.

The main differences can be seen to be the "internalist" orientation of the explanation theory and the "externalist" orientation of the control theory. The internalist argument is that scientists ought to be left to set their own goals; it claims that any interests coming from the larger community will only introduce error into their work.

The externalist position argues that scientists left to set their own goals will serve only themselves or the highest bidder for their services (which amounts to the same thing). Serious scientific error is seen to derive from the sexual, racial, class, economic, and other biases that result from a lack of control by the community being studied. In the externalist vision, science can only be effective when it serves the interests of the community that supports its activities.

Explanation Theory:	**Control Theory:**

a. What are the goals or purposes of science?

To produce understanding and explanations.	To produce control.

b. How is scientific work done?

Bringing ideas about how things work (explanations) and observation of them working into correspondence by a strategy of successive approximation. In the event of non-correspondence between theory and observation, then there must be an error somewhere. The source could be any one or combination of: theory of reality, theory of ideas, theory of observation, theory of error, or the means of observation.	Bringing ideas about how things can be controlled and observation of control schemes into correspondence by a strategy of successive approximation. In the event of non-correspondence between theory and observation, then there must be an error somewhere. The source could be any one or combination of: theory of control, theory of reality, theory of ideas, theory of observation, theory of error, or the means of observation.

c. How is the science industry organized?

1. Isolation: Basic science is isolated from society; interaction is mediated by applied science; basic science gives explanations free to applied science in exchange for subsidies from society. Products of science may influence society and applied science, but isolation of basic science prevents influence in reverse.

1. Non-isolation: Science and society are in constant interaction in mutual influence of all sorts. Terms of exchange between science and society are variable.

2. Responsibility: Scientists take no responsibility for the uses made of their explanations by society. Their job is to produce explanations free of any special interests in society.

2. Responsibility: Scientists and applied scientists are as responsible as any one else for the use made of their products.

3. Effective search activity: must be "self-directing"; the problems science chooses for its attention must come, not from society, but from continuing concerns of science for effective explanations.

3. Effective search activity: must be directed by society: the problems it selects should be those problems for which society needs solutions.

4. Specialization: is necessary because the work involved in finding explanations is no longer comprehensible to all science workers.

4. Specialization merely reflects the variety of groups in society that need explanations and means of controlling nature or others.

5. Free and open communication on all matters scientific among scientific workers is necessary to coordinate search work and allow the accuracy of explanations to be scrutinized.

5. Free and open communication between society and science is necessary to guarantee that scientific effort concentrates on useful work. It implies free and open communication among scientific workers, but this alone will not guarantee accurate explanations or control schemes that work. Pattern of communication will mirror interests being served by scientists.

6. Scientific error: is avoided by keeping interests other than those of scientific accuracy out of the scientific workplace.

6. Scientific error: is avoided by passionate commitment of scientists to controlling nature and society to solve problems of human existence.

7. Objectivity: Ideal is the judge or referee: scientific workers need to be free from any interest in the outcome of tests of their scientific theories.

7. Ideal of objectivity is the lawyer, litigant or competitor: unless scientists have a passionate interest in the outcome of their work, they are likely to misapprehend reality and produce unworkable control schemes.

8. Applied work: must be clearly separated from "basic" science lest the interest in applications influence basic scientific work.

8. Applied work: is in constant interaction with basic work; each influences the other.

9. Training: much training of scientific workers is required. This training has two goals. One is to diminish the trainees' political, economic, family, sexual, and military interests and so on by isolating them from society. The other goal is to inculcate scientific work standards through exposure to scientific culture.

9. Training: amount of training necessary and useful depends upon problem being researched. The amount and type of training are not always easy to specify. It is important to guard against training that only isolates researchers from their communities.

d. How does science change?

Because of its vision of science as isolated and unique, the explanation theory views changes in science as coming from factors internal to science itself. Simple accumulation theory: science changes only by accumulating more and more accurate pictures of reality, means of observation, knowledge of errors and how to avoid them, highly trained and knowledgeable scientific workers.

By definition, the control theory of science does not need any special theory of scientific change as science is not seen to be separate and isolated from society. Scientific change is merely one aspect of general social changes that dispose of the ideas, knowledge, explanations, and control schemes of science, supporting some and discarding others. Disposition of science as a whole

Errors are disaccumulated.

Complex accumulation theory: Solutions to puzzles or confirmations of theories accumulate, but so do unsolved puzzles and anomalies that the theories cannot explain. When the accumulation of anomalies reaches a certain point, a new theory may become dominant, resulting in the discarding of the knowledge based upon the old. In periods of competition between competing theories, scientific workers become divided, error and accuracy become confused, and the accuracy of the means of observation is questioned, as is the adequacy of the scientific training.

depends on society's control scheme for science, which encourages some phases and discourages others.

Accumulation of science is merely one aspect of general accumulation and disaccumulation in the society in which science finds itself. Short of revolutionary change in the society, much expansion of scientific work can be understood as the continuation of work on new problems that resulted from the use of older control schemes of science by society. Scientific accumulation may not necessarily take place because the science used to produce the control scheme may not be applicable to the problems produced by the implementation of the control schemes.

e. Implications

The implications of the above are that social science workers who adhere to the explanation theory framework will be likely to

(a) separate themselves from the community.

(b) take no direction from the community on their work.

(c) accept the judgement of no one but their peers on what work should be done and how well the work has been done.

(d) take no responsibility for the uses to which their science is put.

(e) be highly specialized and highly trained.

The implications of the above are that social science workers who adhere to the control theory framework will be likely to

(a) immerse themselves in the community.

(b) take direction from the community on their work.

(c) accept the judgement of the community on what work should be done and how well the work has been done.

(d) take responsibility for the uses to which their science is put.

(e) be as specialized as necessary but broadly trained.

(f) prefer basic over applied work.

(g) separate any applied work clearly from basic work.

(h) stop work when an accurate explanation has been produced.

(i) ignore policy and practice questions that do not directly bear on the basic scientific work.

(j) be dispassionate in their attitude to knowledge, theory, and so on.

(k) make no judgements about religion, politics, ethics, and community issues.

(f) have no preference for either basic or applied research.

(g) combine applied work and basic work.

(h) stop work when effective control has been achieved.

(i) give high priority to policy and practice questions in both applied and basic work.

(j) be passionate in their attitude to knowledge, theory, applications, and so on.

(k) make judgements about religion, politics, ethnics, and community issues.

1.4 CONCLUSION

What are social science research methods? They are the methods that can be justified by the theory of social science held by the researcher using the methods. The answer, in other words, is that it depends. Different researchers will give different answers, and the same researcher may give different answers at different times.

What social science research methods, then, will be discussed in this book? Since the position of the author is closer to the control theory than the explanation theory, the rest of this book will examine methods of social science research that appear to be consistent with a control theory. Readers who find their values lead them to different positions on these issues are invited to evaluate the author's choices critically.

1.5 SUMMARY

This chapter has introduced the issues and debates involved in defining social science methods. The framework for the debate are three statements not under debate: (1) social science is itself a social activity; (2) methods are prescriptions deriving from theories of science; (3) all these theories prescribe demonstrations over illustrations.

The issues under debate are how and why social science changes and develops; how effective searches can be carried out; what constitutes error and how it can be controlled; and what is and should be the relationship between social science, its sponsors, and its objects of study. These debates revolve around the most fundamental issue: what are the goals of social science and what ought they to be? Students are invited to involve themselves in the debate as a means of understanding and using different definitions of social science research methods.

1.6 EXERCISES

1. Listed below are a series of proverbs, familiar sayings, and conventional wisdom.
    i) *Illustrate* the following statements on the basis of your own experience or knowledge.
    ii) Outline how you would *demonstrate* or prove the accuracy or inaccuracy of the above claims.
    iii) What are the crucial differences between your illustrations and demonstrations?
       (a) Love conquers all.
       (b) Spare the rod and spoil the child.
       (c) A rolling stone gathers no moss.
       (d) Slow and steady wins the race.
       (e) A bird in the hand is worth two in the bush.
       (f) Water always finds its own level.
       (g) The mass media cater to the lowest common denominator.
       (h) You can't fight city hall.
       (i) You can't legislate morality.
       (j) Might makes right.
       (k) Only the fit survive.
       (m) You can be anything you want to be.
       (n) Murphy's Law: if things can go wrong, they will go wrong.
       (o) Those who can, do; those who can't, teach.
       (p) There are lies, damn lies, and statistics.
       (q) The best welfare system is a steady job.
       (r) Where there's an injustice, there's a remedy.
       (s) Parkinson's Law: work expands to fill the time available for its completion.
       (t) Peter Principle: people will be promoted until they find themselves in jobs that are beyond their capacities.
       (u) Seeing is believing.
       (v) What we see is not always to be believed.

(w) The way we see things is affected by what we know or what we believe.

2. Below are a series of definitions of science or social science. These definitions represent positions in the debate over what social science is.
   i) Identify the issues being debated that would lead to these definitions.
   ii) Which of the definitions do you prefer, and why?
   iii) What methods, if any, do these definitions *preclude* social science from using or suggest *must* be used in social scientific work?
   (a) "What makes a science are its aims, not its results." (Homans 1967:4)
   (b) "The scientist has no other method than doing his damnedest." (attributed to P.W. Bridgeman)
   (c) "Real" science allows exact prediction; therefore social science isn't a "real" science.
   (d) Science is a process, not just a product.
   (e) Science is any branch of study concerned with a body of observed material facts.
   (f) "Science is basically a process of interaction, or better still, of engagement." (Morgan, 1983:13)
   (g) Science is "concerned with the realization of potentialities— of possible knowledge." (Morgan, 1983:13)
   (h) "The scientific goal is that of explicit and articulate abstraction and generalization." (Lofland, 1971:5)
   (i) "Science is true, whatever anyone may say; it has for certain minds, if not for all, the intellectual value which is the ultimate test of truth. If a study can have this value and yet violate the rule of logic, the conclusion to be drawn is that those rules, and not science, are deficient." (Campbell, 1952:47)
   (j) "What is distinctive of behavior science, therefore, is basically its subject-matter; the techniques that the subject-matter permits or demands are only derivative. . . .Behavioral science deals with those processes in which symbols, or at any rate meanings, play an essential part." (Kaplan, 1964:32)
   (k) "To understand the nature of science, it is essential to recognize that scientific knowledge at any given time is what scientists agree it is. Because scientific proof is fundamentally based on agreement among scientists, scientific knowledge keeps changing over time." (Babbie, 1986:27)

(l) "It is frequently stated that scientific description is value-free or non-evaluative—in social science just as in physical science. This statement has been seriously questioned, and properly so. It can at best be only partially true." (Seeley, Sim and Loosely, 1956:24)

3. What definitions of social science would lead to the use of the methods described in the statements below?

   (a) "The fact that the social research situation is indeed a social situation, and that the researcher is in it, as well as outside it, poses a subtle and difficult problem in all but the most superficial types of social science inquiry." (Seeley, Sim and Loosley, 1956:21)

   (b) In Seeley, Sim and Loosley's investigation of Crestwood Heights community, friendships between the investigators and their informants were not discouraged, nor even minimized. They claim that friendships could not have been avoided totally. "In any case, even if it had been possible, it is far from certain scientific accuracy would have benefited: much of the material secured could only have been secured in a social relation that was genuinely one of friendship on both sides." (Seeley, Sim and Loosley, 1956:440)

   (c) "Weber gave a place in historical investigation to the imaginary experiment as a means—albeit uncertain—of generating knowledge, and on occasion he utilized such a method in his own work." (Smelser, 1976:149)

   (d) Weber insisted "on taking the subjective meaning that individuals bring to their social situations into account in all sociological explanations." (Smelser, 1976:149)

   (e) Durkheim envisaged " the generation of scientific sociological laws on the principles of objectivity and induction." (Smelser, 1976:149)

   (f) "Only those who are engaged in material transformation have the possibility of knowing reality." (Carchedi, 1983:348)

   (g) "There are many different ways of studying the same social phenomenon, and given that the insights generated by any one approach are at best partial and incomplete,...the social researcher can gain much by reflecting on the nature and merits of different approaches before engaging in a particular mode of research practise." (Morgan, 1983:369)

   (h) "Though the scientific enterprise has a significant element of luck in it, it is not wholly a game of chance, and scientific training surely enhances in some degree the skill of the players." (Kaplan, 1964:16)

(i) "Scientific training is to a significant extent the mastery of techniques." (Kaplan, 1964:19)

(j) "All the sciences, whatever their subject-matter, are methodologically of one species: they can interbreed." (Kaplan, 1964:31)

(k) "Each science...finds some techniques appropriate and others inappropriate and even impossible." (Kaplan, 1964:31)

4. The statements below describe the positions of their authors on various debates over social science. Try to determine if the statements reflect a position closer to the explanation theory or the control theory, or somewhere between them.

(a) "When the dominant political ideology is racist, sexist, classist, and imperialist, these assumptions will necessarily permeate scientific research that tries to be neutral." (Tesh, 1988:176)

(b) "Before we ask after the cause of disease, we must ask what values should guide the search. Values are public issues. Given that people who subscribe to the ideologies of individualism and positivism will probably make reductionistic analyses and come up with individualistic policies, and given that these are usually less effective than broad analyses and socially based policies, we need public discussion about the value, beliefs, and ideologies with which scientists and policy makers begin. This is not an unwarranted intrusion of politics into science. There is no science uninfluenced by politics. This is a plea to get the politics out of hiding." (Tesh, 1988:177)

(c) "Like individualism, science is both a collection of ideological beliefs and an agency for liberation. As an agency for liberation it substitutes democracy for political and religious authority. Demanding evidence for statement of fact and providing criteria to test the evidence, it gives us a way to distinguish between what is true and what powerful people might wish to convince us is true." (Tesh, 1988:167)

(d) "Such considerations offer the possibility of developing a social science that can be liberative as well as functional, guided by a sense of what is possible as much as by what is actual, and which is recognized as being as much a political, moral, and ethical activity as it is a technical one." (Morgan, 1983:8)

(e) "As a scientific doctrine, Marxism essentially consists of the discovery of objective causal relationships. It discovers and analyses the laws which make the system work, describes the contradictions which undermine it from within and signal its destiny. But insofar as it is a work of science and not ideology, Capital will not allow this analysis to be tainted with "value judgements" or subjective choices: instead it makes only "judgement of fact", objective judge-ments, affirmations which in the last analysis are universally valid." (Colletti, 1972:369)

(f) Determinism is an embarrassment for social scientists. It is a funda-mental paradigm for nearly all of our research, yet none of us wants to speak out on its behalf. Closer to the bone, our livelihoods depend on determinism, and yet we hope it isn't true. Crudely put, social research assumes a deterministic paradigm that fundamen-tally denies the existence of free will. (Babbie, 1986:43)

(g) "In his scientific work Marx was concerned to develop concepts which would uncover the reality behind the appearance which concealed it. He did so by critically examining previous efforts to investigate economic, political and social life and demonstrating the failure of previous theorists to account for facts that they themselves would have to treat as relevant...whilst at the same time demonstrating their conceptual contradictions." (Pearce, 1978:52)

(h) "Some of the failings that research methodology seeks to guard against are the following: errors of observation, selective observa-tion, errors of interpretation, incorrect generalization, depen-dence on authority and inappropriate use of evidence." (Binder and Geis, 1983:chap. 1)

(i) "Thus sociology examines the status quo, calls it phenomena, and pretends to take no stand on it, thereby avoiding the necessity to comment on the invidious character of the relationship between the sex groups it studies. Yet by slow degrees of converting statistic to fact, function to prescription, bias to biology (or some other indeterminate), it comes to ratify and rationalize what has been socially enjoined or imposed into what is and ought to be. And through its pose of objectivity, it gains a special efficacy in reinforc-ing stereotypes. Seeing that failure to conform leads to "problems" and "conflicts" as well as other situations it regards as highly undesirable deviant behavior, it counsels a continuous and vigilant surveillance of conditioning that it may proceed on lines of greater proficiency and perfection." (Millett, 1970:328)

(j) "Finally, scientific thinking cannot be, except perhaps in suggesting problems, what nowadays most of us know well enough as wishful thinking. The scientist's own hopes and fears, his own standards of what he would like to have prevail on this earth must be kept as far as possible out of his work, and especially out of his observations of, or dealing with, facts. How far such hopes and fears and standards enter into his choice of conceptual schemes, how far they influence the kind of questions he asks, are difficult problems we may perhaps be permitted to dodge. Sufficient that the techniques of most of the established sciences provide a very effective check on the cruder forms of wishful thinking." (Brinton, 1965:12)

(k) Preamble from the Ethical Principles of Psychologists: "Psychologists respect the dignity and worth of the individual and strive for the preservation and protection of fundamental human rights. They are committed to increasing knowledge of human behavior and of people's understanding of themselves and others and to the utilization of such knowledge for the promotion of human welfare. While pursuing these objectives, they make every effort to protect the welfare of those who seek their services and of the research participants that may be the object of study. They use their skills only for purposes consistent with these values and do not knowingly permit their misuse by others. While demanding for themselves freedom of inquiry and communication, psychologists accept the responsibility this freedom requires: competence, objectivity in the application of skills, and concern for the best interests of clients, colleagues, students, research participants, and society." (American Psychological Association, 1981:633)

(l) "The ultimate goal of the social sciences is to produce an accumulating body of reliable knowledge. Such knowledge would enable us to explain, predict and understand empirical phenomena that interest us. Furthermore, a reliable body of knowledge could be put to use to ameliorate the human condition." (Nachmias and Nachmias, 1981:9)

(m) "It is quite possible to consider that the problems underlying expansion and survival of Canadian society could themselves become fertile grounds for creating a national sociology and a sociology responsive to the critical problems and issues of its constituents. It would be a disservice to the society...if sociologists...continued to propagate the position that sociology is a general, abstract, and value-free science." (Ramu and Johnson, 1976:493-4)

(n) "Black sociologists must develop new techniques and perspectives, as those which are no longer functional are discarded. One of the dominant themes the authors in this anthology address is that there must be a conciliation between culture (theory) and politics (practice) or, as Nathan Hare has described it, the "uniting of the Black academy and the street." Hence, Black sociology must become more political than mainstream sociology has been. Black sociology must also develop theories which assume the basic posture of eliminating racism and systematic class oppression from the society. The myth of "value-free" sociology becomes relevant to the Black sociologist, because he must become "pro-value," by promoting the interests of the Black masses in his research, writings and teachings." (Ladner, 1973:xxvii)

What Is Worth Researching?

Social science is a way of participating in debates on how to solve social problems. Social problems are the product of conflicting policies and practices; they are solved by modifying practice or policy or both. Debates concern the identification of problems, the evaluation of proposed solutions, and the assessment of costs and benefits. They occur because participants want to persuade their opponents to change their policies and practices, if not their minds. The persuasion is done partly by means of cogent argument. Social research is one means of enhancing the relevance, accuracy and amount of information on which cogent argument is based.

2.1 POLICY AND PRACTICE

The distinction between policies and practice intended here is only between more conscious and less conscious "rules."

EXAMPLE: Children may have food preference practices that are mostly unconscious except as a set of likes and dislikes. Their parents are likely to have policies, such as preventing children from eating anything that is poisonous, unclean, non-nutritious, intoxicating, or addictive.

EXAMPLE: Teenagers becoming aware of the promise and danger of sexuality may find that practices for relating to the other sex that they developed in preteen years might involve more danger than they want or exclude them entirely from the promise. The problems are solved partly by modifying their practices and partly by developing policies for how to treat themselves, how to treat others, what kinds of treatment of themselves to tolerate, types of situations to avoid, and so on.

Practices and policies developed for oneself may run into conflict with those developed by others.

EXAMPLE: Children and teenagers are most likely to be aware of how the practices and policies of their parents impinge upon their own wishes. And, of course, many parental policies are specifically designed to do this. For teenagers, the solution to some of these problems is to conform entirely to their parents' wishes or to become clever manipulators of their parents by withholding information, perhaps lying, catching the contradictions in their parents' practices and policies, and requesting equal treatment. Another possibility is frank discussions with the parents, with a democratic setting of policy. Which of these options will work is largely determined by the child-rearing policies and practices of the parents.

EXAMPLE: In abusive families, the children's problems with their parents and the parents' problems with each other may not be solvable by changes in practices or policies short of breaking up the family. It will turn out that there are policies and practices in the larger community governing how family units are disassembled. These larger policies place restrictions of varying degrees on what personal practices and policies can be pursued in breakups without bringing the state's welfare and legal systems into play.

These larger policies and practices can sometimes lead to personal and family problems or prevent solutions to them.

EXAMPLE: One such practice is the police practice of staying criminal proceedings unless the persons directly harmed bring charges. This practice, when applied to situations where the injured person finds it necessary to remain dependent upon the criminal or is required by law to do so may cause the criminal behaviour to continue in that the failure to punish amounts to tacit encouragement. Thus, the persistence of wife battering is seen to be caused partly by the police practice of leaving the wife to lay assault changes against a husband she is unprepared or unable to leave. One possible solution to the problem being tried in some provinces requires a policy change which directs the police to lay assault changes and to proceed independently of the wife.

The above examples illustrate that people live their lives by practices and policies that relate them to their social environment. So also do families, communities, organizations, bureaucracies, institutions, parties, governments, nations, and international organizations. One outcome of the policies and practices are desired results: food, clothing, shelter, education, health, and personal and social development. Other outcomes, when conflict is present, are undesired results: inadequate food, clothing, and shelter; poor health, poor education, inequality, discrimination, insecurity, injustice, oppression, genocide, and conventional or nuclear war.

2.2 SOCIAL PROBLEMS AND SOLUTIONS

Problems are the result of the pursuit of policies and practices that are in conflict with other policies and practices. The conflict can be found within, between, and among individuals, families, groups, communities, organizations, classes, the sexes, bureaucracies, states, regions, empires, and so on. If problems are caused by policy or practice conflicts, then solutions will take the form of new or modified practices and policies that will eliminate, reduce, or change the conflict.

The question of what policies and practices will eliminate social problems is always under public debate in one form or another. But just as a cure may be worse than the disease, a solution can be worse than the problem. The changes proposed may not solve the problem, or they may solve an existing problem but create new ones as bad as the old.

EXAMPLE: People may solve their weight problems by dieting in a way that starves their bodies of essential nutrients and makes them vulnerable to disease caused by micro-organisms.

EXAMPLE: Parents may attempt to solve their problems with their children by the practice of "grounding," which the children may respond to by running away.

EXAMPLE: Communities may solve juvenile crime problems by increasing the size and militance of policing, thereby producing more convicts, overloading the prisons, and increasing the number of adult criminals.

EXAMPLE: A nation state may attempt to settle its foreign policy disputes with neighbours by means of a war, which militarizes the society, results in millions of deaths, creates refugee problems, and in the event of defeat, results in loss of the ability to pursue any kind of foreign policy other than that dictated by the victor nation.

Policies and practices always have some costs and some benefits. Changes in policies and practices are likely to change this distribution. The issues of public debate then are both the effectiveness of proposed changes in policies and practices and the distribution of costs and benefits that result:

1. Will the proposed changes solve the problem?
2. What will the proposed changes cost and who will pay?
3. What does the present problem cost and who pays?
4. What new problems will proposed changes bring?
5. What will these new problems cost and who will be likely to pay?

Many social problems persist partly because it is thought that the solutions proposed would be ineffective, or would create new problems worse than the ones solved. A more important reason is that certain groups (most often the rich, powerful, and privileged classes) benefit more from the persistence of existing social problems than they would from the proposed solutions. When the solution of social problems involves the redistribution of costs toward, and benefits away from, those who benefit from the problem, solutions will be resisted.

2.3 THE DYNAMICS OF PUBLIC DEBATE

First, it should be clear that the word "public" in the term "public debates" is used here in its broadest sense. Virtually any public counts, from families to national parliaments and international forums, public media, associations, professional journals, and so on. Opposing viewpoints or theories are essential if debate is to occur. While these almost always show up in large bodies, they may not in special interest associations. The critical debate may be carried on only between or among such associations.

A public debate is initiated partly by the shifts in power of the proponents of various sides. This happens primarily when the costs of the existing social problems are visited more widely and the benefits more narrowly. Old issues are taken up again by old and new protagonists; old and new proposals for solutions are put forward for debate and action.

The duration of a debate may vary. The more equally balanced the power of the main protagonists, the longer the debate is likely to last. It can also be hypothesized that the more costly the proposed solutions under debate, the greater the resources marshalled in the struggle over the changes.

A public debate may end in a number of ways. One or both parties may change their practices or policies and solve or partially solve the problem. The more powerful group may impose new policies or practices on the weaker group. Token changes may be made that leave the problem, save for appearances, in place. The debate may end in a temporary stalemate, with no changes at all.

Those placed so as to benefit more than they suffer from the existing problems ordinarily defend their position by attacking proposed solutions that would equalize costs and benefits, and their opponents do the opposite. Others, who are affected only indirectly, if any exist, may audit and ajudicate the debate.

Debate on social problems and their solution consists of arguments that freely mix dreams, wishes, suppositions, misunderstandings, falsehoods, threats, false promises, and irrelevencies, and their opposites. The tactics and strategies of debate include pretence, diversions, delays, closure, and attacks on the morality, honesty, or competence of the opposing side.

Nevertheless, public debates are essential sources of information about social problems and the issues that are involved in their solution. The matters that are worth researching are those that will make a contribution to this debate by enhancing the relevance, accuracy and amount of information available.

2.4 RELEVANCE, ACCURACY, AND AMOUNTS OF INFORMATION

Relevance is the most important feature of information exchanged in a debate and the most difficult to determine. From the viewpoint of a strategy of delay and diversion, the relevance of information may be its irrelevance to the issues from which it diverts attention. Where delay and diversion are not involved, however, the relevance of information to a debated issue still requires much attention. Will proposed changes in practice or policy solve the problem? If the solution has never been tried before, there can only be speculation regarding its effectiveness. A small experimental program or limited time trial of a new practice or policy is the only way that relevant information can be obtained. If a solution has been tried elsewhere, relevance depends upon how similar the earlier trials were to the proposed solutions; how similar the magnitude of the problem; and so on. There is no way other than a careful comparison of facts that relevance can be established and argued.

The accuracy of information is important only if it is relevant to the issues being debated. Like relevance, accuracy is mostly a question of care, but in addition it requires some knowledge of how errors can enter into information, and familiarity with the phenomena under debate. In most debates, so much information is exchanged that it is impossible to be sure of its accuracy, or to verify it all. With familiarity comes the ability to spot likely inaccuracies and distinguish large errors that need researching from small errors that do not.

Given relevance and accuracy, at some point the amount of information becomes important. One case is not as convincing as five, which are not as convincing as ten, and so on. Evidence from ten similar cases is not as convincing as evidence from ten different cases: variety in times and places is an important aspect of the amount of information. The amount of information available depends largely on the amount of work.

This is perhaps the time for a warning: the possible contribution of social research to a public debate is the enhancement of the relevance, accuracy, and amount of information exchanged in the debate. Even if diversionary, the information produced by social research, like all social information, amounts to an argument for or against changes intended to solve social problems. Thus, it must be understood that researching the issues in a debate is one way of participating in the debate. And, like any other participant, researchers bring their own interests, dreams, wishes, suppositions, misunderstandings, falsehoods, and irrelevancies to the job in some unknown mixture. Social researchers have contributed to some of the finest progressive experiments in social change and some of the worst kinds of experiments in enslavement, inhumanity, and degradation. Like any technology, social research is no better than the purpose for which it is used.

2.5 CHOOSING RESEARCH TOPICS

Richard E. DuWors, one of the author's teachers, often said, "Researchers had better care about the answers to the questions they are researching, because to get them they might have to do a lot of things they don't like to do." The advice still holds good. While research can be interesting and often exciting, it ordinarily involves a fair amount of drudgery as well. For that reason, it is important for researchers to have personal experience, interest, and practical involvement with the debates and policies they are researching. Then they will bring not only critical insight to the evaluation of the public debate, but enough interest in the solutions to social problems to motivate whatever effort may be required.

In the author's opinion, issues raised in debates about the issues listed below are likely to be worth researching in the next few decades. These problems are persistent if not chronic, and all are important to the way most people live their lives. All have been debated extensively, and all have seen changes in policy and practice. All are issues in many nations of the globe:

sex discrimination, affirmative action, human rights and anti-discrimination policies generally

labour policy, unionization policy, wages and incomes, industrial relations policy, strikes and lockouts, strike-breaking, occupational health and safety, worker's compensation

immigration, emigration, refugee policy

education, employment and unemployment, welfare, guaranteed annual incomes

taxation, tax equity, tax reform, corporate welfare, regional development policy, free trade, foreign ownership

native and Métis land claims and discrimination, minority rights

health services, medicare, hospital services, nursing services

marriage and divorce policy, family violence, wife beating, child abuse, adoption, foster care, reproduction, abortion, birth control, child-rearing policy, daycare crime, juvenile delinquency, justice, access to legal services, prisons, probation, parole, compensation of victims.

defence policy, military policy, foreign policy, nuclear arms policy

The above list is by no means exclusive, nor is the order meant to suggest relative importance. There are many other topics for research that will fit the criteria listed above.

2.6 THE TWO FUNCTIONS OF THEORY

Much of the literature on a research topic interest will be cast in the language of public debate—policies, practices, issues, problems, solutions, costs, and benefits. The language of public debate is primarily a language of action and only secondarily a language of observation. This language has to be translated into the language of theory, which is primarily a language of observation and only secondarily a language of action.

Theory has two complementary functions. One is to enable the policy and practice options of public debate to be translated into matters that can be decided on the basis of observation. In this function, theorizing is part of the process of determining what set of observations will answer the questions posed by public debate on the issues of the day. Here, theories, as sets of hypotheses, serve as guides to *what should be observable*, provided the theory is accurate.

EXAMPLE: According to Wallace, the public debate over military pre-paredness revolves around two basic positions. Proponents of military expansion argue that 'it is not arms races that lead to war, but rather a nation's failure to maintain its military capabilities vis-à-vis its potential rivals and adversaries.' Anti-arms race proponents view military expansion as a contributor to the danger of war: 'the partisans of the "arms race" school do not see the competitive acquisition of military capability as a neutral instrument of policy, still less as a means to prevent war, but rather as a major link in the complex chain of events leading to armed conflict.' (Wallace, 1979:241)

Wallace theorizes that part of what is being debated is two matters of observation: (1) whether serious disputes between nations result in war or not, and (2) whether the presence or absence of an arms race before the serious dispute influences the outcome. His hypothesis is the question "do serious disputes between nations engaged in an arms race have a significantly greater probability of resulting in all-out war than those between nations exhibiting more normal patterns of military competition?"

The other function of theory is to enable what has been researched to be translated into advice as to what changes in policy or practice are likely to solve a problem. This is the form of theory most likely to show up in public debate. In this form, theory is a summary of research findings on the accuracy of the hypotheses.

EXAMPLE: Reporting the results of his research, Wallace argues that military force or violence between great powers indicates great hostility and tension. But these acts, when not preceded by an arms race, led to war in only 3 of 71 cases. "Conversely, when an arms race did precede a significant threat or act of violence, war was avoided only 5 out of 28 times. It is difficult to argue, therefore, that arms races play no role in the process of leading to the onset of war." (Wallace, 1979:252)

Wallace then translates these findings into the language of public debate and action: "The findings support with hard evidence the intuitive fears of those who argue that an intensification of the superpower arms competition could lead to a "hair-trigger" situation in which a major confrontation would be far more likely to result in all-out war." (Wallace, 1979:252) They point to the importance of continuing the struggle against superpower arms built-up.

Theories are at the same time guides for research and summaries of findings produced by earlier and continuing research. As guides for research, theories are the products of public debate. But theories enter that debate as summaries of the findings of earlier research. Any and all policy debate can be translated into theory, and every research finding can be translated into advice on policies.

2.7 WHAT IS A RESEARCHABLE QUESTION?

Researchable questions are those that can be answered in principle and in practice on the basis of observation. Unobservability in practice is the more common problem, but it can sometimes be solved by ingenuity or technology. Questions that cannot, in principle, be answered on the basis of observation are less often a problem, and these problems can often be solved by the careful use of terminology and definitions of terms.

Practical Unobservability:

Given questions that are in principle researchable, observability may be so difficult as to render the question unanswerable on practical grounds.

EXAMPLE: Questions whose answers require the use of records of the past are often practically unobservable. Usually the more distant the past, the greater the problems: records may not have been kept; what records were made may be inaccurate, may have been destroyed or lost, or may be otherwise unobtainable or unusable. And living persons who experienced the events in question may not remember them completely or accurately.

EXAMPLE: The mental activity of people other than oneself is in principle observable, but only indirectly, mediated by language, memory, perception, motivation, and so on. In addition, technology and ingenuity have produced many ways of indirectly observing another person's mental activity: they include hypnosis, "projective" tests, and various electronic devices.

EXAMPLE: Some phenomena cannot be observed directly by the human senses because they are too small, too large, too bright, too dark, too quiet, or too subtle, or otherwise outside the range of unaided human senses.

New technology can extend the limits to practicable observability by extending the range of our senses. And cleverness and ingenuity may find ways of observing indirectly that which cannot be observed directly. Nevertheless, it is well to be aware that, in the short run, there are limits to practical observability. And if the answers to research questions require the observation of what is practically unobservable, answers cannot be obtained until the practical problem is solved.

Unobservability in Principle:

Questions that lead to the formulation of non-falsifiable theories are excluded in principle. A non-falsifiable theory is one that is stated in such a way that no evidence could possibly show that the theory is incorrect.

The lack of "disconfirming" evidence can arise in three different ways: (1) there is no evidence at all; (2) all the evidence that exists is confirming, whereas potentially disconfirming evidence is unavailable, or (3) all evidence that would disconfirm one part of the theory is defined to be evidence in favour of another part.

EXAMPLE: Many theological theories are non-falsifiable. In some interpretations, every good and happy event is taken as evidence of a good and loving god, but unhappy or destructive events are taken as evidence that the god is all-knowing and therefore appears to work in "strange ways."

EXAMPLE: A social science example of non-falsifiable theory is the anti-Marxist claim that Marxism is a "religion" and therefore all Marxist theories are merely statements of faith masquerading in social scientific form. Since statements of faith are intended to be not subject to observational verification, all Marxist theories are thereby removed from serious scientific consideration.

In complementary fashion, some Marxists use the idea of "false consciousness" as a means of dismissing the claims of non-Marxists. Evidence that is troublesome to Marxist theories is sometimes treated as proof of the "false consciousness" of the researchers rather than as proof that the Marxist theories are incorrect.

In the above examples non-researchability means that the research cannot lead to a demonstration or proof. These non-falsifiable theories fail, not because they cannot be researched, but because the research leads only to illustrations. The illustrations can be expanded endlessly, but because all disconfirming evidence has been excluded by a definitional trick, no demonstration of the relative accuracy of the theory is possible.

Some unobservability will not permit even the production of illustrations. A set of terms may be defined as unobservable, and then questions can be asked about their unobservable relationships.

EXAMPLE: Again, theological arguments provide an illustration. In some Christian theology, the "father, son, and holy ghost" are defined as three unobservable spiritual entities. Statements postulating the relationships of these entities cannot produce even illustrations.

In addition to the above there are a whole series of common errors in thinking, speaking, and writing that are analysed by students of argument. Some of the more common fallacies are ambiguous use of terms, double meanings for the same term, innuendo, vague expressions, circular arguments, loaded questions, leading questions, and question-begging definitions. These errors create problems of unobservability in principle. If the error is not noticed, the problem may be discovered when one attempts to design a research project to investigate the statements.

EXAMPLE: A research project investigated the hypothesis that persons with adequate income, lots of friends, and strong interests in hobbies or work "age more successfully" than those without. When planning how to measure successful aging, the researchers noticed that adequate income, friends, and interests define "successful aging."

Non-observability in principle can almost always be avoided by rephrasing the questions addressed, the answers under consideration or the definition of what will constitute evidence for any of the theories. Larger or smaller amounts of rephrasing can produce a reorientation to answers that can be based on observation. As in the example above, the necessity for rephrasing the question may become apparent only after the formulation of the answers as causal theory is well underway.

2.8 SUMMARY

The things that are worth researching are those that can help solve social problems. Social problems—the product of conflict between practices and policies—and their solution are always under public debate. Social theory, as a set of hypotheses about what can be observed, is a product of this debate. At the same time, social theory, as a summary of research findings based on observation, is relevant information for furthering the debate over the solution of social problems. Social research that increases the relevance, accuracy, and amount of information exchanged in the debates is a useful way of participating in them.

2.9 EXERCISES

1. Translate the following statements couched in the "action" language of policy into the "observational" language of theory.
   (a) The aim is to create a greater awareness among Canadians of their present situation, in the hope that a more informed public opinion will make its influence felt on the programs and decisions of the federal and provincial governments. . . . We have enough in common in our concern for an independent Canada to work together effectively on a concrete program to reduce foreign control of the economy, foster the creative arts, assure more Canadian content in the media and in our educational system, and counter the deterioration of our environment. (Rotstein and Lax, 1974:xiv)

(b) However, in the search for an effective policy, we must be careful to avoid a blind anti-American posture which would foster a mood of anti-intellectualism in Canadian universities. The values we seek for Canadian society must not be destroyed by intellectual purges. If Canadian universities are to remain vital and exciting institutions they must continue to welcome those teachers and scholars from abroad who possess expertise unavailable in Canada and who would enrich and enliven the intellectual climate of our universities. Consequently, this paper rejects a policy of legislated or arbitrary quotas for Canadian faculty or any attempt to force out foreign faculty that are already here. (Rotstein and Lax, 1974:196)

(c) "The Council approved a resolution which condemned the inadequacy of government policies on child care in Canada. The resolution stated that the National Strategy on Child Care for Canada does not fulfill the principles outlined in the CAUT Policy Statement on a Child Care System for Canada in that it fails to adequately fund child care, does not create affordable child care services, does not ensure that child care services be non-profit, and does not guarantee universality of access to high quality child care services." (Baxter, 1988:1,19)

(d) When one looks to the future of marital relationships, it is clear that responsibility for settling disputes cannot entirely devolve on the courts. . . . And while this long lineup for mandatory court processing may represent an advance in upholding individual rights, it appears to have been purchased at the additional cost of increasing the load on judicial institutions. . . . The exercise of rights is coming to replace the practise of rites as a principal means of establishing and maintaining social order. The law has become the panacea for all types of everyday social conflict rather than a remedy for the more serious instances which call for authoritative intervention. (McKie and others, 1983:237-9)

(e) Women play an important role in the Canadian economy. It is important for women, as it is for all Canadians, that the nation's economy continue to grow and prosper. Free trade offers opportunities for economic growth, increased employment and incomes, and an improved standard of living. Enhanced security of access to the U.S. market, including assurances against future protectionist actions, will mean increased trade and additional jobs for women.

"The Agreement does not affect the range of social programs currently enjoyed by Canadians, such as medicare, child care, maternity benefits, pensions and unemployment insurance. Nor does the Agreement prevent the introduction of new social programs. Rather, the economic growth created by free trade will provide an expanded financial foundation for our social programs." (Status of Women, 1988:41)

(f) "Women need not stop being tender, compassionate, or concerned with the feelings of others. They must start being tender and compassionate with themselves and with other women. Women must begin to 'save' themselves and their daughters before they 'save' their husbands and their sons; before they 'save' the whole world. Women must try to convert the single-minded ruthlessness with which they yearn for, serve, and protect a mate or biological child into the 'ruthlessness' of self-preservation and self-development. Perhaps one of the effects of this 'transfer of affections' might be an increase in the male capacity to 'nurture': themselves, each other, children, and hopefully women." (Chesler, 1972:301)

(g) "A world of optimal and widespread health is obviously a world of minimal and only occasional medical intervention. Healthy people are those who live in healthy homes on a healthy diet; in an environment equally fit for birth, growth, work, healing and dying: sustained by a culture which enhances the conscious acceptance of limits to population, of aging, of incomplete recovery and ever imminent death. Healthy people need no bureaucratic interference to mate, give birth, share the human condition and die." (Illich, 1975:169)

(h) "The Canadian government moved to severely restrict entry to refugee claimants on January 1, claiming that 70,000 refugees have come to Canada since 1986 in order to escape poverty, not political repression." (Pugh, 1989a:12)

(i) "For many hard-core peace activists peace education is a nice idea, but the benefits are too long-term to deal with the immediate nuclear threat. For some Department of National Defence officials it is naive but dangerous pacifist propaganda—an insidious form of anti-war indoctrination. Some communities and school boards welcome it as an essential element of modern education; other condemn it as a radical (and probably Soviet-inspired) manipulation of young minds." (Macintosh, 1989: 19)

(j) "As the drawbacks of large-scale, technology-centered, and capital-dependent agriculture become clearer, growing numbers of people are seriously examining alternatives to the system. While current trends cannot be reversed overnight, there are hopeful signs that more humane and environmentally sound options are flourishing and may eventually prevail." (Pugh, 1989b:11)

(k) "When the provincial government announced a base funding increase for Ontario universities of only four per cent for 1989-90, less than the rate of inflation, the message was unmistakable. . . . At U of T, the decision means a budget short-fall next year of almost $2 million. . . . President George Connell responded to the announcement by urging the province to protect quality and accessibility through a restructuring of the university system." (*University of Toronto Magazine*, 1989:31)

(l) "Because language appears such a natural instrument with which we can describe reality, its terms and expressions seem to describe the way things are and will always be. But the truth is that these patterns of speech belong to convention and habit. And every time we use prejudicial terms, we actively re-circulate sexist ways of seeing the differences and relations between the sexes. I hope therefore that however much the cards seem to be stacked against us, feminists will keep on about language. For every time someone talks about "piglets", "sluts" and "chicks", the task of achieving equality for women is that much harder." (Coward, 1989:9)

2. The exercises for chapter 3 contain numerous statements couched in the observational language of theory. Translate the statements in set I and set II into the action language of policy and practice.

CHAPTER 3

Theorizing

CHAPTER CONTENTS

Because everything cannot be examined at once, research obliges one to make many assumptions about matters that will not be directly investigated. These assumptions are as important to the findings of the research as those things explicitly examined. Researchers make decisions about what will be assumed and what will be investigated. This being the case, it is desirable to be aware of all the options before making decisions. In this light, theorizing is a kind of consciousness raising. For research planning purposes, theorizing is initially a process of making explicit what options exist. Further theorizing is involved in deciding to assume some things and investigate others by means of observation.

3.1 "PROCESS" THEORIZING

"Process" theorizing is advocated here as a very general form of causal theorizing. The idea of process here is the common sense one that some recognizable phenomenon develops over time, with a number of aspects or dimensions to it, all of which are causally connected in one way or another. What is an effect now may earlier have been a cause in relation to something else. Every element in the process is sometimes determining (a cause), sometimes being determined (an effect). The term "process" is meant to imply a non-mechanical form of causal theorizing. It might be termed "historical causal" or "genetic causal" theorizing.

EXAMPLE: Interaction between individuals is commonly theorized as a process. The actions and words of a husband on one occasion act as causes of his wife's words and actions at the next point in time; these immediately become causes of the husband's next words and actions, which in turn cause the wife's next response, and so on. The husband's words and actions at time 1 are caused partly by his previous interaction with his wife and partly by his interactions with others. Other words and actions may cause the woman to become pregnant, which causes her to seek the advice of pregnancy specialists whose advice causes her to modify her diet and smoking; this modification of her habits causes the birth of a healthy child, whose words and actions then enter the relationship between the husband and the wife as the cause and effect of subsequent development.

EXAMPLE: Interaction between labour and management may be theorized as a process. The availability of labour and other resources causes the construction of a factory, which creates employment, which causes the workers to accept job contracts and produces products that the management sells to pay the workers and provide profits for the owners. Inattention to health and safety, and arbitrary hiring and firing by management cause the workers to organize a union and bargain collectively with the management. The existence of the union increases wages and other costs for management, which decides to buy technology that will decrease the number of jobs; this action causes the union to bargain for a job security clause in its contract; this clause will interfere with management's plan to reduce the work force; therefore management locks the workers out in order to get a better settlement. The lockout causes the workers to go on strike and appeal to other workers for support and strike pay loans. The prolonging of the strike and lockout is costly to both labour and management and forces both to compromise. The partial defeat of both sides heightens the union's militancy, and makes management decide to let the plant run down in preparation to shutting it down and pulling out of the country altogether. This threat causes the workers to appeal to the government to prevent the shutdown; as a result the government offers to forgive the company's taxes for five years in return for keeping the plant operating. The company takes the money, keeps the plant open for three years, and then shuts the plant down and moves to Malaysia where the government has offered interest-free loans, outright grants, and no taxes in perpetuity. The shutdown causes workers and the government to search for a way to keep the plant open, and on and on. Each of the events in this process is caused by preceding events. The union causes management action, which causes union action in turn. The process is a causal one, in which event is causally determined. But the fact that the union's actions are caused by management, which in turns causes new union actions, means that later developments in the process are determined partly by immediate causes and partly by earlier stages of the process. In addition, the actions of the union are only partially caused by the management action, and vice versa. The activities of other corporations, other unions, the employment market, and the state also operate as causes, and in turn they are affected by the activities of both union and management.

Features of process theorizing

As the above examples illustrate, process theorizing amounts to telling stories about how events happen and relationships develop, with much attention to postulating causal connections among the events. This kind of theorizing makes causality central without requiring commitments to single causal roles for any element in the process. All causes are themselves caused (which makes them effects) and all effects influence other effects (which makes them causes).

Another feature of process theorizing is that is it open-ended. The starting and ending points of theoretical stories have to be chosen on reasonable grounds. And stating one causal connection suggests another, which suggest a third and so on.

EXAMPLE: The above story about the marriage started some time after the marriage and ended after the birth of the child. It could as easily have started before their marriage, with their births, with the marriage of their parents, or with *their* births. The story could have ended with the maturing of the child or the death of the parents or at any other time. The story could have taken up the kind of jobs held by the parents, what kind of income this provided, what kind of education they had started or completed, what kind of pregnancy specialists were available, and so forth. When education, jobs, and health activities are brought into the story, other stories are suggested about the development of changes in these institutions that shape the options available to the parents at any point. The options available are also determined by the place of residence of the couple. In the socially backward United States, gaining access to medical facilities for giving birth may cause a family financial crisis. In Canada since the socialization of medicine these crises no longer occur.

The open-ended feature of process theorizing brings the problem of boundaries: when should causal stories start and end and what should be included and excluded? Each of these decisions is a crucial determinant of the theory produced. Each requires an explicit defence. Since there are no fixed answers here, the defence is based on whatever research or other information is available. When hard information runs out, the defence will be based on plausibility.

The general principle for deciding what to include and exclude and where to start and end in process theorizing is to err on the side of inclusion and longer episodes, rather than the reverse. The argument behind this principle is that one of the main purposes of theorizing is to make explicit the assumptions to be employed in research; larger boundaries at this stage will bring more assumptions to light.

Guidelines for process theorizing

1. Consider each cause as an effect and ask: What are its causes? Stop when the causal influence on the effect of primary interest is so indirect as to be trivial.
2. Consider each effect as a cause and ask:
   (a) What does it cause?
   (b) What are the other causes of these effects? Stop when the influence of the effect of primary interest (treated as a cause) on other effects is trivial.
3. Examine the connections between the answers to the above questions.

Aids to theorizing

Initially, much theorizing can be based on one's experience. Process theorizing is more or less what most people do in everyday life. Other people's experience can enhance the theorizing considerably. Interview people connected to or concerned with your question, informally or formally. Read current material in the popular media: radio, TV, the daily press, and magazines. Examine popular books and academic journals and monographs. In general, use the resources of public and research libraries.

Some of this material will have already been used in determining what is worth researching. In this theorizing phase, note every causal claim made or implied and use them to complete or augment your own theorizing. At the same time, be critical. Keep lists of assumptions that each claim seems to require.

If done with even moderate thoroughness, this work will more than likely produce a great deal of contradictory claims, which will be very important for bringing order to your work.

3.2 ORGANIZING THEORETICAL MATERIAL: ALTERNATIVE THEORIES

Alternative theories are apparently irreconcilable cause and effect claims. Irreconcilable means simply that if one claim is true the other cannot be. The importance of irreconcilability is that it locates critical points of theoretical difference. In one way or another, these points are the result of gaps in research or other information. The gaps in research may result from (1) contradictory research findings, (2) events or developments that move faster than they can be researched, or (3) the fact that the necessary research is very difficult or very expensive. Whatever the case, *irreconcilable alternative theories identify points where more research is essential*.

Theories may be irreconcilable with regard to

1. the causal status of two variables,
2. whether a cause is a cause or not,
3. the direction of a relationship, or
4. any combination of the above.
1. Claims about the causal status of two variables may take the form that one variable is an effect and therefore cannot be a cause, or vice versa. This type of irreconcilability is infrequent for obvious reasons: the two claims might be reconciled as a mutually determining cause and effect pair, or as alternating determinants.

EXAMPLE: It might be argued that changes in social conflict cause changes in crime, and that if this is true then it cannot be true that changes in crime lead to changes in social conflict. However, it is more credibly argued that at time 1 changes in social conflict bring about changes in crime at time 2, but these changes in crime bring about a change in social conflict at time 3.

Certainly intense social conflict (such as strikes or racial strife) may lead to illegal activities, and crime (such as violations of industrial health and safety regulations) can lead to strikes. Marital conflict can lead husbands to assault their wives criminally, which can lead to further intensification of the marital conflict.

2. The claim that some phenomenon is a cause of an effect cannot be reconciled with the claim that it is not. This type of irreconcilability is not very common, because the conflict can be reconciled by admitting multiple causes of an effect and assessing the relative contribution of each cause.

EXAMPLE: Automobile companies claim that their products do not cause accidents, whereas some victims of automobile accidents claim that vehicle failure was the cause of their accident. The alternative theories could be reconciled here by admitting vehicle failure, flaws in the driver's skill or judgement, and road conditions to the status of causes. The job of research would be to assess the degree to which each cause contributed to accidents.

A variation on this kind of irreconcilability takes the form of arguing that a cause is only an apparent cause and that proper research would reveal the true cause and would show the apparent cause to be only apparent.

EXAMPLE: The germ or micro-organism theory of disease claimed, for example, that diseases were caused, not by sinful behaviour but by exposure to infection by micro-organisms. With microscopes and appropriate research designs, it could be shown that with no infection there was no disease, and that infection was quite independent of behaviour, except when behaviour, sinful or not, brought a person into contact with sources of infection.

Even this irreconcilability may be resolved by theorizing that an apparent cause is really a cause, but only indirectly: sinful behaviour may heighten the probability of contact with the sources of the infection, or weaken the immune system's ability to neutralize them.

3. Contradictory claims about the direction of a causal relationship are usually irreconcilable. If the claim that increases in social conflict cause increases in crime rates is true, the claim that increases in social conflict causes decreases in crime rates must be false, and vice versa.

3.3 SIMPLIFICATION

Following the above advice, a student should be able to

1. formulate a process theory,
2. identify conflicting claims or ambiguities about the working of the process,
3. organize all the theoretical material into two or more alternative theories on the basis of the conflicting claims or ambiguities, and
4. thereby pinpoint those matters requiring research.

A process theory formulated as above will ordinarily be something more than can be researched in a single project. For policy as well as research purposes, the entire theory is usefully seen as a set of cause and effect claims. The smallest element of a process theory that can (1) be researched and (2) provide at least some information useful for policy purposes is a single cause and effect relationship (when a cause changes how does the effect change, and by how much?). However, the smallest element in the theory that can be researched *with any confidence in the results* is not a single cause and effect relationship, but *a single effect with all of its major causes*. This is the result of a simple fact: causes, whether observed or not, influence effects. And the influence of unobserved causes can appear to be the influence of observed causes. In order to have any confidence in the accuracy of a description of the influence of cause A on effect B, it is necessary to have information of the influence of all other causes of effect B. If the results of a research project suggest that changing one cause will have a desired effect, it is always necessary to know what is to be done with the other causes: are they to be held constant, and if so, how? If they have to be changed, how much and in what way? Causes may be distinguished in terms of how *controllable* or *manipulable* they are with the available "social technology."

EXAMPLE: Some factors that might be treated as causes, such as ageing or maturing, race, ethnicity, or sex, cannot be controlled easily, even in the long run, given current social capabilities and technology. Other things that might be treated as causes, such as income, place of residence, school attended, and people associated with, are controllable in the short or medium run by relatively cheap and well-known methods.

What is the value of researching the influence of uncontrollable causes? One answer is to provide estimates of how well an effect might be managed by controlling the controllable causes.

EXAMPLE: What is the point of knowing if age, ethnicity, or sex is a cause of juvenile delinquency when there is no possibility of controlling them so as to control delinquency? One obvious answer is to provide estimates of how effective the control of controllable causes (recreation, policing, charging, sentencing policy and practice) can be in diminishing juvenile delinquency. The more important the uncontrollable causes, the smaller will be the decreases in juvenile delinquency brought by changes in the controllable causes.

The other answer is that when the causes that are difficult and expensive to control are the more important, the policy implications are useful for containment, even when prevention appears unlikely. Troublesome age, sex, and ethnic groups might be monitored more closely for delinquent activity by police than less troublesome groups.

Note: Although it is common to talk as if things like age, sex, and ethnicity cause juvenile delinquency, it should be understood that this is a shorthand way of saying that a whole set of sex, age, and ethnic policies and practices are the causes, and not that sex, age, or ethnicity is a cause per se.

For the purposes of planning research projects, the practical problem is to decide
1. what effect(s) will be investigated,
2. what set of causes must be observed, and
3. what set of causes can be left unobserved.
Unobserved causes have to be assumed to be constant or inoperative or so unchanging as to be irrelevant. What assumptions about cause can be made safely without compromising the results of the research? How many and what causes can be left unobserved without throwing doubt on the accuracy of the findings based on observed causes?

Alternative theories impose basic limits on what can be safely assumed. Alternative theories represent the organization of conflicting views of the process in question. It will be recalled that scientific demonstration requires that the relative accuracy of competing alternative theories be evaluated. Research that investigates only one of the alternative theories can produce only illustrations. Research is a very expensive way to produce illustrations.

What alternative theories specify is alternative causes, directions, strengths, time periods of operation, and so on. The accuracy of one theory cannot be proved or demonstrated by assuming what is critical to an alternative theory. Because one theory is supported not does mean the alternative is inaccurate, except when the only difference is the direction of a causal relationship. Alternative theories may be partly accurate and partly inaccurate. Unless what is essential to each alternative is observed, no demonstration of relative accuracy is possible.

As stated earlier, everything cannot be examined at once; therefore the researcher is obliged to make assumptions about those matters that will not be investigated directly. These assumptions are as important to the findings of the research as those things not assumed but examined by observation. The purpose of process theorizing should now be clear: it allows one to make explicit statements about what is being assumed. Further theorizing is involved in deciding to assume some things and investigate others by means of observation.

Policy goals and research capabilities may be in conflict here: how much simplification, introduced to keep a research project manageable, will still be useful for modifying a simple policy or practice that doesn't work?

There are also practical problems in simplifying a theory for research purposes: how much simplification can be justified in light of what is already known? If existing research has demonstrated relationships between three causes and an effect, can a fourth cause be usefully researched without controlling or measuring the first three? The answer is a matter partly of research design and partly of theory. The research design part of the answer is that clever researchers may be able to design a study in which the values of the first three causes are known to be constant or to vary only slightly or to be measurable with a minimum of effort.

The theoretical part of the answer is based on an assessment of the importance of the first three causes. Weak determinants are safely ignored, but moderate ones less so. To ignore strong determinants would be an oversimplification of a theory for research purposes.

EXAMPLE: In theories where conflict is important, the activities of each party immediately determine the activities of the other. Any theory that ignores one of the parties clearly oversimplifies. Some of these will be obviously nonsensical and easy to spot, such as theories of changes in one boxer's behaviour that ignore the behaviour of his opponent.

Other similarly nonsensical theories seem to be less easy to spot, for some attempts have been published: theories of labour unions that ignore management, theories of the middle class that ignore the ruling and working classes, theories of crime that ignore the law and the police, theories of women's behaviour that ignore men's, theories of victims that ignore victimizers, theories of voters that ignore candidates, and so forth. In short, where a simplification requires one to ignore what is obviously necessary for understanding and control, the point of oversimplification has been reached.

Choosing assumptions and choosing hypotheses

For planning research, it is essential to assign cause and effect status as a description of how the researcher will proceed with the investigation. It commits the researcher to seeing some things as causes and other things as effects. It also commits the researcher to particular policy implications: the implications are that in order to control the specified effect, one must manipulate or make changes in the specified causes.

EXAMPLE: Researching genetic inheritance as the cause of criminality or poverty commits the researcher to the policy implication that criminality or poverty can be reduced by preventing the reproduction of genetically defective persons. Durkheim investigated anomie, fatalism, and altruism as causes of suicide and thereby committed himself to the policy implication that anomie, fatalism, and altruism would have to be controlled in order to reduce suicide rates.

It is important to be aware of the indirect as well as the direct policy implications of cause and effect research choices. For example, if alcoholism is seen to be a cause of wife battery, the direct and immediate policy implication is that the alcoholism should be cured to control wife battery. But notice that such a theory also argues indirectly against viewing wife battery as something that criminal prosecution will stop. Both the question of (1) what effect the battery has on the alcoholic consumption of the batterer and (2) the effect of not criminally prosecuting the batterer are put aside. Blaming alcoholism also implies that men do not have to take individual responsibility for this particular crime.

Choosing assumptions and hypotheses, then, is partly a matter of choosing a sensible and defensible set of policy and practice implications. Where the policy and practice implications are inadequate, more attention to theoretical alternatives is the likely remedy.

Finally, researchers also need to consider the concrete implications for policy and practice of each possible outcome of the project. For two alternative theories the possible findings are: theory A is true, theory B is false; B is true, A is false; both are true; both are false. If the implications of any of these possibilities are ridiculous, trivial, or impossible, it's time to repeat at least some of the theoretical work.

In summary, choosing hypotheses and assumptions simultaneously involves choosing policy and practice implications. A powerful test of the adequacy of a researcher's work is the adequacy of the policy and practice implications of the theorizing.

Some simplification guidelines

1. Do not simplify in a way that ignores the most fundamental features of phenomena.
2. Do not simplify so as to ignore central parts of alternative theories.
3. Do not simplify so as to ignore important causes.
4. Proceed from the more important to the less important—if it's unimportant, don't do it at all.
5. Proceed from the simple to the less simple.

Ordinarily, earlier investigations will investigate the causes postulated to be the strongest determinants of an effect. Causes seen to be less important might be ignored here. The reverse is not the case, however. Projects investigating weaker causes of an effect cannot afford to ignore stronger causes—stronger causes must be either controlled or measured in some way. Failure to do so is likely to produce results that are simply errors and, consequently, inaccurate evaluations of theories.

3.4 SUMMARY

Theorizing is a way of making explicit what will be researched and what will be assumed while doing it. Process theorizing, a form of causal theorizing, is recommended here. The voluminous products of process theorizing can be organized into alternative theories that identify those matters where research is critical. It is necessary to simplify the alternative theories because everything cannot be researched at once, but oversimplification must be guarded against. In simplification the researcher becomes committed, by default, to specific policy and practice implications. Care must be taken to see that these are desirable rather than otherwise.

3.5 EXERCISES

Listed below are numerous examples of social science theoretical statements. The statements were chosen to represent the wide variety of things that are theorized about, ways of stating theories, policy applications, and interests. For convenience they are grouped into single statement theories (set I), multiple statement theories (set II), and sets of alternative theories (set III).

The questions below are to be asked for each of the single- and multiple-statement theories (sets I and II). The basic exercises should be attempted before the additional questions. Some of the additional exercises assume that the basic questions have been attempted. Students should do only the exercises on those examples that are of interest or importance to them.

Basic Exercises

1. Using the guidelines for process theorizing, expand each of the following statements into process theories.
2. Specify the policy implications of each of the statements.
3. Specify alternatives for each theory.

Additional Exercises

4. Outline the most important (a) *direct* policy implications and (b) *indirect* policy implications of the theories.
5. (a) If the theories are stated formally, translate them into less formal process theories: (i) first tell one or more of the stories implied by the theory and (ii) highlight the causal relationships between successive events in your story.
   (b) If the theories are already informally stated process theories, translate them into formal statements. (For an example of a highly formal theory statement, see Hirschi and Selvin's theory of delinquency in set III.)
6. (a) Extend the boundaries of the theories forward and backward. Specify what happens to cause the initial causes and what happens after the effect is caused.
   (b) What parts of the process, in your understanding, have been excluded from the theory? Do you agree with these exclusions? Would you exclude some of the material now included?
7. Identify all the causes in the theories and rank them according to controllability. In other words, which of these causes are relatively easy to control by known techniques and which are less easy? Which can be controlled in the short run, the medium run, the long run?
8. Outline a simple project for researching some part of a multiple-statement theory. List the assumptions you will have to make.

9. Rank the causes in the theories from most important to least important. What implications does this ranking have for your first research project to investigate this theory?

Set I Single-Statement Theories

(a) Social conflict is more intense, the less integrated the community involved in the conflict.

(b) The smaller and more primitive the society, the more homogeneous its culture tends to be.

(c) The more that men are exposed to actual combat in battle, the less convinced they are of the ideological value of the war.

(d) The first labour unions in a country are more likely to be formed by skilled than by unskilled workers. White-collar workers are more difficult to organize into unions than blue-collar workers.

(e) The most deprived groups in the society are the most likely to engage in salvationist religions. (Statements (a)-(e) from Berelson and Steiner, 1964)

(f) The more paternalistic the value system of elite groups in a community, the greater their involvement in community affairs.

(g) The higher the degree of industrialization in a community, the more decentralized the decision-making structure. (Statements (f) and (g): from Clark, 1968)

(h) The stratification order, cultural beliefs, and interracial conflict influenced the content of Canadian narcotics legislation. (Cook, 1969:45)

(i) Low-income and high-income farmers are not as active in the organization activities of the [agrarian] movement as middle-income farmers. (McCrorie, 1971:40)

(j) Basic personality characteristics are probably not [the most important determinant of] an individual's responses to placebos. (Liberman, 1964:245)

(k) The "capture theory" stipulates that regulatory agencies that were established ostensibly to regulate economic and social behaviour in various fields, were "captured" by the regulated and cease to regulate in the public interest. (Schultz, 1981:314)

(l) The pattern of sex differences indicated females to be more appropriately assertive in their overt behaviour than males. Males were more aggressive. In their cognitions, females were more likely to deny their impact on others, while males were more likely to deny the impact of others on themselves. Potency training was suggested for females, assertiveness training for males. (Smye, Wine and Moses, 1980:164)

(m) The higher the class origin of college students, the less the prestige they assign to elementary and high school teaching.

Set II Multiple-Statement Theories

SARI TUDIVER'S THEORY OF FEMINISM IN THE UNIVERSITY

Feminist faculty...operate in a hierarchical, largely male-dominated, generally conservative workplace. Despite an ideology of academic freedom, [women's studies courses] operate under serious constraints and feminists often experience harsh consequences. Thus, most male academics (this is true even of politically progressive males) continue to avoid the huge feminist academic literature in their fields or dismiss it, unread, as unobjective. Few integrate questions pertaining to women and their experience into their course materials. Many remain suspicious, perhaps recognizing that to do so would necessitate rethinking their analytic framework, assumptions and methods of inquiry.

Such individuals sit on tenure and hiring committees, as heads of departments and deans and control the number of women (not to mention feminists) hired, given tenure and promoted. The particular danger to women's studies courses is that where they are not taught by progressive feminist scholars, they can easily become special topic courses about women rather than settings for feminist education. Similarily, as research about women gains popularity with funding agencies, conservative academics compete with feminists, often successfully, for funding of research.

But the problem is much larger. Perhaps the most serious constraint to feminist education in the university lies in the non-democratic, authoritarian structure of the university itself. One consequence of this structure is that female faculty often see themselves having interests and concerns different from women clerical and support staff. (Tudiver, 1981:283)

MURPHY'S THEORY OF TEACHER MOBILITY

1. The greater the student's readiness to learn, the more satisfied the teacher will be with his professional status.
2. The higher the socio-economic status background of the pupils in a school, the greater their readiness to learn.
3. The greater the ease of establishing compliance, the greater the satisfaction of teachers with their professional status.
4. The difficulty of establishing compliance will be related to the SES background of the pupils in the school in a curvilinear fashion, with the lower, upper, and middle stratum being the decreasing order of difficulty.
5. There is horizontal mobility resulting from teacher dissatisfaction, with teachers leaving schools with lower status clientele to work in schools with higher status clientele. (Murphy, 1977:49)

BERELSON AND STEINER'S THEORY OF FERTILITY

In their review of the fertility literature, Berelson and Steiner (1964) found studies investigating the following causes: prosperity/depression, rate of social change, development/underdevelopment, status of women, socioeconomic status, size of place of residence, religious affiliation, minority status, size of family of origin, family mobility and, finally, season.

The direction of relationships between these causes and fertility is summarized below.

1. Fertility is higher during prosperity and lower during depression.
2. Fertility is lower during periods of rapid social change than in periods of slow social change.
3. Fertility is lower in industrialized societies than in non-industrialized societies.
4. The more equal women are to men, the lower the fertility rate.
5. In societies where women are more equal to men, women employed in the paid labour force have lower fertility than those not so employed.
6. The higher a group's socioeconomic status, the lower its fertility.
7. The greater the size of the place of residence, the lower the fertility: big city residents have the lowest fertility; rural farm residents have the highest.

8. Catholics have higher fertility than Protestants, and Protestants have higher fertility than Jews.
9. Couples who descend from large families have higher fertility than those who descend from small families.
10. The greater the degree of geographical or social mobility, the lower the fertility rate.
11. Fertility is higher in late summer and early fall than in other seasons.

BERELSON AND STEINER'S THEORY OF PREJUDICE AND DISCRIMINATION

In their review of the prejudice and discrimination literature, Berelson and Steiner (1964) discovered a number of causes of prejudice and discrimination, and, given the presence of prejudice and discrimination as causes, a variety of effects. The statements below summarize the direction of the relationships between prejudice and discrimination and some of the causes they reviewed.

1. The less the competition between groups, the lower the likelihood of prejudice.
2. The greater the threat from a minority group, the greater the prejudice and discrimination in the majority group.
3. People with more education have less prejudice and discrimination than those with less education.
4. The stronger the prejudice, the greater the resistance to anti-prejudice information.
5. Personal contact between members of different ethnic groups leads to a reduction of prejudice and discrimination, but only when the prejudice is initially not very high.
   Given that prejudice and discrimination are in existence (as causes), the statements below describe how these causes influence various effects.
6. "Prejudice and discrimination against minority groups are partly maintained by a reinforced spiral of built-in cause and effect: the disapproved group is deprived, and as a result of the deprivation it is further disapproved." (Berelson and Steiner, 1964:523)
7. Prejudice and discrimination lead to stereotyping by both majority and minority groups.
8. Strong prejudice and discrimination lead to guilt among members of the majority over their treatment of the minorities.

9. Minority groups subject to prejudice and discrimination are more
   likely than the majority to engage in crime.

SOROKIN'S THEORY OF WAR, REVOLUTION, AND REFORM MOVEMENTS

Their interrelation has been studied little. Nevertheless, there seems
to be a tangible correlation between these two phenomena, especially
between an unsuccessful war and revolution. Such a war is in a great
many cases followed by revolution (in 1917-18 in Austria, Turkey,
Hungary, Germany, Russia, Bulgaria, Greece, and so on); in 1905 in
Russia; in 1912 in Turkey; in 1870-71 in France, and in a great many
other cases in various countries during the previous centuries. On
the other hand, many revolutions have led to wars. Generally, they
tend to breed each other. The reasons for this are quite comprehensible. An unsuccessful war means that the society's organization could
not meet the test of war, and that it consequently needs a reconstruc-
tion. Through its calamities it breeds a dissatisfaction in the masses,
and stirs them to revolt against the existing conditions especially
against the political regime. Hence, revolution as a result of a military
defeat. On the other hand, revolution itself tends to change so
radically the existing relationships within such a society and outside
of it that it endangers the most important interests of many social
groups within, and outside of, that society. Such an antagonism is
likely to result in civil or international war as the final method of
solution for such antagonisms. Hence war as a result of revolution
and their functional relationships. This correlation has been studied
very little, but its existence seems to be probable. (Sorokin,
1957:346-7)

HAYWOOD'S REVIEW OF THEORIES OF ROME'S FALL

The most common point of view in the past asserted that there must
have been a definite cause or group of causes which made Rome
decline and finally fall....One scholar has found that Rome was
undernourished because of its low productivity; another that it had
circulatory trouble because of the failure of the supply of precious
metals for currency. One of the most recent theories is that the
Romans as a people were ill physically; their vitality was sapped by
repeated and violent incursions of the plague.

Other scholars have brought forward theories. . . . There is a racist theory that the people of Rome declined because the Romans received too many people of "inferior" stocks among their citizens. . . . The Marxist view, on the other hand, is that the oppression of the many by the few caused the decline.

Those who specialize in politics have tended to ascribe Rome's decline to the increasing inadequacy of her political institutions. Moralists have found in the decline and fall a most satisfying example of what happens to a people guilty of luxury and immorality.

Gibbon offers two reasons for Rome's fall. He speaks of the triumph of Christianity and the barbarians, and in another place he asserts that the vast fabric sank of its own weight. (Haywood, 1958:1-3)

LEXCHIN'S THEORY OF DRUG COMPANIES AS "PUSHERS"

The research efforts of the drug industry are also distorted. The development of drugs is biased toward producing the ones with greatest sales potential, and not necessarily the greatest social benefits. In order to sell their products, the companies generate a constant bombardment of advertising directed at doctors. Physicians rely on this advertising for much of their knowledge about drugs. When the reliance is superimposed on an initially deficient base of knowledge, the result is overuse and misuse of drugs, often leading to injurious consequences.

In another effort to expand the use of drugs, the industry has even tried to create new diseases that require drug treatment. This process is easily observed in the cases of Valium and Ritalin and is one that is called "medicalization." What this term means is that problems that were formerly social or family ones now become diseases for doctors to deal with; however, most of these problems cannot be solved on an individual basis. When people are depressed because they are unemployed, the answer is not to give them an antidepressant, but that is the choice many physicians make. Drug advertising encourages doctors to view loneliness or marriage breakdown as medical problems. Medical education is grossly deficient in equipping doctors to help people with these problems. The easiest solution for doctors, especially when they are trying to see a patient every ten minutes, is to take the advice in the ads and prescribe a pill. (Lexchin, 1984:15-16)

LEXCHIN'S THEORY OF HIGH BLOOD PRESSURE (HYPERTENSION)

Besides stress reduction, is is known that many cases of mild and even moderate hyptertension can often be treated successfully by other non-drug methods. These include weight reduction, muscle relaxation and yoga, among others. Unsurprisingly, drug ads never mention these other forms of therapy. But most research, too, ignores them. Instead large amounts of money and scientific talent are devoted to discovering newer and, sometimes, more effective drugs. Concentrating time, money and scientific expertise on drug therapy is done at the expense of other modes of treatment. The other therapies outlined here are less costly to the patient and do not carry the side effects of drugs. However, research into new antihypertensives is a good investment for the drug industry. About 11 percent of the Canadian population over twenty years of age has high blood pressure, by commonly accepted criteria. High blood pressure is a life-long disease and that means life-long pill taking. Also the drug companies know the economics of a physician's practice. With visits lasting an average of ten to fifteen minutes, it is much easier to write a prescription than to start enquiring into a patient's dietary habits or to set up a physicial fitness program. Consequently, for the majority of doctors, the treatment of hypertension begins and ends with drugs. By 1977, four of the 25 most frequently prescribed brand name drugs in Canada were those used in therapy of high blood pressure. (Some of the four are also used in treating other diseases, and their frequent prescribing may, in part, be due to these other diseases.) (Lexchin, 1984:212)

PORTES AND WALTON'S THEORY OF INTERNATIONAL CLASS FORMATION

Once we have shed our national blinders postindustrial society dissolves in a nationally interpenetrated global economy with its own division of labor that concentrates production in the enclaves of cheap labor, secondary markets, and easy access, while concentrating its financial, managerial, and technical direction in the metropolitan core.

Class formation on a global level cuts across national boundaries, placing geographically distant groups in similar strata despite their local furnishings. The working class of core countries, for example, does not benefit systematically from upgrading associated with the export of less skilled, dirty work. Cheap labor abroad enhances profit, although working under primitive labor relations. Obviously, in the particular setting these are apt to be desirable jobs. A small fraction of the Third World labor force is upgraded and drawn closer to the material position of workers in the advanced countries, thus widening the gap between formal and informal sector workers in the periphery. At the same time this process differentially affects U.S. workers. Many are displaced and unemployed whereas a lesser number may be reabsorbed at a higher level. Nevertheless, the main effect in the long run is to degrade the labor process in general, leading to an accentuation of worldwide class inequality. Polarization, stemming from the fact that core and periphery workers increasingly share a common situation, is engendered further in the periphery as a dependent bourgeoisie allies with multinational business. The fact that there are winners and losers at both ends of the core-periphery relationship reemphasizes the new global basis of stratification. The emerging pattern is one of internationally stratified classes rather than of countries. (Portes and Walton, 1981:184)

ILLICH'S THEORY OF HOSPITAL DEVELOPMENT

As the doctor's interest shifted from the sick to sickness, the hospital became a museum of sickness. The wards were full of indigent people who offered their bodies as spectacles to any physican willing to treat them. The realization that the hospital was the logical place to study and compare "cases" developed towards the end of the 18th century. Doctors visited hospitals where all kinds of sick people were mingled, and trained themselves to pick out several "cases" of the same disease. They developed "bedside vision" or a clinical eye. During the first decades of the 19th century, the medical attitude towards hospitals went through a further development. Until then, new doctors had been trained mostly by lectures, demonstrations and disputations. Now the "bedside" became the clinic, the place where future doctors were trained to see and recognize diseases. The clinical approach to sickness gave birth to a new language, which spoke about diseases from the bedside, and to a hospital reorganized by disease for the exhibition of diseases to students.

The hospital, which at the very beginning of the 19th century had become a place for diagnosis, now turned into a place for teaching. Soon it would become a laboratory for experimenting with treatments, and towards the turn of the century a place for healing. By now the pesthouse has been transformed into a compartmentalized repair shop. (Illich, 1975:113-4)

RUSSETT'S THEORY OF PEACE SCIENCE

In the scholarly role of pursuing "pure science," one looks primarily for variables that will explain a substantial portion of the variance in given behavior. One is searching, in other words, for a "powerful" theory that will, when carefully articulated and tested, in crude statistical terms, produce a high R-square. As a practitioner of "pure science" one is not so readily concerned with whether that variance can actually be controlled; that is, whether the explanatory variables are themselves readily "manipulable" by policy makers. The first step is understanding, and perhaps prediction. A "peace scientist" will of course care about finding practical means of promoting peace, but will not necessarily expect the immediate application demanded by a policy maker, nor need to serve the vested interests which constrain a policy maker's choice of policy goals and instruments. (Russett, 1979:9)

RUSSETT'S THEORY OF POLICY MAKERS

The policy maker, quite the contrary, is primarily concerned with what s/he can manipulate. His or her eyes are much more likely to light up in reaction to an explanation that identifies something that can be controlled, than by one that identifies broad historic forces over which the policy maker has little control. Manipulability is of prime interest, prediction next, and "mere understanding" of little import. By this characterization, the policy maker is likely to be much more interested in anything that can explain how a crisis might possibly be resolved short of war than in knowing about forces that brought about the crisis, and over which s/he has little control. Or at least over which s/he is willing to have little control. The role of "pure scientist" macroanalyst may not be a popular one even if such a scientists's findings are accepted. Suppose one were to show that large, bureaucratically unwieldy states are more war-prone, or that great powers with system-wide hegemonic interests are more likely to be involved in world-endangering crises, or that the dynamics of capitalism or communism produce expansionist, aggressive and war-prone behavior. Would a policy maker of such a government want to take the steps that would reduce the power of his/her state, or fundamentally change its socioeconomic system, even if the steps could be identified? I think this perspective makes a substantial contribution to understanding why macroanalysis is not so well regarded in some circles, and less well-regarded the closer one draws to the circle of the prince. (Russett, 1979: 9-10)

SCHORR'S THEORY OF INTELLECTUAL PROBLEMS OF SOCIAL SCIENCE

A worrisome intellectual problem is that social scientists take a narrow view of problems that require a broader view. That is, they approach problems by way of a single discipline. It is barely necessary to repeat what has been said so often, but it is perhaps useful to illustrate how this limitation affects policy development. For example, "culture of poverty" explanations of the behaviors of poor people draw vitality from two sources that are peripheral to the evidence. One source of vitality that should bring no surprise is that this set of ideas defines the problem in a way that supports current values. The other source of vitality is that social scientists are expert in description of attitudes and status situations. They are largely inexpert on such matters as nutrition and in understanding what makes social patterns change over time. So "culture of poverty" reflects the expertise of the researchers more than it explains the situation or prospects of poor people. Yet this notion is the major support for social service and educational stategies in dealing with poverty.

Another intellectual problem in the applicability of social science is the value that is placed on elaboration. Our universities may be directly responsible for this. Students are taught to abandon unlearned common sense and, with it, simplicity. Somehow the necessary search for rigor in thinking is converted into overvaluing the complex and technical. Therefore, simple matters may be overlooked. For example, the significance to social behavior of nutrition and shelter were all but ignored in post-World War II research. When one seeks a policy recommendation from people so disposed, the result is either a retreat to the need for more research or a hopelessly involved recommendation. This is not to plead for reductionism but only to name the parallel error of elaborationism.

We have been cataloguing intellectual difficulties in bringing social science to bear upon social policy, and perhaps it is already obvious how closely involved with these difficulties is the self-interest of social scientists. If social scientists are trained in elaborationism, it is because their professors are most secure with that. It is the surest route to academic success for faculty and students as well. The National Academy of Science and Social Science Research Council put the point as follows: "Many academic scientists value the prestige that their contributions to basic research and theory give them in the eyes of their peers more than whatever rewards might be obtained from clients who would find their work useful. (Schorr, 1975:32-33, 35)

Set III Alternative Theories

BASIC EXERCISES

1. Where relevant, do the exercises for set I and set II for the alternative theories below.
2.
   (a) Are any of the alternative statements reconcilable?
   (b) If they cannot be reconciled, describe the most important differences in the statements. Identify these differences according to the types of ways theories may be irreconcilable (see the section entitled "Organizing Theoretical Material").
   (c) What are the most important points on which the theory statements apparently agree?

ADDITIONAL EXERCISES

3. In light of your answers to question 3 above, what hypotheses are most in need of research?
4. Using the discussion of simplification in the text, identify a set of hypotheses for the initial investigation of the alternative theories. (Assume little research has been done on the theories so that you are beginning from scratch.)

5. Suppose (i) all alternatives are correct; (ii) all are wrong; (iii) one is correct and all others wrong (consider each alternative as correct and all others as wrong, in turn).
   (a) Given the differences and similarities in the alternative theories, are each of these outcomes possible?
   (b) Are the policy implications of all of these outcomes credible—that is, not ridiculous, trivial or impossible?

6.
   (a) Outline a strategy for a series of projects to research one of the alternative theories completely and exhaustively, ignoring the alternative theories. Initial projects should investigate the most important causes; later projects should investigate less important causes.
   (b) Now outline a strategy for a series of projects to research two alternative theories simultaneously and exhaustively. Compare the two strategies. Which do you think is the most effective for (i) evaluating the theories (ii) producing findings useful for policy and practice application?

Theories of suicide

Durkheim's Sociological Theory

Egoistic suicide is caused by "excessive individualism." It varies inversely with the degree of integration of the social groups of which the individual forms a part.
(a) Suicide varies inversely with the degree of integration of religious, domestic and political society.
(b) Political and national crises increase the degree of integration.

Altruistic suicide, the opposite of egoistic suicide, is caused by "insufficient individuation."

Anomic suicides are caused by insufficient social regulation of individual activities. (This cause is independent of excessive or insufficient individuation.)
(a) Suicide varies directly with the rapidity of economic change.
(b) For men, anomic suicide varies directly with the rate of divorce.

The above causes may be combined with one another to produce composite types. Characteristics of several types may be united in a single suicide. Durkheim lists the combined types as egoistic-anomic, egoistic-altruistic, and anomic-altruistic.

Each social group has a collective inclination for the act of suicide. "It is made up of the currents of egoism, altruism or anomy running through the society under consideration. . . ." (Durkheim, 1951:299)

DeCatanzaro's Sociobiological Theory

1. Suicide is tolerated by evolutionary selection when it has no effects on the gene pool. Suicide of individuals who are relatively incapable of passing their genes to future generations would not be selected against by biological evolution.
2. Suicide is due to the extraordinary development of learning and cultural evolution so that human behavior is rendered independent of biological constraints of evolution.
3. Suicide is due to the breakdown of adaptive mechanisms in extremely stressful novel environments, i.e., environments other than those in which human nature was moulded.
4. Kin and group selection: in limited circumstances, suicide is tolerated by evolution when it has beneficial effects on other surviving individuals who share the suicide's genes.
5. In summary, self-destructive behavior patterns each involve complex synergies of culture, stress and diathesis [predisposition]; the synergies overlap but differ for the various patterns. (deCatanzaro, 1981:11)

Theories of pornography

The Feminist Theory

1. Pornography expresses patriarchal (dominance of men over women) attitudes toward women—their objectification, degradation, and sexual assaultability.
2. The link between male sexuality and aggression toward women derives from men's learning of patriarchal values.
3. The effect of pornography on male consumers is to teach or reinforce patriarchal attitudes toward women—objectification, degradation, sexual assaultability.
4. The wider the availability of pornography, the higher the rates of incest, rape, and sexual assault of women.

5. As challenges to the social and sexual dominance of men over women increase, the amount and violence of pornography increases as a form of political backlash.

The "Liberal" Theory

1. Pornography is an expression of sexuality. Sexuality has traditionally been suppressed, at least in Western societies.
2. Any link between sexuality and aggression toward the other sex is accidental.
3. The effect of pornography on its consumers is to release their repressed sexuality harmlessly.
4. The wider the availability of pornography, the lower the rates of incest, rape, and sexual assault of women and children by men.
5. As freedom of speech is extended in democratic societies, pornography becomes more widely available.

Theories of crime

Teevan's theory

Certainty, severity and celerity (swiftness) of punishment and criminality are negatively related. (Teevan, 1972:41)

Vold's Theory

1. The problem of criminological theory...is not primarily a concern with the explanation of the behavior as such, but rather concern with the question of why control of that behavior is attempted through law and police methods. (149)
2. Many aspects of the behavior penalized as criminal are quite directly and simply reflections of economic and cultural patterns common in the nation generally. (151)
3. There are categories of offenses in the U.S. (drunkenness and related offences, vagrancy and begging, gambling, prostitution, drug and narcotic law violation) that cannot be explained in terms of personality factors or presently known categories of individual differences.
4. The cultural definition of the behavior is not only antecedent to and the principal element in the explanation of the particular legal codes in effect, but cultural definitions similarly prescribe the role of how to be a criminal violator...(154)

5. Theories in terms of personality differences are quite inadeq rate and inapplicable for the explanation of the many important economic and cultural elements involved in these crimes.

6. ...The whole political process of law making, law breaking, and law enforcement becomes a direct reflection of deep-seated and fundamental conflicts between interest groups and their more general struggles for the control of the police power of the state.

7. There are many situations in which criminality is the normal, natural response of normal, natural human beings struggling in understandable normal and natural situations for the maintenance of the way of life to which they stand committed.

8. Group conflict is strictly limited to those kinds of situations in which the individual criminal acts flow from the collision of groups whose members are loyally upholding the in-group position. (Vold, 1958)

Sutherlands's Theory

The problem in criminology is to explain the criminality of behavior as such. Criminal behavior is a part of human behavior, has much in common with non-criminal, and must be explained with the same general framework as any other human behavior.

The following paragraphs state...a genetic theory of criminal behavior on the assumption that a criminal act occurs when a situation appropriate for it, as defined by the person, is present.

1. Criminal behavior is learned.

2. Criminal behavior is learned in interaction with other persons in a communication.

3. The principal part of the learning of criminal behavior occurs within intimate personal groups.

4. When criminal behavior is learned, the learning includes
   (a) techniques of committing the crime, which are sometimes very complicated, sometimes very simple;
   (b) the specific direction of motives, drives, rationalizations, and attitudes.

5. The specific directions of motives and drives is learned from definitions of the legal codes as favorable or unfavorable.

6. A person becomes delinquent because of an excess of definitions favorable to violation of law over definitions unfavorable to violation of law.

This is the principle of differential association. It refers to both criminal and anticriminal associations and has to do with counteracting forces. When persons become criminal, they do so because of contacts with criminal patterns and also because of isolation from anticriminal patterns.

7. Differential associations may vary in frequency, duration, priority, and intensity.
8. The process of learning criminal behavior by association with criminal and anticriminal patterns involves all of the mechanisms that are involved in any other learning.
9. While criminal behavior is an expression of general needs and values, it is not explained by those general needs and values, since noncriminal behavior is an expression of the same needs and values. (Sutherland, 1947:6-7).

Hirschi and Selvin's theory of delinquency

1. The larger the family, the more likely the child is to become delinquent.
2. Criminality among other members of the family is fairly strongly related to delinquency.
3. Church attendance is negatively related to delinquency.
4. No good evidence has been collected to suggest that club membership is related to delinquency, either positively or negatively.
5. Poor workers are more likely than good workers to be delinquent.
6. Delinquency is negatively related to social class.
7. Taken as a whole, these studies suggest a relation between poverty and delinquency.
8. Employment of the mother outside the home is not related to delinquency.
9. There is no relation between health and delinquency.
10. The better the child's performance in school, the less likely he is to become delinquent.
11. Truancy and delinquency are highly related.
12. Children from broken homes are at least slightly more likely than children from intact homes to become delinquent. (Hirschi and Selvin, 1967:25)

Theories of prisons

Cousineau and Veevers' theory

The size of prison populations might be expected to vary directly with changes in the crime rate, in the processes of detection and conviction, in the disposition of convictions, in the length of sentences, and in the use of parole to modify the length of sentences. (Cousineau and Veevers, 1972:237)

Vogel's theory of prisons

The overall trends and year-by-year correspondence between economic conditions and imprisonment establish quite clearly the relationship between capitalism and incarceration—prisons under capitalism are, as Marx pointed out long ago, dumping grounds for the industrial reserve army. In very few respects are the social consequences of the un- and underemployment of people under capitalism as clear as they are in the fluctuations of the prison population. . . .

The relationship between economic relief and incarceration was inverse—the more money that was spent on economic relief, the lower the rate of incarceration. This special relationship, like the overall relationship between unemployment and incarceration, underscores the economic basis of the prison question in America.

The heavy concentration of minority people in prison should come as no surprise in view of this simple fact: the unemployment rate of black males is typically twice that of white males. . . . The predictable result of this differential oppression is a disproportion of national minority people in America's prisons. . . .

The three waves of [prison] uprisings—1929-1930, 1952-1955, and 1968-1971—all took place during periods of economic recession and immediately after periods of relative prosperity when both the rate of new prisoners received and total prisoner populations were relatively low and stable. In all three periods the massive uprisings took place when the prisons of the nation were beginning to fill up again.

During these periods of rapid influx, the prisoner population undergoes significant changes. Masses of young people in the prime of life are being dumped into prison by the economic pressures of the stagnant economy, and they are more likely to react against the oppression.

During the initial periods of build-up, the prisons are least prepared to handle these people.

In short, economic crises in capitalist society at large lead to
massive incarcerations, which in turn lead to penal crises. (Vogel,
1983:34, 37, 38-39)

Scott and Scull's theory of penal reform

Penal practices appear to follow a cyclical, vacillating pattern
between comparatively enlightened humane treatment and treatment which is brutal and repressive.

It is our hypothesis that society's treatment of its criminal members
at any given time is probably a function of (a) the size of the surplus
labor force at that time; and, (b) related to this, the extent of the
demand for labor. During periods when the surplus labor force is
large, and the demand for labor small, the methods employed for
dealing with criminals tend to be brutal and repressive; conversely,
when the surplus labor force is small or non-existent, and the demand
for labor large, social reform movements develop which emphasize
what are said to be more humane, considerate methods of treatment
and care.

At least two mechanisms link economic conditions to penal practices. The first is direct, by virtue of the fact that criminals comprise a
'captive' group which can serve as a source of labor to be exploited
during periods of economic growth, and controlled and repressed
during periods of social unrest accompanying downswings in the
economic cycle. The second is indirect, by virtue of the effects which
economic depression and labor surplus have on public attitudes
about the value of human life. (Scott and Scull, 1978)

Theories of voting

Hartman's theory

"The emotional political appeal is a better vote-getting instrument
than the rational political appeal." (Hartman, 1936:113)

Terry and Schultz's theory

1. Social class influences party preferences.
2. Age influences party preference.
3. Religious affiliation influences party choice.
4. Ethnicity influences party preference.

5. Males tend to vote NDP more than women, while women are more likely to vote Conservative than men.
6. The NDP and Liberal party have greater success among urban than among rural voters; the Conservative and Social Credit party do better in rural areas and small urban centres, respectively.
7. Region is related to party choice.
8. The tendency to vote for any particular party is strengthened by previous identification with that party.
10. A voter's level of knowledge and information influence his party preference. (Terry and Schultz, 1973)

Brodie and Jensen's theory

Canada's federal party system provides a somewhat perplexing case for students of politics in liberal democracies. Some sociological theory, drawing on Western European experience in particular, predicts that as changes in social structure induced by urbanization and industrialization occur, the traditional electoral cleavages of religion, language and region are eroded by the politics of class. In so-called "modernized" party systems, class cleavages delineate the electoral support base of the parties as well as their major policies and electoral platforms. From this perspective, then, the Canadian federal party system does not appear to have modernized. Instead, religion, language and region—each considered to be a traditional electoral cleavage—continue to mark the partisan division of the Canadian electorate. In addition, the programs and policies of the Liberal and Progressive Conservative parties, the two major parties in the federal system, reveal few real and consistent differences in the class interests that they claim to protect and advance. Both depict themselves as guardians of the "national interest". The result is that they are most clearly distinguished by the differences in electoral support that they gain from Canada's major ethnic groups and regions. (Brodie and Jenson, 1981:189)

Karlins and Abelson's theory of persuasion

Opinions that people make known to others are harder to change than opinions they hold privately.

People who are most attached to a group are probably least influenced by communications that conflict with group norms.

The impact of a persuasive appeal is enhanced by requiring active, rather than passive, participation by the listener. (Karlins and Abelson, 1970)

CHAPTER 4

Causal Theorizing and Research Hypotheses

CHAPTER CONTENTS

4.1 THEORY AND HYPOTHESIS

The connecting links between a theory and a research project are research hypotheses. The theories discussed so far are broad in scope but limited in detail. Research hypotheses are versions of theories poorer in scope but richer in explicit detail. Theories state what any and every instance of a process should look like. Research hypotheses state what the process should look like in particular times and places.

EXAMPLE: The class theory of juvenile delinquency states that as the social class of neighbourhoods decline their delinquency rates will increase. The research hypothesis version might state that between 1960 and 1985 (a particular time period), for communities in Metropolitan Toronto (a particular set of communities), where average family incomes have declined from 50% above the poverty level to less than 5% above it (a particular level of decline in the cause social class of neighbourhoods), juvenile delinquency rates will increase by 10% or more (a particular level of increase in an effect).

Getting from theory to research hypotheses involves "detailing," or *specification*. There are conventions for what to specify and how to make the specification. These provide a practical check list of the work involved in planning the evaluation of a theory by means of observation.

The smallest part of a process theory useful to specify is a simple causal theory like the ones discussed in the previous chapter. These simple causal theories concentrate on one central effect and its causes; they ignore the influence that the central effect might have on its causes or on other effects.

EXAMPLE: In the simple theory of crime, changes in unemployment are seen to cause changes in crime, but those changes in crime that might cause changes in unemployment are ignored.

EXAMPLE: In simple theories of immigration, higher wages for professional labour in the United States causes emigration of Canadian professionals, but the influence of the emigration on wages in Canada and the States is ignored.

EXAMPLE: Simple theories of divorce see increases of divorce rates to be caused by liberalization of divorce laws, but they ignore any influence that higher divorce rates might have on changes in the law.

4.2 SPECIFYING SIMPLE CAUSAL THEORIES

For simple causal theories, the items below have to be specified:
1. an effect
2. a list of causes
3. *how* the effect is influenced by the cause (the "direction" of the relation between each cause and the effect)
4. *how much* the effect is influenced by each cause (the "strength" of causal determination of the effect)

---

*(These theories are sometimes referred to as *recursive* causal theories because the causal process is seen to be recurring (happening over and over again), with no alternation of cause and effect status: effects remain effects, and causes remain causes.)

5. one or more types of case the theory applies to
6. the time frame of the causal determination process
1. Specification of the effect is the most important part of any simple causal theory, since all other information in the theory revolves around it. The critical part of specifying an effect is *detailing its 'variability' and how it changes over time*. Much of the specification is common sense.

EXAMPLE: The variability of smoking behaviour may be specified as "smoking/non-smoking." Among cigarette smokers the variability might be specified in terms of number smoked per day.

EXAMPLE: The variability of crime may be specified in terms of (a) the frequency of the occurrence of legally prohibited behaviour, (b) the number or proportion of individuals apprehended for such behaviour, (c) categories or types of crime in a particular country, (d) variation in these categories in different countries, and so on.

EXAMPLE: Variability in economic systems can be specified in terms of types of productive units, the types of things produced, the rate of productivity of the system, the type of consumption units, the rate of consumption, the proportions of workers and managers, the rates of strikes, lockouts and boycotts, and so on.

EXAMPLE: Variability in relations between the sexes can be specified in terms of the division of reproductive and productive labour, the equality of access and incumbency in different types of occupations, the division of income, rates of wife battery, rates of sexual assault, rates of prosecution for these crimes, and rates of marriage and divorce.

2. For causes as for effects, it is essential to specify the variability of a cause and to detail how it changes. An important aspect of this specification is the qualitative and quantitative dimensions. Changes in quantitative causes and effects are increases or decreases. Changes in qualitative causes and effects are category changes or classification changes (e.g., employed—unemployed, single—married—divorced, member—non-member, guilty—innocent, citizen—immigrant.)
3. *How* an effect is influenced by a cause specifies what kind of change (increase or decrease or category change) in an effect is expected for a given change (increase or decrease or category change) in a cause.

Where both the cause and the effect are quantitative, the terms positive or negative can be used to describe how an effect is influenced by a cause. If an increase in a cause brings an increase in an effect (or a decrease brings a decrease), the direction of the relationship is said to be positive. If a decrease in a cause brings an increase in an effect (or an increase brings a decrease), the direction is said to be negative, or inverse.

EXAMPLE: Amount of education is often thought of as a cause of amount of income: the higher the education, the higher the income, or education is positively related to income.

EXAMPLE: The social class theory of crime and delinquency postulates that the lower the social class of a neighbourhood, the higher the crime and delinquency rate. In this case social class is said to be negatively or inversely related to crime and delinquency.

Where either the cause or the effect is a qualitative variable, the terms positive and negative have no meaning, so the categories of the qualitative variable have to be specified in order to describe how the effect is influenced.

EXAMPLE: Sex is a qualitative variable, and wages are quantitative. In order to describe how sex influences wages we have to say that men have higher wages than women.

If both cause and effect are qualitative, describing the influence of the cause on the effect requires using the categories of both cause and effect.

EXAMPLE: The influence of union membership on political party preference might be described by the statement "union members vote more frequently for the New Democrats than for Liberals, Conservatives or other parties." This is equivalent to the statement that non-members of unions more frequently vote for Liberals, Conservatives, and other political parties than for New Democrats.

How a cause influences an effect is crucial for application purposes. It communicates what kind of change in the cause variable is necessary in order to bring about a desired change in the effect.

EXAMPLE: If a major cause of employee turnover is the number of overtime hours, it is essential to know whether increasing or decreasing the overtime will increase or decrease the turnover rate.

Even where the causes are qualitative variables, like sex, that cannot be easily changed, direction information is necessary to policy application.

EXAMPLE: For example, where sexual discrimination is a cause of wage inequality, the direction of the relationship between sex and average wages (women's higher or lower than men's) must be known. Because even though sex cannot be changed, discrimination can. The direction of the relationship will determine whether anti-discrimination policies (such as affirmative action) will attempt to improve the wage situation of women or of men.

The specification of the direction of the relationship between cause and effect is essential for evaluating possible errors in methods when researching a theory. If the direction of relationship observed is different than expected, this is a signal for either rethinking the theory, re-examining the methods, or both.

4. Stating the relative influence of each cause on an effect often takes the form of an informal ranking of the causes from the most to the least influential. Causes with even less influence are omitted from the list altogether. The basis for deciding to include or exclude items from a list of causes is an estimate of relative causal influence.

A more formal specification might take the form of stating that a cause determines an effect totally, strongly, moderately, weakly, trivially, or not at all. A formal ranking using numbers might take 100 to represent the complete determination of an effect. If a cause accounted for half of the variation in an effect, it would be said to have 50% determination of the effect. Each cause would be assigned a percentage to express the strength of its determination of the effect.

One final point on detailing the relative strength of causal determination. The simple listing of causes of an effect assumes that the influence of each cause can be simply *added* to the influence of another. A list of causes can be thought of as containing implicit plus signs: cause 1 + cause 2 + cause 3 determine the effect. This kind of theory may be referred to as additive. There is another possibility: the influence of one cause may *multiply* the influence of another. This possibility is specially important where some of the causes are qualitative variables.

EXAMPLE: A familiar example is the age and sex of drivers as causes of traffic accidents. Generally, adolescent and young adult drivers have higher traffic accident rates than older drivers; male drivers have higher rates than female. The accident rates for young male drivers, however, is much higher than would be predicted on the basis of merely adding the influence of age and sex together. The influence on traffic accident rates of being male seems to multiply the influence of being young.

As stated above, listing causes is the convention for indicating that the theorist is assuming that causal influences are additive. If multiplicative causal influences are to be postulated, explicit means of indicating this will have to be employed.

5. The type of case the causal theory applies to must be specified. To this point we have talked about causes and effects without directly specifying the type of case or unit of observation on which the causes and effects are to be observed. This kind of talk is not necessarily confusing because the causes and effects can plausibly be thought of as operating at one or more levels.

EXAMPLE: Juvenile delinquency can be seen as a characteristic or attribute of an individual, a neighbourhood, a community, an ethnic or racial group, a province, or a country.

EXAMPLE: Sex can be seen as an attribute of individuals, groups, organizations, occupations, or communities.

EXAMPLE: Unemployment can be thought of as a feature of a country, a region, an industry, an occupation, a profession, a level of education, a community, a corporation, or a person.

In everyday conversation the type of case referred to may be implicit and assumed or made partly explicit through the use of masculine and feminine pronouns. The investigation of individuals is quite a different undertaking from the investigation of occupations, which is quite different from nations. For research purposes, then, the type of case must be specified.

Specifying the type of case the theory applies to is a serious research decision, and major choices are involved. One way of thinking about the choices is in terms of the *level of aggregation*.

EXAMPLE: In social science the individual person is ordinarily the lowest, or "zero level," of aggregation used. Many other types of cases such as families, groups, or clubs, are seen as aggregates of individuals. These aggregates may be aggregated again into neighbourhoods or communities, and these aggregated yet again into cities, regions, provinces, countries, empires, blocks of nations, continents, or worlds.

EXAMPLE: Types of jobs may be aggregated into occupations, groups of occupations into industries, industries into sectors and sectors into economies.

The choice of a level of aggregation is fundamental—it sets boundaries on virtually every research design option. Researching a causal theory of unemployment or reproduction on individuals will be a much different job from researching it on a community, region, religious group, nation, or other aggregate. Cause variables as well as effect variables may be transformed from qualitative to quantitative.

EXAMPLE: Being unemployed and being pregnant are observable as qualitative attributes of an individual: you either have a job or you don't; you can't be a "little bit pregnant." At a higher level of aggregation, however, these qualitative attributes become observable as quantitative. Unemployment or pregnancy rates in a community may vary from 0% to 100% of the aggregate of individuals at risk and both can increase or decrease.

In addition, causes important to the way aggregates operate may be quite unimportant at the individual level.

EXAMPLE: The size of a nation's population, for example, may be an important determinant of level of development, but the size of an individual is unlikely to be an important cause of personal development. All the causes and effects in the theories under investigation must be specified as attributes of the type of case chosen.

6. It is essential to specify the time frame in which the causal determination process is thought to operate because it determines the minimum time boundaries for a research project. Causes may determine effects instantaneously or over considerable periods of time, but each specification must be at least plausible.

EXAMPLE: The causes of seasonal changes in suicide rates, for example, must themselves change seasonally. Business cycles usually occur over a number of years. The causes of these cycles must themselves be changing at roughly the same rate. A steady upward trend in crime rates over a decade cannot plausibly be caused by seasonal changes in unemployment rates. National rates of unemployment change by the day, week, season, and year, by business cycles (usually a few years in length), by decade, and by era. Any causal theory of unemployment changes would obviously have to specify which of the above time frames was being examined.

There is also the question of how long it takes for a change in a cause to bring about a change in an effect.

EXAMPLE: Unemployment may be a cause of crime, but since the Second World War in industrialized nations that have unemployment insurance and welfare systems, unemployment does not reduce a person's income to zero. To the degree that crime is promoted by severe income shortages, the changes in crime that are caused by changes in unemployment will not be instantaneous. They will lag by whatever time it takes for unemployment insurance, welfare, and other sources of income to be depleted.

The time frame specified then must, at a minimum, include the period necessary for observing a change in the cause and a change in the effect, plus the period necessary for the cause to work its influence on the effect.

4.3 RESEARCH HYPOTHESES

A simple causal theory, detailed as above, can be seen as a *composite hypothesis* that postulates that, for the type of case specified, within the time period specified, the specified changes or variation in the effect are determined by the specified changes or variation in the causes. Without the specification, the theory cannot be researched. Alternatively, we can say that any researching of a theory necessarily involves specification whether it is made explicit or not.

The composite hypothesis can be broken down into its components. Each cause paired with the effect constitutes a component hypothesis. Each of these postulates that, for the type of case specified, within the time period specified, (1) variation or change specified in the effect is *partly determined* by specified changes or variation in a cause, and (2) the form of the determination will correspond to the specified direction of relationship. A component hypothesis can be separated from its composite (theory) but not from what has to be assumed in order to research it. The tiresome reiteration of the term specification above emphasizes the importance of making the assumptions explicit. For each component hypothesis, the composite hypothesis is a statement of the assumptions involved in researching it. Single hypotheses, in other words, are always attached to a theory. Or we could say that hypotheses always come in sets.

A simple causal theory specified as above constitutes the minimum possible amount of detailing work for a research project. A research project may concentrate on a component hypothesis, but the implication of the theory is that all the causes must be dealt with in one way or another. Perhaps they can all be measured, or perhaps there is information for some time period and some cases about the values of three causes that permits the researcher to concentrate on the fourth. However the problem is solved (for it is largely a design problem from here on), the researcher must manage to research the composite as well as any component. Of course it might be argued that there are matters of strategy involved here. A researcher might reasonably ignore less important causes while investigating the causes postulated to be the strongest. But it would seem like folly to investigate weaker causes of an effect while ignoring the stronger.

4.4 SPECIFYING LESS SIMPLE CAUSAL THEORIES

In the specification of simple theories, causal relations among the set of causes is mostly ignored. The causes, however, may influence not only the central effect, but also other causes in the list. One less simple specification would detail the influences among a set of causes (of the effect of interest). This specification can be carried out like that already discussed. Such a specification will also consider whether the direction and strength of the relationships among the causes correspond to expectations.

EXAMPLE: Causes may be distinguished from each other by how immediate or direct they are as determinants of the effect. The social class of a juvenile's parents might be a cause of the juvenile's committing crimes, but it is probably a less direct cause than the activities and friendships of the juvenile, and the opportunities he or she encounters for criminal activities. Parental social class then might be seen as a direct cause of the juvenile's peer friendships but an indirect cause of his or her delinquent behaviour.

EXAMPLE: The degree of industrialization and the system of labour-management relations in a country are possible causes of strikes and lockouts, but they are less direct causes than the wage, promotion, hiring and retirement policies followed by the corporations or the militancy of the unions involved.

Where causes differ in the immediacy of their determination of an effect, it is common to think of "chains" of causation. Indirect causes determine the direct causes, which in turn determine the effect. Direct causes may be spoken of as "intervening" causes, and said to intervene between the effect and its indirect causes.

$$A \rightarrow B \rightarrow C$$

B is an effect of A; B is a *direct* cause of C
A is an *indirect* cause of C
B is an intervening cause between A and C

More difficult to handle are those theories where simple specification requires the researcher to ignore important aspects of the way a process works. The cost of simplicity here is too high. Simple specifications will not serve as useful guides for research where one is interested in an effect that becomes an important and immediate cause of changes in one or more of its determinants. This situation is sometimes represented as a causal arrow with two points. If two variables D and E alternated their causal status, this relationship would be represented as $D \longleftrightarrow E$.

A
B $\rightarrow$ (D $\longleftrightarrow$ E)
C

D is a cause of E; E is a cause of D
A, B and C are causes of D and E

EXAMPLE: Berelson and Steiner's theory states that "prejudice and discrimination against minority groups are partly maintained by a reinforced spiral of built-in cause and effect: the disapproved group is deprived, and as a result of the deprivation it is further disapproved" (Berelson and Steiner, 1964). Other statements in their theory identify causes of disapproval and deprivation.

This theory could be partially diagrammed as below.

Relative   prejudice
social $\rightarrow$ $\rightarrow$ (disapproval $\longleftrightarrow$ deprivation)
position   discrimination

The simplest of the less simple theories involves at least two variables that alternate as cause and effect. Specification of such theories requires (in addition to that required for simple theories) the following information:
1. two variables that alternate between cause and effect status.
2. the time period for one alternation of causal status.
3. how the effect is influenced by the cause and how it influences the cause. (Two directions are required for each pair.)

4. how much the effect is influenced by the cause and how much it influences the cause. (Two strengths are required for each pair.)

It should be clear that the amount of information to be detailed here is considerably larger than that required for a simple specification.

4.5 SUMMARY

Research hypotheses are detailed specifications of causal theories. For simple causal theories the researcher must specify (1) an effect, (2) a list of causes, (3) one or more types of case the theory applies to, (4) the time frame of the causal determination process, (5) *how* the effect changes when a cause changes, and (6) *how much* the effect changes when the cause changes.

Less simple causal theories involve variables that alternate between cause and effect status. Specification here requires (in addition to those items for simple theories) detailing (7) two variables that alternate between cause and effect status, (8) the time period for one alternation of causal status, (9) *how* the effect is influenced by the cause *and vice versa*, and (10) *how much* the effect is influenced by the cause and vice versa and the direction of the relation between cause and effect pairs (two are required for each pair), and (11) the relative importance of each cause and effect as determinants of the other.

4.6 EXERCISES

1.
   (a) From the exercises in chapter 3 select theory statements (or suitable portions of them) and specify them using the guidelines for simple causal theories outlined in this chapter. Where appropriate, do the specification for the community where you now live.
   (b) Change the level of aggregation of your specification. What other features will have to be re-specified?
   (c) Now change the time frame of your specification, forward or backward. What other features will have to be re-specified?

2. Select another example theory from those listed in chapter 3. Specify the time period you think would be required for a change in each cause to have an influence on the effect. What would a suitable time period for a project investigating the theory?

3. Select a multiple-statement example theory from the exercises of chapter 3 and, using arrow diagrams, diagram the cause and effect

relationships. Be sure to include any connections among the causes in your diagram.

4. Find an example theory statement from those listed in chapter 3 in which a pair (or larger group) of variables is considered to be "mutually determining" (that is, they alternate their status from cause to effect and back again). Diagram the theory using arrow diagrams.

5. Select a multiple statement theory from the exercises of chapter 3.
   (a) Rank the relative importance of the causes as determinants of the effect.
   (b) Briefly outline how you might research the hypotheses linking the two or three most important causes to the effect.
   (c) Choose one hypothesis containing a cause that you have ranked as relatively unimportant. Outline how (and when) you could justify a project focusing primarily on this hypothesis.

PART 2

RESEARCH PROJECT DESIGN

CHAPTER 5

Introduction to Research Project Design

CHAPTER CONTENTS

5.1 WHAT DRIVES RESEARCH?

Research is primarily *driven* by the need for information for policies and practices. People undertake research because they want to get a description of the relationships between causes and effects that will be useful for policy and practice application. Most often we want to know what happens to the effect when we change the cause. If we increase or decrease the cause (1) will the effect increase or decrease? and (b) by how much?

EXAMPLE: Studies of capital punishment and murders are undertaken in order to find out if capital punishment decreases the number of murders. Suppose a country has experienced an apparent increase in the number of murders. If the government introduces a death penalty for murder, will the murder rate decrease? And if it does, by how much will it decrease? And will any decrease be permanent or temporary?

EXAMPLE: Studies of human rights legislation and affirmative action are undertaken in order to determine if they decrease inequality. Will a bill of rights prohibiting discrimination decrease inequality in the workplace? Will preferential hiring of women or minority racial or ethnic groups reduce inequality? And if either or both reduce inequality, by how much will it be reduced? For how long will either have to be in effect to achieve equality?

The information about cause and effect relationships useful for policy application is commonly referred to as *Direction* and *Strength*. The direction of a causal relationship tells whether an increase in the cause increases or decreases the effect. The strength of a causal relationship tells by how much the effect will change for a given change in the cause. Research projects all have the goal of describing the direction and strength of causal relationships. Should more or less labour, more or less time, more or less money, more or less effort, more of one kind of activity, less of another, be applied to remedy the problem motivating the research? We might say that the goal of social research is to provide information useful for determining what policy options exist, and how effective they are likely to be.

5.2 WHAT CONDITIONS RESEARCH?

Though social research is driven by the need for information for the purpose of policies or practices, it is strongly *conditioned* by the need for *accuracy*. The reasons for this concern can be appreciated by considering what can happen as a result of basing a policy or practice on inaccurate findings. If research gets the direction of the relationship between a cause and an effect wrong, then any policy or practice based on the findings will have the opposite effect of what is desired.

EXAMPLE: Suppose research on capital punishment and the murder rate concludes incorrectly that capital punishment decreases the homicide rate, and a death penalty is introduced on the basis of the research. Since the research got the direction of relationship wrong, murders will continue at the same rate as before the death penalty, and the possibility of executing innocent people is increased.

EXAMPLE: If research on affirmative action programs incorrectly finds that such programs increase the amount of workplace inequality, then not instituting such programs will result in more inequality.

If research gets the strength of the relationship between a cause and effect wrong, then the policies and practices based on the research findings will be inefficient.

EXAMPLE: Suppose the introduction of a death penalty will actually reduce the homicide rate by .1%, but some research finds that the introduction of a death penalty will reduce the homicide rate by 10%. The error might lead to the introduction of a death penalty, where the accurate results would not. Furthermore, the change in the homicide rate after the death penalty was introduced will be much smaller than expected. In fact, no reduction might show up at all: causes that have such small influence on effects can easily be overwhelmed by changes in other more important causes.

EXAMPLE: Suppose that affirmative action programs actually have strong influence in decreasing the workplace inequality of women, but a research project finds weak or moderate influence. Based on the inaccurate research, the amount of resources necessary to correct the disadvantage of women would be overestimated. At the end of the period thought necessary for correcting the discrimination against women, the affirmative action program might be contributing to discrimination against men.

If the research gets both the strength and direction of causal relationship wrong, then a policy or practice based on it may be disastrous.

EXAMPLE: Suppose research showed incorrectly that destroying the police records of adolescents when they reached the age of majority permitted the adolescents to lead non-criminal lives, whereas in fact the adolescents without records increased their criminal activity, at least for a few years. A program of destroying juvenile records then would result, not in fewer criminal careers, but in higher crime rates as well as a reduced ability to apprehend and convict those whose records had been destroyed.

In short, the desire for accuracy in social science research is understandable: mistaken beliefs about how the world works lead to mistaken policies and practices designed to modify the world. Policies and practices based on inaccurate findings are ineffective, counterproductive, or worse.

5.3 THE PRINCIPLES OF REPETITION AND WEIGHT OF EVIDENCE

Can inaccurate research results be avoided? They could be if infallible or error-free methods existed, but as yet none have been discovered. It seems there are no infallible procedures, no error-free methods, no techniques that can be employed without the possibility of mistakes. If there are no perfect methods, then error-free findings cannot be guaranteed. Could very careful work with fallible methods guarantee accuracy? Apparently not: the history of social science is replete with careful research that was seen to be incorrect by later workers. Care is essential, of course, given that all methods are fallible, but it is not enough by itself to guarantee accurate findings.

EXAMPLE: In the 1950s the research team of Sheldon and Eleanor Glueck examined a sample of juvenile delinquents and found that many of their mothers worked outside the home. The Gluecks concluded (incorrectly) that mothers working outside the home was a cause of juvenile delinquency. It was shown later that in middle-class families, children of mothers employed outside the home were no more likely to be delinquent than the children of mothers who worked in the home. There was no technical misuse of research methods in the Gluecks' study.

Since error-free methods cannot be found, and careful work with fallible methods cannot by itself guarantee accuracy, researchers have adopted a strategy based on the *repetition* and *weight of evidence* principles.

The *repetition* principle directs researchers (and everyone else) to withhold their confidence in research findings until they are repeated. Until repeat findings are produced, it is impossible to know whether the findings are repeatable or not. If findings are not repeatable, it may be because the first set of findings was inaccurate. The general idea is quite simple: if no error is made in using a set of techniques to arrive at findings, then a repeat use of the same techniques ought to produce the same findings as the original (unless the identical error is repeated also). A third repetition ought to corroborate the first two, and so on. On the other hand, if errors are made in the original or repeat uses, then the findings will be different.

In other words the principle of repetition tells you do it again if you think you made a mistake. In effect it asks how you know if you made an error unless you can do it again. Whether an investigator thinks an error was made or not, repetition is a good idea. The principle is no more complicated than it sounds. It explains the amount of attention given to detailed description of research methods in social science reports. Without this description, detailed repetition by other researchers is not possible.

The *weight of evidence* principle is a technique for dealing with the possible diversity of findings that use of the repetition principle may produce. Five different studies may produce five different findings, or four similar and one different, or three similar and two different and so on. The principle says: the greater the agreement among repetitions, the greater the confidence in the accuracy of the repeated findings. Where findings are diverse and contradictory, the principle counsels witholding confidence in any of them while seeing which findings, if any, can be repeated. It should be noted that the weight of evidence principle doesn't direct that diverse findings should prevent changes being made in policy and practice. It does suggest that any changes be made very tentatively and the results monitored closely.

The strategy arises from observing scientific success and failure over the long run, as well as success and failure of changes in policy and practice based on the scientific findings. The strategy demands not only careful work, but detailed descriptions of research methods, critical evaluation of the uses to which any observational technique is put, and perhaps even scepticism about the possibilities of accuracy.

Both principles are apparently very simple, but there are a number of questions involved in applying them.

1. What counts as a repetition?

Projects by other researchers should be included, but what if the same person carries out the repetition? Should such a study be given as much weight as one carried out by someone different?

Should careful but informal observation that appears to be relevant count as a repetition?

Suppose the findings lead to a change in policy or practice; should the results of this application be counted as a repetition? Should this kind of evidence be given the same weight as formal research studies?

Repetition studies should all investigate the same effect variable, but if they investigate different causes do they count as repetitions? How many of the causes have to be the same?

If one study investigates an effect using individuals as cases, and a second investigates the same effect using families as cases, are they repetitions? If a third uses cities as cases, is it a repetition of either of the first two?

EXAMPLE: The Gluecks studied employed and non-employed mothers as a cause of juvenile delinquency. Another project examined social class as well as mothers' employment as causes of juvenile delinquency. Is the second project a repetition of the first?

EXAMPLE: One study found that the lower the social class origin of college students, the higher the prestige they assign to a teaching career. A second project found that the greater students' "readiness to learn," the more satisfied teachers will be with their professional status. Can these two projects be seen as repetitions?

EXAMPLE: One study compared the homicide rates of states with and without capital punishment for a five-year period. Another study compared homicide rates in these same states before and after capital punishment laws were introduced or abolished. A third study looked at variation in homicide rates before and after well-publicized executions for murder. Can any of these studies be regarded as repetitions?

2. How similar do the methods have to be in order for studies to be considered repetitions?

Should the same sample of cases be used in each repetition? Should identical measurement techniques be employed? Are identical data analysis procedures necessary? Does each of the cause and effect variables need to have the same ranges of variation in each repetition? If all methods are fallible, should similar findings produced by different methods be given more weight than those using identical methods?

EXAMPLE: Weber studied European state bureaucracies and concluded that formalized rules were an efficient way to organize the co-ordination of specialized tasks. Alvin Gouldner studied an industrial firm and concluded that bureaucratic rules were inefficient compromises between workers and management. Should these studies be considered to be repetitions?

EXAMPLE: Researchers investigating "human capital" theory examined the *supply* of skilled and unskilled workers and found that the higher the skill level of the workers, the better they were paid. They conclude that workers are rewarded better, the more they can offer in the workplace. Researchers examining the *demand* for workers find that there are restrictions on (a) the number of jobs paying higher wages and requiring skilled workers and on (b) the mobility of workers from "bad" to "good" jobs. Are these studies repetitions?

EXAMPLE: One study of blue-collar workers in a particular factory used questionnaire and interview responses to measure job satisfaction. A second study of the same factory measured job satisfaction using rates of lateness, absenteeism, sick leave, and employee turnover. Are these studies repetitions?

EXAMPLE: In the above example, the questionnaire and interview study found average job satisfaction was high, while the rates of absenteeism study found low rates of job satisfaction. Would you weight these studies equally?

3. How alike do the findings of repetition studies have to be in order to count as similar findings?

Obviously the direction of relationship between the cause and the effect has to be the same, but does the strength of each relationship have to be identical? What if two causes have the same strengths but two are different? What if the measured strengths are different, but the relative strengths are the same? What if one study investigates more causes than another?

Should different weights be given to very similar than to less similar repetitions?

EXAMPLE: One Canadian study of jobs found that for each year of increased education, wages increased an average of 5%, but male workers got on average 40% more than women. Another study found that a year of education was worth 8% more wages on average and being male was worth 17% more than being female, but that workers with a European background got an average of 45% more wages than workers of native background. Do you think these two sets of findings should be regarded as similar?

The kind of questions discussed above lead to three versions of the repetition principle: *replication, triangulation,* and *extension* principles. These principles advise that confidence in the accuracy of findings should be withheld until replication, triangulation, and extension repetitions are produced. This development of the repetition principle is required because there are at least three sources of inaccurate findings that have to be guarded against.

Replication usually refers to a repetition that is a detailed replica of another study, except for the sample. Replication guards against findings that are unique to a particular sample. If the procedures in a second study are exact duplicates of those used in a first study, then the findings ought to be exact duplicates also, unless the findings of the first study were unique to the sample.

EXAMPLE: One medical researcher finds that after a specified dose of acetylsalicylic acid (aspirin) was administered to a sample of high school runners who reported shin splints, 73% reported reduced discomfort. A second researcher following the replication principle obtained another sample of high school runners who reported shin splints, administered the same dose of aspirin, and then obtained reports of discomfort. The second researcher found that 78% reported reduced discomfort. Can any part of the findings be seen as unique to each sample?

The *triangulation* principle was formulated because there are inaccuracies that replication alone cannot guard against. For example, if a study used a method incorrectly or the findings were a product of the particular methods used, an exact replication of the project (on a different sample) would only reproduce the error. The two studies would support the conclusion that the findings were not a unique product of the sample but would not guard against the possibility that the findings were a peculiar outcome of the methods employed.

Triangulation ordinarily refers to a repetition study in which the causes and effects investigated are the same, but different procedures are employed. The sample of cases may or may not be the same. If similar findings are produced by repetition studies that use some different procedures, it may be concluded that the findings are not unique to the procedures employed in any of the studies.

EXAMPLE: A third medical researcher suspects that the first and second samples of shin-splint sufferers in the example above would have reported reduced discomfort if given anything that a doctor claimed would work. Selecting a third sample of shin splint victims, the researcher administers starch pills in place of aspirin. Thirty-four % of the third sample report reduced discomfort. What would you conclude about the accuracy of the findings of the first two researchers? How would you combine the methods of the first two projects and the third into a single study?

EXAMPLE: A fourth researcher suspects that since discomfort was measured only with self-reports, the findings of the first three researchers might be partly the result of inaccurate measurement of pain severity, so infra-red sensors are used in addition to self-reports to ascertain the severity of the shin pain before administering a pain remedy. In addition to aspirin and starch pills, some runners are given no treatment. The sub-sample of runners given each treatment were chosen randomly. Eighty % of those given aspirin, 40% of those given starch pills, and 25% of those given no treatment reported reduced discomfort. What do these findings suggest about the accuracy of the first three studies? What use could be made of the measurements of discomfort based on infrared sensors?

Note that care is required in the use of triangulation because every research project involves the use of a combination of procedures. Which of the procedures are likely to be sources of error (and therefore worth triangulating) depends on what is being investigated, as well as on the other procedures used. In the above shin-splint example, the researchers concentrated on the accuracy of the measurement of the pain and the percentage reporting reduced discomfort. No attention was given to other sample characteristics, other measurement problems, or data analysis procedures.

The triangulation principle was formulated because there are inaccuracies that replication alone cannot guard against. The extension principle was formulated because replication and triangulation are necessarily limited to re-investigations of hypotheses. Resources devoted to replications and triangulations are resources that cannot be used for examining other hypotheses from the alternative theories under investigation. Extension refers to a repetition study that examines extensions of the theories already investigated. It directs researchers to withhold their confidence in the findings of research on alternative theories until some significant part of the potential formulations and derivations explicit or implicit in them have been investigated.

Extension studies can be done in three basic ways: (1) effects are investigated as causes, (2) causes are examined as effects, (3) hypotheses investigated on one type of case are investigated on other types of case (which usually requires some reformulation of the hypotheses). Are hypotheses that are accurate for families, say, also accurate for communities (and vice versa)? Are political theories that are accurate for national states also accurate for municipal governments? Are theories of bureaucracy accurate for the workers in the bureaucracy?

EXAMPLE: The feminist theory of patriarchy suggests that some time in the prehistory of human society, men established a patriarchy, a structure of relations that prevented women from participating fully in the major institutions of human communities. It points also to the historical and contemporary manifestations of patriarchy. It suggests the possibility of matriarchal and egalitarian social organization in ancient and contemporary preliterate communities. It provides a set of postulates about what kind of changes will be easy to accomplish and what kind will not. It provides hypotheses about how patriarchy was maintained in recent historical times in spite of challenges. It suggests hypotheses about where political opposition to women's equality and liberation will come from, how it will be organized and financed, and what its tactics and ideology will be.

In one sense the feminist theory of patriarchy is very simple: it postulates that the subordination of women to men in historical and contemporary human society is a social conspiracy. On the other hand, the observable manifestations of the patriarchy theory are perhaps innumerable. The principle of extension directs the withholding of confidence in the theory of patriarchy until a good number of its possible formulations are stated, debated, researched, and shown to be better than alternative explanations of the same things. (At the same time, a lot of earlier work that ignored women will have to be redone in the light of the challenge of feminist theories.)

EXAMPLE: The "labelling" theory of crime postulates that the activities of authorities in apprehending and processing individuals through the criminal justice system is an important cause of subsequent criminal activity by these individuals. The effect of the processing is to label some individual lawbreakers publicly so that subsequent criminality is encouraged by the fact that some of their non-criminal options are cut off. It points to patterns in the activities of police forces, courts, and prisons as perpetuators, if not provocateurs, of criminal activity. The larger community is also implicated through its co-operation or lack of co-operation with the authorities. In short, the labelling theory of crime points to observable patterns of behaviour in law administration, policing, police policy, adjudication, sentencing policy, prison policy, and even the social psychology of apprehended and non-apprehended lawbreakers as both causes and effects of crime. Clearly until a good number of these phenomena are investigated, it is justifiable on the principle of extension to withhold confidence in the accuracy of labelling theory.

5.4 EXISTING RESEARCH LITERATURE AND PROJECTS

In the long run the replication, triangulation, and extension principles are complementary, though they may be contradictory in the short run. Each research report represents different amounts of attention to the three principles. The collection of all these project reports constitutes a literature—a mixture of extensions, replications, and triangulations that develops around the search for information on which to base policy and practice. A literature includes all sources of information on the question addressed. In addition to work that sees itself as social scientific research, census materials, government survey reports, government commission reports, labour, business and consumer reports, and statistics, international organization reports, judicial inquiries, histories, textbooks, newspapers and magazines and policy and practice statements in any form should be included.

The reason for being inclusive rather than exclusive in defining a literature is entirely practical. A review of the literature is the information foundation on which research projects are designed. The more inclusive the literature reviewed, the better the information from which new projects can be planned. There is no point in replicating studies that have already been adequately replicated, triangulating studies already adequately triangulated, or extending studies already adequately extended.

EXAMPLE: "An examination of existing published reference sources... indicated that the field of Canadian criminal justice history could be defined as encompassing an immense range of substantive topics, an abbreviated list of which might include: the history of policing and law enforcement; the history of crime, deviance, and dependency; the history of the legal profession, the courts, and the administration of criminal justice; the history of forms of 'private justice' (such as duelling and vigilantism); the history of civil disobedience, labour unrest, and rebellion (such as the Winnipeg General Strike or the Riel Rebellion)." (Smandych and others, 1987:x)

A second reason for defining a literature inclusively rather than narrowly is as an aid to common sense. Each of the groups that contribute to a literature—academic researchers, government workers, consumers, producers, labour, managers, lobby groups, journalists, and so on, have preoccupations that need to be put in perspective. Academic researchers as a matter of professional training may be more interested in precision of measurement, for example, than an informed common sense would warrant. It is important to counter this preoccupation with the views of managers, workers, and consumers whose concern with accuracy of measurement is practical: large differences always affect practice and policy decisions; small differences, no matter how precise, usually do not.

5.5 DESIGN DECISIONS I: REPLICATION, TRIANGULATION, EXTENSION

A very important decision researchers make in planning their projects is whether to design a replication study, a triangulation study, an extension study, or some combination of these.

1. If a replication only study is chosen, the research is left with only one design decision: how to choose a sample of cases and time periods. All the other design decisions have already been made by the researcher whose study is being replicated.

EXAMPLE: A replication study of the impact on employment of technological change (computer use) in the financial industry of a middle-sized Quebec city has only one design decision to make: what other city or cities should be chosen as the sample cases for the research. All the other design decisions have been made: what time period before and after the introduction of computers to use, measurement of the "amount" of use, how to measure employment in the financial industry before and after computers are introduced, how to measure employment increases in industries directly related to the financial industry, and what methods to use to analyse the results.

2. If a triangulation only study is chosen, most design decisions are also already made. The researcher need only decide how to select a sample, which additional measurement or data analysis techniques will be used in the triangulation, and how to do the data analysis and triangulation.

EXAMPLE: A study of food prices concluded that the greater the competition between big food retail chains in the city or region, the lower the average price of a standard food basket. If a triangulation is planned, the researcher needs only to select a sample of regions or cities—which could be the same as in the initial study. Since many, if not all, of the measurements done in the first study will also be done in the triangulation, few design decisions are involved here. If the researchers are suspicious of the measurement of competition and the standardized food basket, they will have to decide what other indicators exist or can be created, and how to apply them.

3. If an extension only study is chosen *all* design decisions have to be made.

EXAMPLE: The theory of retail competition and prices points to three medium- and long-run outcomes of price competition: (a) competition stabilizes and prices remain low, (b) one of the competitors wins, the others lose, and the winner gains a monopoly, (c) the competitors form a oligopoly, which usually amounts to an agreement that they will stop competing in prices and that each will accept a negotiated share of the business. For outcomes (b) and (c) prices will not remain low; indeed they are likely to rise until the profits lost in the earlier competition are made up and to stay high as long as there is no competition. A study of the medium- and long-run outcome of the retail competition in the previous example would be an extension study. The researcher would have to decide what time periods to choose, what sample of cities or regions to observe, how to measure the outcome (monopoly, oligopoly, or stable competition) of earlier "unstable" competition, how to measure prices, how to measure changes in food preferences, how to control for inflation, how to control for price changes that are not related to competition in the sample markets, and so on. Finally, the procedures for analysing the measurements would have to be designed.

The choice among replication, triangulation, and extension will be made on the basis of a critical review of a literature. I advised above that the literature should be inclusive rather than narrow, but how inclusive? There are no rules here other than common sense. Textbook tables of contents, bibliographies, and card catalogues can be initial guides to the categories of literature to search. (Of course, the review process, once started, will provide the means for modifying these initial guides, because most reports include references to other parts of the literature.)

How is a critical review carried out? Common sense will be adequate for all but the most technical matters. You want to end up being able to recognize which findings are strong enough to base policy and practice on, and which are not. They might be divided into four groups:

1. findings that need *no* further investigation
2. findings that need *some* further investigation
3. findings that need *a lot of* further investigation
4. questions that have not yet been directly addressed in the literature.

Have the findings been sufficiently replicated? Count the replications and note particularly the variation in them. Have the findings been sufficiently triangulated? Again, count them and note if the triangulations change the results a lot or a little. Replicated and triangulated findings with *little* variation in the results may be judged to need *no* further investigation. The less the replication and triangulation, or the greater the variation in them, the greater the need for further replication and triangulation investigations. Has a theory been sufficiently extended? Note how many important questions have *not* been directly investigated. The greater the number of important uninvestigated questions, the greater the need for extension studies. When replication, triangulation, and extension are all in short supply, the greater the need is for studies that combine these features. In short, apply the *weight of evidence* principle to the collective body of work reviewed. Design a study that is most likely to produce the information that is needed for policy and practice applications.

5.6 REQUIREMENTS FOR EVALUATING
HYPOTHESES BY OBSERVATION

It was argued above that a very important decision regarding project design is whether to design a replication, triangulation, extension, or combination study. The next most important decision is how the actual project will be done. The decision has many facets because a large number of details have to be designed and executed. In one sense the many details constitute a single decision because each detail is related to all the others, but they can be grouped into four main sets of decisions. Each set corresponds to one of the requirements for making conclusions about hypotheses on the basis of observations.

Recall the goal of research—to produce descriptions of the relationships between causes and effects that are useful for policy and practice application. We want to know what will happen if we increase or decrease a cause: will the effect increase or decrease, and by how much?

EXAMPLE: *Prevention* magazine (April, 1988:112) reported, "Women who consumed the recommend dietary allowance of calcium (800 milligrams per day) decreased their risk of high blood pressure by 22 percent compared to women who consumed less than 400 mg. per day."

This statement reports the relationship found between the *measurements* of a cause (calcium consumption per day) and the *measurements* of an effect (risk of high blood pressure). Both measurements were done on a *sample* of women. The example makes it clear that in order to describe a relationship between a cause and an effect a sample of cases is needed and each case in the sample has to be *measured*. But two other things are also necessary. First, note the *different values* of the cause (800 mg/day and less than 400 m/day) and the *different values* of the effect (difference in risk of high blood pressure) stated in the conclusion. These values are crucial parts of the description of the relationship between the cause and the effect.

Second, note that the relationship between the measurements is *summarized*: the risks of blood pressure of the high- and low-calcium consumers is not reported, but the difference between them is. The summary takes this form for entirely practical reasons: it tells what happens to the effect when the cause is changed: increasing the cause decreases the effect. By how much? Doubling the cause (from 400 to 800 mg/day) decreases the effect by 22%.

EXAMPLE: According to Overton (1988), the Newfoundland government of the 1930s attempted to limit its spending on relief (welfare). The level of payouts to the unemployed was determined by what the unemployed could force out of the government "by protest, raids, and riots. . . . And violence seems to have been one of the few things which did move governments which were bent on limiting relief as much as possible." (Overton, 1988:164)

Here we see the same four features required to state a conclusion. First there is a *sample*. In this project there is one *case* (Newfoundland), observed over a *period of time*—the decade of the 1930s. In this time period *measurements* are taken of the effect (level of public relief support) and the cause (degree of violence of political actions needed to increase support levels). The different values of the cause (political means, protests, raids, and riots) and different values of the effect (raising, lowering, no change in level of support) are critical parts of the conclusion. Data analysis here consists of a *summary* of what happens to the effect when the cause is changed: the more violent actions produce increases in the level of support; the less violent ones do not. Since the emphasis is on which form of political action had any influence at all on the level of support, the question by how many dollars level of support was raised is not reported in the conclusion (but it does appear elsewhere in the report).

The elements highlighted in the above examples and discussion specify the four requirements for drawing conclusions from observations about the accuracy of hypotheses.

1. A sample of cases or time periods.
2. Measurements of the values of the causes and of the effect variables taken for each case in each time period selected.
3. variation in the values of the measured causes and effect.
4. Data analysis of the measured values to provide a description of how the effect is changed by changes in the causes.

Designing a research project involves deciding how each of the requirements will be met. Findings become impossible if even one of the requirements is not met. Or, to make the same point in reverse: if findings are used to draw a conclusion regarding the accuracy of a hypothesis, then each of the requirements *must* have been met.

5.7 PHASES OF THE RESEARCH PROJECT

The project design process can be thought of as a series of phases, named for the requirements being attended to. In each phase the researcher decides how one requirement will be met. In the sampling phase, the question is what cases or time periods to select. In the measurement phase, the question is how to measure each cause and effect variable. In the data analysis phase the question is how to organize and display the measurements to summarize the relationship between the cause and the effect. In the variation phase decisions are made regarding what values of the cause and effect variables need to be observed. (Of course, as will be discussed later, decisions made in different phases have to be consistent with each other.)

One way to see the connections among the phase designs is to consider the end point of a project, then figure out what decisions would have been made to get to this end point. The end point is always a display of data showing the observed relationships between the cause(s) and the effect.

EXAMPLE: Wallace (1979) investigated the hypothesis that arms races cause war. The alternative would be the opposite, that military unpreparedness causes war. Since the alternative theories here are direct opposites, a single cross-tabulation of the causes and the effect tests both alternative theories. If Wallace's hypotheses were correct, the high and low percentages would appear as Table 5.1. If the alternative theory were correct, the high percentage and low percentage would be interchanged. If neither alternative theory was correct, all percentages would be more or less equal.

Table 5.1

	Arms Race	No Arms Race
War	High %	Low %
No war	Low %	High %
Number of cases	?	?

Whatever the actual data turns out to be, the data analysed in this way provides an evaluation of the alternative theories. In addition, the percentages can tell if war is the more likely outcome of an arms race, and how much more likely.

Sample of cases or time periods: To arrive at the above data display, a sample of cases has to be chosen. Since pairs of nations are usually the kind of units that declare and execute wars and get involved in arms races, the type of case involved here is pairs of nations.

Measurement: The display above requires the measurement of the cause (presence or absence of an arms race) and the effect (presence or absence of war).

Variation: The display above requires that at least one case appear in each cell of the table. This means that some of the sample pairs of nations have to have an arms race and a war, an arms race and no war, no arms race and a war, and no arms race and no war. Another way of saying this is that it is necessary to observe variation in both the cause and the effect.

Sample of cases and time periods again: where can pairs of nations that engage in arms races and wars be found? How many cases are needed?

Measurement again: If cases are found, how can the presence or absence of arms races and war be measured?

What Wallace actually did was use historical records to find nations that had "serious disputes" with other nations. Each pair of nations with a serious dispute became a sample case. Each nation could appear several times, depending upon the disputes it had had with its neighbours. He searched the historical records from 1815 to 1965, using only nations that were considered as great powers at the time.

The data produced by Wallace is presented in Table 5.2.

Table 5.2

	Arms Race	No Arms Race
War	23	3
No war	5	68
Number of cases	28	71

In Table 5.3, the numbers are converted to percentages. The theory that arms races cause wars is supported. Wars occur more frequently when an arms race is present than if it is not. How much more often? War is 78% (82% − 4%) more likely when there is an arms race, or we can say that without an arms race it is 78% (96% − 18%) more likely that there will be no war.

Table 5.3

	Arms Race %	No Arms Race %
War	82	4
No war	18	96
Total percentage	100	100
Number of cases	28	71

EXAMPLE: Marchak (1973) investigated the hypothesis that union membership would diminish wage discrimination against women. One alternative theory would postulate that wage differences could be explained by differences in education, experience, and job commitment between males and females.

If the first hypothesis were true, the data would appear as in Table 5.4.

Table 5.4

| | Non-members | | Union Members | |
Wages	Males	Females	Males	Females
High	High %	Low %	High %	Medium %
Low	Low %	High %	Low %	Medium %

If the union causes discrimination against women to diminish, then union women, compared to non-union women, should show medium percentages of high and low wages, or no difference from the men. But how could the researcher know that the differences were not caused by the union women having more education, experience, and so on than the non-union women? If all the cases in the above display were, for example, high school graduates, then education would be removed as a cause of wage discrimination. To arrive at the above display we need the following:

1. Sample design: A sample of workers is needed.
2. Variation design: The sample will have to include both male and female workers, of whom some are in unionized workplaces and some

are not, some of whom have high wages and some low. The data would be more convincing if all the workers had the same kind of jobs and in addition all had the same amount of education, experience, and so on.

3. Measurement design: The effect (wage discrimination) and all the causes—union membership, sex, type of job, education, experience, and so on—have to be measured.

What Marchak actually did was sample workplaces first—all were white-collar workplaces in British Columbia—and then sample workers in them. Equal numbers of unionized and non-unionized firms were selected. Workers were sampled in each workplace according to occupational skill levels. Table 5.5 shows Marchak's actual data: all cases are high school graduates, without further formal schooling.

Table 5.5

Wages	Males	Females
High	79 %	18 %
Low	21 %	82 %
Total %	100 %	100 %
No. of cases	70	84

In the above table, which includes both union and non-union members, 61% (79% − 18%) more men have high wages than women. What influence does unionization have? Compare differences between men and women inside and outside the union as in table 5.6.

Table 5.6

| Wages | Non-members | | Union Members | |
	Males	Females	Males	Females
High	94%	24%	64%	9%
Low	6%	76%	36%	91%
Total %	100%	100%	100%	100%
No. of cases	34	50	36	34

The percentage of union females obtaining high wages is 55% (64% − 9%) less than the percentage of union males, while the percentage of non-union females with high wages is 70% (94% − 24%) less than the percentage of non-union males. This suggests that unions do diminish wage discrimination, by about 15%. The data does not provide as clear an answer as that in the mock-up table because unionization also affects the percentages of males with high wages.

5.8 PHASES OF THE RESEARCH PROJECT: ARTIFACTS AND CONTROL

To this point we have concentrated on how to design a project that includes everything necessary to permit the production of findings. We need now to consider what can go wrong. Research projects should produce *facts*—descriptions of the things observed. But sometimes the methods of observation influence the content of the observations. Content added to, or subtracted from, an observation by the means of observation is an *artifact*. When we have some idea of what artifacts can be produced by the methods used, we can modify our designs to control them.

The *major* potential artifact that the variation phase can produce is an "inadequate variation" artifact. This artifact can be controlled only by planning. The major possible artifact of the sampling phase is a "biased sample." The general method for controlling sample bias is to measure factors suspected of causing the biases.

The measurement phase can produce two main artifacts: random measurement error and systematic measurement error. Random measurement errors are generally controlled by using repeat measurements, a kind of "internal replication"—replication within the project. Systematic measurement error is generally controlled by measuring the suspected sources of error, a kind of internal triangulation.

The major artifact produced by the data analysis phase is "mis-weighting" of the cases. The common control strategy is, again, a kind of internal triangulation. Alternative weighting schemes (which amount to alternative computation formulas) are applied to the same data.

At the beginning of this chapter we discussed the use of replication, triangulation, and extension as means of satisfying doubts about the accuracy of the findings of *different* projects. As suggested in the previous paragraph, the principle of replication and triangulation can be applied *within* a project to control possible artifacts in the measurement and data analysis phases. The internal use is the same as the external use: if no artifacts are present, the findings should be the same.

EXAMPLE: Different data analysis techniques applied to the same set of observations should provide very similar descriptions of the relations between the causes and the effect. But if different descriptions are produced, then the differences must be artifacts produced by the techniques.

In contrast, the measurement of possible biases in the sample phase compares the findings of the project to those of other projects. A sample is biased if the cases or time periods are selected so that one theory is supported more strongly than an alternative. But it is usually impossible to determine whether a sample is biased or not, except by comparing the findings of different replication or triangulation studies in existence or forthcoming. If the findings are different, then the measures of possible biases in each study can be compared to determine which of them are the sources of the different findings. (Note that if the findings are the same, the possible biases of the different samples become merely "sample characteristics." The greater the variety in these sample characteristics, the more confident one can be in the accuracy of the findings.)

Potential variation artifacts are controlled by planning. Variation artifacts are produced when the observed variation is inadequate for evaluating the hypotheses being investigated. One place the problem can become apparent is in the data analysis work. Every data analysis has minimum sample size requirements. If too few cases or time periods are measured, it will be impossible to draw conclusions about causal relationships. Even if the minimum sample size is met and exceeded, inadequate variation may erode one's confidence in the findings.

EXAMPLE: In the calcium-blood pressure study referred to above, the conclusion stated that "women who consumed the recommended dietary allowance of calcium (800 milligrams per day) decreased their risk of high blood pressure by 22 percent compared to women who consumed less than 400 mg. per day." Variation in the values of the cause variable ranged from less than 400 to 800 mg/day. If the sample had consisted of one woman at one point in time, then no variation in either the cause or effect variable would be observable and no relationship between them could be described. The minimum sample size is at least two cases, or one case observed at two different points in time. How much confidence could be placed in a study with only two cases or time periods? Ordinarily very little. One would suspect that the findings might be changed dramatically or even reversed with the addition of even one or two more cases or time periods. The same suspicion would apply even if the sample were fifty cases, but only two or three of these took less than 400 mg/day while 47 or

48 took 800 mg/day. In sum, independently of the adequacy of the sample size, inadequate variation can erode one's confidence in findings.

5.9 DESIGN DECISION II: DETAILS OF PHASE DESIGNS

The first design decision is the choice among replication, triangulation, and extension. Subsequent design decisions involve planning the research project in detail. Below we discuss the principal types of decision required for designing a research project.

In the *variation* phase the goal is to observe adequate variation. But is adequate variation necessary for every cause and the effect? For example, in the calcium-blood pressure study, is it necessary to observe variation in calcium consumption *and* variation in blood pressure? In the long run, the answer is yes, but as will be seen in the next chapter, if *at least one cause or the effect* has adequate variation, useful findings can be produced. If a variation had been observed in the calcium consumption of the sample women but all had the same blood pressure (no variation), it could be concluded that the level of calcium consumption is not a cause of high blood pressure.

The principal decisions, then, are whether to concentrate on adequate variation in a cause or in an effect. Most variation designs are implemented by "guiding" the sampling process: cases or time periods are included or excluded selectively to ensure that adequate variation is observed. In some situations, the variation observed is left completely contingent on "random sampling"—this is a kind of unguided selection process. The main choices for the variation phase are then among cause, effect, and sample-contingent strategies.

In the sampling phase one goal is to choose a set of cases or time periods. The choices range from case studies (a single case and multiple time periods) to surveys, or censuses (multiple cases at a single point in time), and everything in between. The number of cases or time periods must be large enough to meet the requirements of the variation design.

A second goal is to avoid sample biases. Can a characteristic of a sample be proved to bias the sample? In the calcium consumption-blood pressure study, one characteristic of the sample was that all the cases were all women: can this be proved to bias the findings of the study? Using the data from the study it cannot; but if the findings of other studies and samples are compared, it can, provided that suspected biases are measured and reported in *every study*. The evidence for and against sample biases comes from a comparison of different studies. In sample design, then, the control of sample biases requires the researcher to anticipate what sample characteristics *might* be biases, and to measure them so that the question can be settled.

Where there are no close replication or triangulation studies for comparison, the analysis of sample bias waits upon their completion. In some designs it is possible to address the bias question in another way. A census is a complete enumeration of the cases in a defined boundary at a particular time. If census information exists, it is possible after selecting a sample to assess its *representativeness* by comparing sample and census characteristics. If they differ, then the sample is biased in the sense of being unrepresentative of the population.

The goal of *measurement* design is to obtain measurements of each cause and effect appearing in the hypotheses. Indicators are observable and recordable variables, and at least one must be chosen for each cause and effect. Each indicator must be applied to each case or time period sampled, and its value noted and recorded. Two or more single indicators may be added to form a combination indicator. When this is done, attention must be given to the manner of combination.

The other goal is to avoid random and systematic error in the measurements. This usually means more measurement. Where a random error or measurement error is suspected, the remedy is usually to average *repeat* measurements (internal replication). One remedy for systematic error is to find indicators for the suspected sources. The application of these indicators adds to the total amount of measurement work. (And recall that the investigation of sample bias may also involve the use of additional indicators.)

The goal of *data analysis* is to produce a description of the relationships between causes and the effect: how the effect changes when the cause is changed, and by how much. There are more or less standard techniques for doing this. Which technique is the right one depends upon whether indicators for the causes and the effect are treated as qualitative or quantitative. (Note that researchers are not entirely free to treat indicators as qualitative or quantitative, because some indicators are inherently qualitative—sex, religion, ethnicity, for example.) There are four different possibilities, three of which are in common use.

Cause Indicator Treated as	Effect Indicator Treated as	Mean Differences Technology
1 Qualitative	Qualitative	Percentage Differences
2 Qualitative	Quantitative	
3 Quantitative	Quantitative	Regression/correlation

(The technology for the the fourth possibility—qualitative effect and quantitative causes—is often complicated. Many researchers choose to treat the quantitative causes as qualitative and use the technology for 1 above.)

The second goal is to avoid mis-weighting artifacts. Each technique for describing causal relationships weights the observations differently. If the same observations summarized by two different techniques produce different findings, the findings must be artifacts of the techniques.

EXAMPLE: The two most common kinds of averages are means and medians. When the researcher suspects that mean differences contain artifacts of the weighting scheme inherent in this form of average, median differences can also be computed. If the findings are different, both techniques are suspect. Since the data are the same, the different findings must be a product of the different weightings employed. They are artifacts of the methods used rather than facts about what was observed.

Table 5.7 summarizes the principal decisions facing the designer of the research project.

Table 5.7

Phase	Major Options
Variation	cause strategy effect strategy sample contingent strategy
Sampling	(1) sample size (no. of cases or time periods) (2) extent and method of investigating sample bias

Measurement	(1) single or multiple indicators
	(2) extent of internal replication or triangulation

Data Analysis	(1) qualitative or quantitative technology
	(2) extent of internal triangulation

In the following chapters the questions involved in each design phase are addressed in detail.

5.10 SUMMARY

Social science research is *driven* by the need for information on how causes influence effects, because this is essential for useful information about policies and practices. It is *conditioned* by the desire for accuracy. A general strategy for ensuring accuracy can be based on the *repetition* and *weight of evidence* principles. It directs researchers to withhold their acceptance of research findings until the same findings are repeated by other projects. The principles of *replication, triangulation*, and *extension* (r/t/e) are three important forms of the general principle of repetition.

Conditioned by the repetition principle, the drive for useful policy and practice information produces a *literature* of existing research and a program of ongoing research. A literature is composed of research project reports that repeat, triangulate, and extend each other and provides a context for planning research projects. The most basic decision to be made in designing a research project is whether to plan a study that *replicates, triangulates* or *extends* the existing work in the literature.

R/t/e choices are made on the basis of *weight of evidence* assessments of a literature—the content of the findings is weighted according to the number of replications, triangulations, and extension appearing in the literature.

Given the r/t/e decision, designing a research project that will produce a factual description of cause and effect relationships has several requirements: suitable *variation conditions*, a *sample of cases or time periods, measurement* of the causes and effect, and *data analysis* of the measurements.

About half of research project design consists of planning how to meet these requirements of variation, sample, measurement, and data analysis. The other half consists of attempting to control *artifacts* or errors in this work. Since artifacts cannot always be avoided or controlled, it is important to plan for an assessment of the possible influence of artifacts on the project findings.

5.11 EXERCISES

Exercise 1 has three parts (A, B, and C). Students and instructors can devise suitable forms of the question for topics that interest them.

The exercises can each be done independently of the others. However, much can be gained if each type of exercise is done for a particular topic. For example, if 1A is done, the topic of controlling the use of performance-enhancing drugs in sports should be the subject of exercises 2, 3, and 4 in succession. It is also recommended that the entire set of exercises be done for at least two different, preferably very dissimilar topics.

1A. i) To reduce the use of performance-enhancing drugs in sport, would you increase or decrease
    (a) salaries and benefits paid to elite athletes
    (b) salaries and benefits paid to coaches
    (c) funding of sports facilities
    (d) funding for drug education of athletes, coaches, and trainers
    (e) funding for ethics education of athletes, coaches, and trainers
    (f) funding for other facets of the sports industry?
  ii) How much increase or decrease do you think would have a noticeable influence on the use of performance-enhancing drugs in sport?
 iii) Your answers to the above questions are hypotheses about how people in the sports industry use performance-enhancing drugs. How would you investigate the accuracy of your hypotheses?

1B. i) To make Canadian industry more competitive would you
    (a) hire better-trained managers
    (b) hire better-trained workers
    (c) instal the latest technology
    (d) pay workers less; pay managers less
    (e) keep unions and union activity out of the workplace
    (f) bring in immigrant labour and "guest workers"
    (g) hire foreign-trained professional labour
    (h) hire foreign-trained teachers
    (i) get rid of foreign-owned branch plants
    (j) lower interest rates
    (k) increase funding for research and development

      (l) reduce funding for social programs, e.g., welfare, medicare

      (m) introduce other changes?

  ii) How much change in the above items would have a noticeable influence on the competitiveness of Canadian industry?

 iii) How would you investigate the accuracy of your ideas for increasing competitiveness?

1C.   i) To reduce crime rates would you

      (a) enlarge police forces

      (b) raise the pay of police officers

      (c) change the criminal code, e.g., remove victimless crimes from the code

      (d) reduce unemployment

      (e) increase recreation funding for juveniles

      (f) increase funding for safe homes for juveniles

      (g) decrease costs of education to students

      (h) increase the severity of punishment for crimes

      (i) increase the swiftness of apprehension for crimes

      (j) increase funding for legal aid

      (k) increase alternatives to incarceration

      (l) institute separate justice systems for native people

      (m) introduce other measures?

  ii) How much change in the above would have a noticeable effect on the crime rates?

 iii) How would you investigate the accuracy of your ideas for reducing crime?

2.   i) Select a topic and find abstracts from eight articles on the subject. *Sociological Abstracts* is a good source of abstracts.

  ii) Arrange the abstracts in order of their date of publication.

 iii) On the basis of the information in the abstracts, classify each article either as a replication, triangulation, or extension of articles published previously, or as unrelated to previous articles.

 iv) Decide which findings need more replication, triangulation, or extension and which do not.

  v) If you were to carry out research on the topic selected, what hypotheses would you investigate?

 vi) Would you investigate the hypotheses with a replication, triangulation, or extension study?

 vii) Find eight more article abstracts on the topic and analyse them according to the instructions in (ii) to (v). Would you change your answers to questions (vi) and (vii)? If you would, specify the changes.

CHAPTER 6

Variation Design

CHAPTER CONTENTS

6.1 WHAT ARE VARIATION CONDITIONS?

Variation conditions are the amounts of variation observed in all the causes and effects measured in a project. If every observed value of a cause or effect is identical, then the variation condition for that cause is "no variation."

EXAMPLE: A project to investigate the influence of the death penalty on homicide rates looks at the experience of a single country over a period of years. If the same rate of homicide is observed year after year, the variation condition for the effect is no variation. If there is no death penalty during these same years, then the variation condition is similarly no variation.

EXAMPLE: The military spending of nations was examined as an effect of left-wing and right-wing government policy. Military spending for one year was measured on a sample of nations. If all of the nations had right-wing governments, the variation condition for the cause is no variation. If all of the nations spent 58% of taxes on the military, the variation condition for the effect is no variation.

If the observed values of a cause or effect are different, the variation condition for that variable is the amount of variation. The amount may be described as "some," "little," "much," etc. (Later we will see that the amount of variation can be described with numerical values.)

EXAMPLE: If the rate of homicide is observed to fluctuate between 40 and 50 per 100,000, then the variation condition is "some variation." If the death penalty is introduced during the years selected, then the variation condition is similarily some variation.

EXAMPLE: If some nations had right-wing governments, while others had left-wing governments, the variation condition for the cause is some variation. If some nations spent 30% of taxes on the military, others spent 50%, and still others spent 70%, the variation condition for the effect is some variation.

6.2 WHY ARE VARIATION CONDITIONS IMPORTANT?

Variation conditions are crucial determinants of research findings. One class of variation conditions precludes findings altogether, and another class permits only the finding of no causal relationship. The third class permits a variety of findings, but only within the limits of the variation conditions.

If no variation is observed in a cause but some is observed in an effect, the only possible finding is that the cause has no influence on the effect. The opposite is also true.

EXAMPLE: If the rate of homicide is observed to fluctuate from year to year during a period when there is no death penalty, the only possible conclusion is that the death penalty does not influence that particular range of fluctuation. Conversely, if a death penalty is introduced but the homicide rate does not change, then the most plausible finding is that this cause has no influence on the effect and that other causes do.

EXAMPLE: If all the sampled nations had right-wing governments but that military spending varied from 30% to 70% of taxes, the only possible finding is that the variation observed in military spending is not caused by right-wing government policy.

If variation is observed in the cause and the effect, the accuracy of an observed causal relationship is limited to the amount of variation observed in *both* the cause and the effect.

EXAMPLE: A survey of families examined the influence of family income on the number of children in the family. It was postulated that the larger the yearly income, the smaller the number of children. Observed variation in yearly income ranged was $15,000 to $25,000, and the number of children reported varied from 0 to 4. The average number of children was 3.2 for the $15,000-$19,000 income group, and 2.1 for the $20,000-$25,000 income group. The finding was that the hypothesis was correct: on average, the larger the income, the smaller the number of children. But we know from census data that annual family incomes can be both much less than $15,000 and much more than $25,000. It is possible that the relationship between children and income is different at the high and low end of income than it is in the middle. The conclusion is accurate *only* for the range of variation observed.

EXAMPLE: The influence of type of industry on the presence or absence of unions was investigated for the automobile, textile, steel, paper, and financial industries; it was discovered that all except finance were heavily unionized. The finding of the project was that type of industry is not an important cause of the presence or absence of unions. Clearly this conclusion is determined by the restrictions in the categories of industry observed. Further research (without the restriction) would show that in the trade, service, and farming industries, for example, there are few or no unions. The original conclusion is based on the restricted range of variation observed in the types of industry considered. Its accuracy is limited to that range.

Finally, if no variation is observed in *either* the cause *or* the effect, then a causal relationship cannot be described.

EXAMPLE: If the nations that were observed for a study of the influence of arms races on war did not include any nations that had experienced either an arms race or a war, the relationship between the cause and the effect cannot be described. The same non-finding would result if all nations had had no wars—all arms races, all wars—all arms races, all wars—no arms races. What we mean by causal relationship is the observable connection between the different values of the cause and the different values of the effect. When no different values are observed, no connection between them can be observed.

Variation conditions are important because observed causal relationships are *always* subject to variation conditions attached. Since variation conditions are determinants of research findings, it is essential to decide which conditions will be imposed.

6.3 VARIATION CONDITIONS AND SAMPLING

Variation conditions are usually imposed by the sampling process. In the sampling phase, cases or time periods are selected for measurement. By choosing suitable cases or time periods, the researcher can determine what values of the causes and effects will be observed and measured.

EXAMPLE: A researcher wishes to discover if urbanization and women's employment are causes of changes in the fertility in industrialized countries. Canada, the United States, most European nations, and a few others qualify as possible cases. What time periods might be selected? Any time period from the late 1960s to the present (1988) exhibit decreases only. However, if the period selected includes the past five decades for any of these countries, the variation observable in the fertility rates will include the baby boom period, in which increases become observable as well.

The desired variation conditions for the effect are imposed by choosing the appropriate cases and time periods. If the 1965-1980 period is chosen, variation in the effect is restricted to decreases. But if the 1935-1965 period is chosen, both increases and decreases are included. The variation conditions imposed upon the cause would be contingent on what was happening to urbanization and women's employment in the period.

EXAMPLE: In nations there are provinces or regions and groups with different changes in fertility from the country as a whole. In non-industrialized nations, for example, the middle classes might show decreases in fertility while other classes might show increases. In North America some religious communities and racial or ethnic groups have fertility patterns at odds with the larger society, at least for some time periods. Some native communities in Canada had fertility rates that continued to increase after the baby boom of most non-native groups had run its course.

By selecting communities within a nation rather than the entire nation as the type of case, different variation conditions are imposed on the causes and the effect. The time periods could be chosen so that the changes in the causes (urbanization and unemployment) or the effect (fertility rate) or both the cause and effect are observable.

Variation conditions may also be imposed by subjecting the cases selected to different treatments, or "stimuli." In research projects referred to as experiments, variation conditions are usually imposed both by the selection of cases or time periods and by different treatments.

EXAMPLE: In an experiment to evaluate the hypothesis that exposure to anti-prejudice information causes decreases in expressed prejudice, Middleton (1960) showed the movie *Gentleman's Agreement* to one-half of a sociology class in a southern U.S. college. Expressed anti-black and anti-Jewish prejudice was lower after the students has seen the movie than before. The other half of the college class (the "control" group) did not see the movie. The control group showed decreases in expressed prejudice also, but not as much as the group that saw the movie.

By selecting college students, the researcher imposed a limited variation in age, social class, education, and literacy. No variation was observed in Jewish/non-Jewish background—Jewish background students were asked not to participate. There were no black students in the class. Observable variation in anti-prejudice information was imposed by selecting a particular movie and exposing one group to this treatment and the other to no treatment.

Further restriction in expressed prejudice was imposed by selecting a southern U.S. location in the 1950s for the study.

6.4 THE STEPS IN VARIATION DESIGN

There are three steps in variation design. First a *strategy* is selected.

Second, cases or time periods are chosen. Third, plans are made for assessing the adequacy of the variation observed.

Variation design strategies are ways of determining which causes and effects will have observable variation and which will not. The options for a researcher are to design variation "in" to design it "out," or to make it "contingent." There are two basic strategies that design variation into causes and effects—the cause strategy and the effect strategy. The sample contingent strategy makes observed variation contingent on the sample selection process. Designing variation out is best thought of as a substrategy to be combined with the basic strategies. The most important feature of a design must be what variation is observed rather than what is unobserved.

a. The cause strategy

In the cause strategy, variation is designed into a cause by selecting those cases or time periods that have the desired values.

EXAMPLE: To investigate the hypothesis that unions (the cause) have an influence on wages (the effect) one researcher selected some workplaces with unions and some without and compared the average wages of workers in the two types of workplace. If the hypothesis is accurate, the workplaces with unions will have higher wages. If the hypothesis is wrong, either there will be no difference in wages or the non-union workplace will have higher wages.

EXAMPLE: A second study chose the same unionized workplaces but observed the wages before and after they were unionized. If the hypothesis is correct, the wages should be higher after unionization than before.

In both examples above, note that the cases or time periods were selected in order to guarantee the observation of variation in the cause. No attempt is made to guarantee observable variation in the effect— variation in the effect is *contingent* on the cases or time periods chosen to design variation into the cause. In these examples, the strategy guides the sampling process. Observable variation is obtained by selecting the cases or time periods with the different values required. In experiments, another type of cause strategy, observable variation is obtained less by selecting the cases or time periods and more by manipulating the experience of the cases chosen.

EXAMPLE: In the Middleton anti-prejudice experiment described in an earlier example, variation in the cause variable was obtained, not by selecting particular individuals, but by dividing the sampled individuals into two groups and manipulating their experiences differently. One of the groups was shown an anti-prejudice movie, but the other was not. If the anti-prejudice movie has the expected influence on the effect (expressed prejudice), then the group shown the movie (the experimental group) should express less prejudice after the showing than the group that didn't see the movie (the control group). If the hypothesis is wrong, the control group will express the same amount of prejudice as the experimental group or less.

b. The effect strategy

In the effect strategy, variation is designed into an effect by selecting those cases or time periods that have the desired values.

EXAMPLE: To investigate the hypothesis that baby booms (an effect) are caused by decreases in women's employment, Canada is selected for observation between 1920 and 1960 because this period encompasses the low fertility rates before the boom and the high rates of the boom. If the hypothesis is true, low values of women's employment should be found with high levels of fertility and vice versa. If the hypothesis is false, either no differences in women's employment will be observable, or high employment will be found with high fertility.

EXAMPLE: The hypothesis that a high-fat diet is a cause of heart disease (an effect) was investigated by choosing a sample of hospital patients forty years of age and over, half of whom had been admitted for heart disease and half who had not. If the hypothesis is true, the heart disease patients should report having eaten more fat than the non-heart disease patients. If the hypothesis is false, their diets should be the same, or the heart disease patients will have eaten less fat.

In both examples above, note that the cases or time periods were selected in order to guarantee the observation of variation in the effect. No attempt is made to guarantee that the variation in the cause would be observed.

c. The sample contingent strategy

With the exception of the experiment, for all of the above examples the cases or time periods were chosen in order to guarantee the observation of variation in a cause or an effect. The strategy is implemented by guiding the sampling process: observable variation is obtained by choosing cases or time periods with the different values required. In the sample contingent strategy no attempt is made to guide the sampling process. Whatever variation is observed is contingent on the sampling of cases or time periods.

EXAMPLE: Studies of voters' preferences for political parties and candidates are often carried out before elections in democratic countries. In North America a popular method is the random selection of telephone numbers. Voters who answer the phone are queried on a number of cause variables (including age, sex, marital status, and occupation) and the effect variables (such as party preference, candidate preference, and intention to vote). In this strategy, observable variation is entirely contingent on the random selection of telephone numbers. In other words, no attempt is made to make sure that men as well as women, young people as well as old, married as well as unmarried, are included in the sample. The guiding of the sampling process stops at the point of choosing the list of phone number and the time at which the telephoning takes place.

d. Variation design substrategies

Substrategies in variation design concentrate on designing variation out of causes and effects. Recall that if the variation in a cause is set to zero the relationship between that cause and any other cause or effect is set to no causal relationship. (The same is true for an effect with zero variation.) Designing variation out of causes and effects may serve a number of purposes: (1) various minor nuisance causes may be removed from consideration, (2) alternative theories may be disposed of, and (3) consideration may be limited to one particular type of case or time period, such as children, voters, the aged, natives, immigrants, convicts, parolees, or victims. Any variable that is made constant by designing all variation out becomes a "design constant."

EXAMPLE: To determine if sexual discrimination is a cause of differences between men's and women's wages, a study was undertaken of office workers. Since variation was required in sex, both male and female workers were included. Since education and experience differences might also be causes of wage differences, only workers with the same education (completion of high school) and the same experience (none) were chosen.

By designing variation into sex while designing variation out of education and experience, the accuracy of the sexual discrimination hypothesis could be investigated without the possibility that education and experience causes would confound the findings.

EXAMPLE: To determine if arms races cause wars, Wallace selected only pairs of nations that had serious disputes, defined as a dispute in which the parties threatened military action. By this restriction Wallace designed variation out of international disputes, removing from consideration those minor disputes that are less likely to be seen as important causes of war. Variation in the cause (arms race or no arms race) and the effect (war or no war) was left contingent on the choice of time period, 1820-1965.

EXAMPLE: In the investigation of expressed anti-Jewish prejudice discussed in an earlier example, the researchers asked Jewish students not to participate. This meant that there was no variation in the Jewish/non-Jewish variable. That was done, because it is most unlikely that any movie about anti-Jewish prejudice would have any effect on students from Jewish backgrounds. If they were included in either the experimental or control group, the result would probably be confusing findings.

6.5 CHOOSING STRATEGIES

Strategies are chosen on three bases. The first basis is the variation required to evaluate the hypothesis being investigated. The second is the facts about what variation exists for observation. The third basis is the principles of variation design. We will look at each basis in turn.

a. What ranges of variation are required?

Determination of the necessary ranges of variation involves a close examination of what the hypotheses state.

EXAMPLE: Suppose one hypothesis states that sex determines criminality and that male crime rates are higher than female. Sex is a two-valued cause. Crime rate is an effect with many values, but since the exact difference in crime rates between males and females is not stated, any difference will suffice. Since the hypothesis claims there will be a difference, all that is needed is a crime rate for males and females. The nature of the difference between them, if any, will suffice as an evaluation of the hypothesis.

EXAMPLE: The hypothesis that the replacement of the Juvenile Delin-quents Act (JDA) by the Young Offenders Act (YOA) will bring about changes in the trying and sentencing of non-adult offenders requires only that the replacement occur. However, whereas there will be ample records for observing the influence of the JDA, it will be some time before the influence of the YOA produces enough records for comparison.

EXAMPLE: The hypothesis that high blood pressure can be reduced by increasing the daily intake of calcium cannot be investigated effectively until both the levels of blood pressure and amounts of calcium intake under consideration are specified. As stated, any levels of blood pressure and calcium intake are relevant, but we know that there are definite upper and lower limits to both the cause and the effect.

EXAMPLE: It has been hypothesized that native peoples are incarcerated in Canada at a greater rate than non-natives because they engage in plea bargaining less often than non-natives. The investigation of this hypothe-sis requires native and non-native persons charged with similar offences in the criminal justice system. In other words, to discover if differences in plea bargaining (rather than other differences) are a cause of higher rates of native incarceration, variation in types of charges to natives should be similar to those for non-natives.

b. What ranges of variation exist?

EXAMPLE: What kind of sex differences are there in crime rates? In what places do large and small differences show up? Are there changes over time in the differences between the male and female rates? Are there crimes that only males or only females are charged with? Factual answers to these questions are important determinants of variation design.

EXAMPLE: To investigate the influence of the YOA one needs to know the exact date that it came into effect and have a detailed analysis of the differences and similarities between the two Acts. In addition to these facts, it would be necessary to estimate how long it would take for differences to show up in enough records to justify an analysis of them.

EXAMPLE: Some of the facts needed in selecting a variation design strategy for the calcium/blood pressure hypothesis would be (1) how blood pressure and calcium intake vary according to age, sex, occupation, region of residence, etc. and (2) the calcium content of foods, liquids, and diet supplements, and how much of this is likely to be taken up in digestion.

c. What are the principles of variation design?

There are two principles of variation design. The first states there must be observable variation in either the cause or the effect. The second states that the range and distribution of the observed variation set the limits on the accuracy with which the relationship between the variables can be described.

The first principle means that without variation in at least one variable, it is impossible even to describe a relationship between variables. The term relationship means the pattern of joint occurrence of all the values of two variables. With only one value of each variable observed, no pattern is observable.

As stated above, if there is observable variation in only one variable, it is possible to observe a relationship between the variables. Of course, that relationship is always the same: no causal relationship between the variables. The importance of observing such relationships is that they evaluate the accuracy of causal hypotheses.

The first variation design principle is the basis for the cause-and-effect variation design strategies described above. If variation is designed into the cause variable, the first principle of variation design guarantees that some evaluation of the causal hypothesis will result. If no variation is observed in the effect variable, the researcher can conclude that the causal hypothesis is inaccurate. If variation is observed in the effect variable, then the pattern in its relationship will also permit the evaluation of the causal hypothesis. It is possible that the relationship observed will be different from that predicted by the hypothesis, but that is useful as an evaluation. In short, the first principle of variation design guarantees that an evaluation of the hypothesis will result.

The first variation design principle can be stated in a number of different but equivalent forms:

1. If no variation is observed in either of two variables, it is impossible to observe a relationship between them.
2. If variation is observed in only one of two variables, the only observable pattern of relationship is that indicating no causal relationship.
3. In order to observe anything other than the no relationship pattern between two variables, it is necessary to observe variation in both of them.

The cause, effect, and condition variation design strategies are simple applications of the first principle of variation design. But there are further applications if we turn the condition around, so to speak. *In order to guarantee that no causal relationship exists between two variables, make sure that no variation is observed in one of them.*

EXAMPLE: Suppose, for example, we are investigating sex as a cause of income differences. Since we know that variable education is a cause of income differences, we want its influence removed so that any observed differences in income between men and women can be attributed unambiguously to sex. Now, if we select individuals who all have the same education, we will set the causal relationship between education and income to zero, or no causal relationship. So, even though it is thought that education has a causal effect on income, we will have a set of observations from which that causal effect has been removed. Whatever the causes of observed variation in income, we know it is not education. In short, we design variation into the cause and/or effect variables that we want to investigate, and we design variation out of the causes we want to eliminate from consideration. Both strategies derive from the basic principle of variation design.

The second principle of variation design states that the range and distribution of observed variation set the limits of accurate description of the relationship between variables. The second principle makes explicit what we all know: you can't describe what you haven't observed. As explained earlier, the range of variation refers to the spread of the observed values of a variable. Obviously, if any range of the possible variation in a variable is not observed, its relationship to other variables cannot be described.

The distribution of the possible values of a variable also determines the limits of accurate description of relationships. If only the extremely low and extremely high values of a variable are observed, middle values cannot be addressed in the description.

Generally, the ranges of values, observed and unobserved, of a variable determine the limits of accurate relationship descriptions. Excluded values play no role in the descriptions.

6.6 WHAT CAN GO WRONG IN VARIATION DESIGN?

Either or both of the principles of variation design may be broken.

a. Offending the first principle

In projects investigating one cause and one effect, the first variation design principle can be offended only with extraordinarily bad luck; therefore the situation is not worth discussing. However, perfect correlation between or among causes (also referred to as collinearity) is fairly easy to produce in a research project if the number of variables being investigated is large in relation to the number of cases or time periods observed. Suppose that, in the investigation of the discrimination vs. the education theory of income differences between men and women, only two cases are chosen. Recall that variation was designed into sex, so with two cases, one is a male, one a female. With such a design and a sample size of only two individuals, there are only two possibilities for education: (1) either no variation is observable (both are graduates or both are non-graduates); (2) education is collinear with sex. Table 6.1 shows all the possibilities.

Table 6.1

Education	Sex M	F	Education	Sex M	F	Education	Sex M	F
grad	1	0	grad	1	1	grad	0	0
non-grad	0	1	non-grad	0	0	non-grad	1	1

Although attention is given here is to collinearity in the relationships among the causes, it should be noted that the same situation holds for the effect variable: either no variation is observable, or the variation is perfectly correlated with sex, with education or with both.

Clearly, then, the number of cases in relation to the number of variables being investigated is a crucial determinant of the variation conditions imposed. When the number of cases is equal to, or smaller than, the number of cause variables, collinearity or near collinearity becomes one of the variation conditions imposed. One rule of thumb for avoiding the collinearity condition is to make sure that the number of cases is always larger than the number of variables appearing in the theories under investigation and as much larger as is feasible.

b. Offending the second principle

The second variation design principle makes variation design more than a trivial exercise. If only the first principle were important, variation design would be quite simple: researchers would merely have to make sure that variation was observed in either the cause or the effect to ensure the design would evaluate alternative theories. The second principle should warn the researcher against naive enthusiasm for such simple solutions to design problems. The difficulty of variation design posed by the second principle is this: until we know how a cause and effect are related over the entire range of variation of both, we cannot construct a design that will provide an unambiguous evaluation of the theory.

The possibility of threshold effects and non-linear relationships means that designs which exclude any range of possible variation may be misleading. When relationships between an effect and two or more causes are under investigation, as will ordinarily be the case, the design problems are compounded in direct relation to the number of causes being investigated.

Thresholds are points where the relationship between two variables changes. The direction of the relationship may change, the strength of the relationship may change, or both may change. Thresholds may exist anywhere in the range of variation of a variable.

EXAMPLE: A simple physical example of thresholds is the freezing and boiling points of water. If we didn't know that water freezes at 0 degrees C or that at sea level water will not boil until its temperature reaches 100 degrees C, we might observe water temperatures from 5 degrees C to 97 degrees C, observe neither boiling or freezing, and then conclude that the temperature of water has no effect on its state. Now this conclusion would be accurate enough if we specified the temperatures observed, but it illustrates the importance of observing the maximum range of variation in variables before stating general conclusions about their relationship.

EXAMPLE: One experiment to investigate the feminist theory of the effect of exposure to pornography on attitudes toward sexuality found no difference between the control group and the experimental group after it had been exposed to some video pornography. They concluded that exposure to pornography had no influence on attitudes toward sexuality. The second principle of variation design tells us that such a conclusion is accurate only for the range of observed variation in both variables. The amount of exposure to pornography and the degree of violence and degradation depicted in the pornography that are necessary to make a difference in attitudes toward sexuality might be greater than the amount of exposure the experimental group received. Given the ubiquity of "soft-core" pornography in the advertising, newspapers, and even television situation comedies that influence all of us, it may take a more prolonged exposure to more violent and degrading pornography than was encompassed in the experiment to produce changes in sexual attitudes. The values of the attitude toward sexuality are also critical: if they are already affected by exposure to pornography, a small increase in exposure will be unlikely to influence them further. If attitudinal responses to pornography are subject to thresholds, the experimental findings cannot serve as general evaluations of the theory, but only as statements about the relationship of attitudes and exposure for the range of variation encompassed.

EXAMPLE: Some thresholds in social science may involve, not high or low amounts of one variable, but the conjunction of specific values of two or more variables. If we are to believe popular accounts of criminal investigations and trials, suspects are evaluated in terms of three variables: means, motive, and opportunity to commit a crime. The absence of any one of these removes a suspect from the list of prime suspects, while the presence of all three operates as a threshold to place a suspect on the short list. Investigative work consists of finding evidence that establishes the presence or absence of these variables for any individual.

EXAMPLE: Individual development is another everyday example of threshold effects in operation. "Reading readiness," for example, is something observed by every primary school teacher and many parents. Attempts to teach reading before the child is ready leads to frustration for teacher and child and very little learning by the child; teaching attempts after readiness is achieved are dramatically more successful. Reading readiness is a threshold composed of the conjunction of many processes of individual development, including motor skills, control of eye movement, attention span, and social and conceptual skills. It is highly correlated with age and most often occurs between five and eight years, but it is earlier in some and later in others, and for the mentally handicapped it may not occur at all. Many of the apparently startling changes in individual behaviour in puberty also appear to be threshold responses: dramatic changes in behaviour that occur only after certain social, physical, and intellectual developments have taken place.

Whereas threshold relationships may apply to relationships between qualitative or quantitative variables of any type, non-linear relationships occur only between pairs of quantitative variables. A linear relationship between two variables is one that may be described as a straight line: an increase in the cause variable results in an increase (or decrease) in the effect variable; and the amount of change in the effect for a given change

Figure 6.1

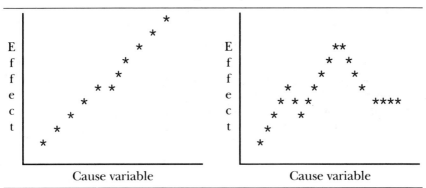

in the cause is always the same. In Figure 6.1 the first plot illustrates a linear relationship. The second plot shows a non-linear relationship between variables: at one (or more) points in the relationship the direction changes. At some points, a given amount of change in the cause produces a specific amount of increase in the effect; at other points, the same change in the cause produces decreases in the effect, or greater or lesser amounts of change in the effect.

6.7 ASSESSING VARIATION ADEQUACY

A variation design is a plan, and unanticipated problems may arise when its execution is attempted. Cases and time periods selected may be unavailable, or necessary information may be unobtainable or obtainable only at too high a price. In short, things can go wrong, and until a good part of the data is collected, it is impossible to determine what the consequences will be. An assessment of the variation design is a routine part of data analysis.

The purpose of the assessment is to determine if the variation design principles are met in practice. Recall that if the first principle is not met, a condition for the observability of a relationship between variables has been violated—no relationship can be observed. If the first principle is met, the second principle then becomes operative. Here the researcher attempts to determine if the observed variation is an adequate basis for drawing conclusions about the accuracy of the hypotheses under investigation. The ranges of included and excluded variation in both cause and effect variables are examined and measured. These are the bases for evaluating

1. the relationship of the observed ranges to known maximum or critical ranges,
2. the possibility of thresholds and non-linear relationships, and
3. generally, the usefulness of the relationship observed for evaluating alternative theories.

a. Primary assessment

In primary assessment the first task is to determine that the planned ranges of variation have been realized:

1. Variation designed in should be observable.
2. Variation designed out should not be observable.
3. Design constants should all have the same value.
4. Sample contingent variation should be observable.
5. Sample contingent constants should be noted particularly.

Unless the execution of the plan has obviously gone astray, (1), (2), and (3) will be routine. Items (4) and (5) need special attention. Sample contingent variation is often troublesome: there may be too little observable variation, or what is observable may not include the desired ranges.

Unplanned constants are a possibility whenever variation is left contingent upon random selection of cases/time periods. Unplanned constants are not a disaster unless the goals of the project require that the contingent variation be observable. Relationships between constants are unobservable because they violate the first principle of variation design. Remember that, whether planned or unplanned, the set of constants in the date identifies the set of causes and effects between and among which no relationships can be observed.

The second task in the primary assessment of variation design is to compare the observed ranges of variation to known critical or maximum ranges of variation. The point of the comparison is to judge the usefulness of the observed variation for evaluating the hypotheses investigated.

EXAMPLE: Suppose a study of daily calcium intake and blood pressure using a sample of individuals found that calcium intake ranged from 200 to 235 mg and found no relationship between calcium intake and blood pressure. No matter what the findings are, the range of observed variation in the calcium intake is probably too small to have much effect on blood pressure, and the highest value is below the recommended daily intake.

EXAMPLE: Researchers investigated exposure to television cartoons as a cause of children's attitudes toward violence. Cartoons were first grouped according to average amounts of violence in an average episode; then children were surveyed with regard to how often they watched each type of television cartoon. The child with the lowest exposure watched violent cartoons three times a week; the child with the highest exposure watched four times a week. The researchers concluded that the range of variation in exposure was too small to produce differences in attitudes toward violence.

b. Secondary assessment

Secondary assessment addresses the same questions as primary assessment, but now triplets and larger groups of variables are the concern—one effect and two or more causes. Secondary assessment is necessary because violations of the second principle of variation design can occur when two (or more) highly correlated causes are present.

EXAMPLE: A study of white-collar workers investigated the hypothesis that wage variation is caused by sexual discrimination and the alternative hypothesis that it is caused by education differences. Variation was designed into sex. When the data was collected, both causes and the effect had observable variation. The average income for men was $2,000 higher than the average for women. The average income for high-school graduates was $2,000 higher than for non-graduates.

In order to determine if sex was a stronger cause of income differences than education, education was controlled while the relationship between sex and income was examined. Controlled here means that cases were grouped according to whether or not they had completed high school: within these subgroups, there is no variation in the high school completed/not completed cause, and it can therefore have no influence on the effect. The result is shown in Table 6.2.

Table 6.2

	High School Completed		High School Not Completed	
	Males	Females	Males	Females
Average wage	$16,000	-	-	$14,000
Number of Cases	50	0	0	50

What the table shows is that within the completed/not completed subgroups, observable variation in sex disappears. As a result, we would have to conclude that no causal relationship exists between sex and income in the group of workers who completed or failed to complete high school. (The same conclusion would result if sex were controlled while looking at the relationship between education and income.)

This conclusion violates the second principle of variation design in that the description of the relationship derived from the table is limited by the restriction of sex variation produced by controlling education. The limited variation of sex results in an inaccurate description of the relationship between sex and education.

There are two possible explanations for the disappearance of sex variation when education is controlled: (1) no matter what cases are selected, females always have less education than males; or (2) all females *in this particular sample of cases* have less education than males. In contemporary North America we know that women do not always have less education than men, so the better explanation for the disappearance of variation in sex when education is controlled is (2): it is a product of the sample of cases selected. Had variation been designed into education and sex simultaneously, the problem would not have occurred.

The discovery that variation in one cause disappears completely when another cause is controlled is a useful one if there is any reason to believe that this means that there is a perfect correlation between two causes. This is an important finding in its own right, and one that will influence theories and programs of research. When this is not the case, however, the discovery merely means that the goals of the research project cannot be met: causal relationships that a project was designed to investigate are set to zero, even when it is known that this is inaccurate. The conclusions are variation artifacts produced by the variation design.

In the discussion so far, we have talked about perfect correlation between two or more causes. However, even if the correlation is not perfect, but almost perfect, the condition is troublesome. While the relationships between causes and effects are not constrained to zero, the strength and direction of the relationship may be based on only one or two observations. If these observations are changed, then both the strength and direction might change.

EXAMPLE: Continuing with the previous example, suppose the data looked like that in Table 6.3. Note that the number of women in the high school completed group now contains one case and the men in the high school not completed group included two cases.

Table 6.3

| | High School Completed | | High School Not Completed | |
	Males	Females	Males	Females
Average wage	$16,000	17,000	14,000	14,000
Number of cases	48	1	2	49

Looking at the high school completed group, we would conclude that women have higher average wages than men. Looking at the high school not completed, we would find that average male wages were equal to average female wages. But notice that the first conclusion is based on the difference between forty-eight men and one woman. If this woman happens to be much higher than the average for women, the conclusion is suspect. If a woman with lower wages than average happened to be the one in this sample that completed high school, the opposite conclusion would result. Similar observations apply to the male cases in the group that did not complete high school.

Because the correlation between sex and education is not perfect, the relationship between sex and income may be something other than zero or no relationship. However, the nearly perfect correlation makes the relationship unstable: the findings are entirely dependent upon two or three cases. Two or three different cases might produce opposite findings. The conclusions might be just the product of a single error in the measurement of wages or education. These are not findings in which anyone could have much confidence.

In short, secondary assessment examines variation in causes remaining when other causes are controlled. It searches for violations of either of the variation design principles produced by the variation conditions imposed by the project design.

6.8 SUMMARY

Observed causal relationships always come with variation conditions attached that are fundamental determinants of the observed relationship. Variation conditions are the amounts of variation observed for each cause and effect being investigated. Variation conditions are imposed through the selection of cases or time periods for observation. The three major strategies of variation design are the cause, the effect, and the sample contingent strategies. Various substrategies may be employed within these strategies.

Variation design strategies are selected on three bases: the ranges of variation required, the ranges of variation that exist, and the principles of variation design. The first principle of variation design is that there must be observable variation in either the cause or the effect under investigation. The second principle states that the limits of accurate description of the relationship between causes and effects is determined by the range and distribution of observed variation in both.

Projects that offend either of the principles will be ineffective. The first principle can be broken by selecting too few cases in relation to the number of causes and effects being investigated. The second principle can be broken by failing to encompass enough or appropriate variation, overlooking thresholds, and so on.

The adequacy of variation design is assessed in two steps. In primary assessment the researcher determines that the variation is sufficient for each cause and effect pair under investigation. In secondary assessment the aim is to determine whether variation is sufficient for describing relationships among larger groups of variables, such as multiple causes and a single effect.

6.9 EXERCISES

1. Below are a list of hypotheses and a variation design for investigating them. Identify the variation designs as cause, effect, or sample contingent designs.

   (a) Hypothesis: Fertility is higher in stable times than in periods of sharp social change.

      Variation design (i): the birth rates of Vietnam from 1950-1976 (the period of the Vietnamese War) were to be compared to the crude birth rate from 1976 to the present (post-war period).

(ii): European countries selected for their high fertility and low fertility rates will be examined for rates of social change in their political, religious, economic, educational, and military institutions.

(iii): Random samples of families will be interviewed with regard to their fertility behaviour and major changes in their circumstances—job loss or changes, residence changes, income changes, family crises, community crises, major successes or failures in achieving family goals.

(b) Hypothesis: Fertility is higher in times of prosperity (low unemployment) than in non-prosperous times (high unemployment).

Variation design (i): The birth rates of the Maritime provinces (where there is relatively high unemployment) are to be compared to the birth rates of the Prairie provinces (where there is relatively low unemployment) from 1950 to 1980.

Variation design (ii): Random sample of individual women who have completed menopause. Through interviews, respondents' income history and reproductive history will be recalled and recorded.

Variation design (iii): The unemployment rates in the baby boom (when there was high fertility) and after the baby boom (when there was low fertility) are to be compared.

(c) Hypothesis: The more direct the competition between members of majority and minority groups, the stronger the prejudice of the majority against the minority, and the more hostile the minority are towards the majority.

Variation design (i): Attitudes of (non-immigrant) residents of neighbourhoods with high concentrations of immigrant households are to be compared with those of residents with no immigrant households.

Variation design (ii): Anti-Catholic attitudes of Protestants in communities with 5% of fewer Catholics are compared to attitudes of Protestants in communities with 30-50% Catholics; vice versa for anti-Protestant attitudes of Catholics.

Variation design (iii): Workplaces are selected where 95% or more of workers claim the same ethnic origin and are compared with other workplaces where more than 50% of all the workers belong to a single ethnic group. Workers' attitudes toward the minorities in the workplace are measured by means of a questionnaire.

2. (a) Select single hypotheses from the exercises for chapter 3 and construct the following five variation designs for each:
   i) cause strategy with variation in the cause over time
   ii) cause strategy with variation in the cause over space
   iii) effect strategy with variation in the effect over time
   iv) effect strategy with variation in the effect over space
   v) sample contingent strategy.

   (b) Select multiple-statement theories from the chapter 3 exercises and attempt to construct the same five variation designs.

   (c) Select two alternative theories from the exercises in chapter 3 and attempt to construct the same five variation designs.

3. The hypotheses below are to be investigated with the accompanying variation designs. (a) Do they use cause, effect, or sample contingent strategies? (b) What kind of variation error do the designs contain? (c) How could it be remedied?

   (i) Hypothesis: The larger the family, the more likely the child is to become delinquent.

   Variation design: Families with more than six children are to be located and their delinquency rate computed.

   (ii) Hypothesis: Criminality is caused by small cranial capacity.

   Variation design: Obtain measurement of the cranial capacity of prison inmates.

4. Here are some conclusions about causal relationships. What variation conditions ought to be attached to these conclusions to make them credible?

   (i) Immigrants from Europe and the United States obtain higher wages than immigrants from nonwhite origins. (Satzewich and Li, 1987:239).

   (ii) "Minority communities and women don't need affirmative action. They need profound social change." (Bonacich, 1987:110)

   (iii) "The findings show that a university education no longer yields the same opportunities for upward social mobility." (Harvey, 1984:283)

(iv) While the number of police officers killed shows no trend, the rate of police officer killings per 1,000 has decreased markedly. (Hackler and Janssen, 1985)

(v) "People who are close to women inventors, including their husbands, collude in trivializing women's attempts to invent." (Cummins and other, 1988:390)

5. Select alternative theories from those listed in the exercises for chapter 3, elsewhere in this book, or from other sources. Specify the minimum amount of variation required for drawing a useful conclusion about the relationship between each cause and effect in the alternative theories. Specify your answer for (i) a cause strategy and (ii) an effect strategy. Which of these strategies appears to be the more effective type of study to start with?

6. Below are descriptions of the amount of cause and effect variation observed in a sample of cases. What possible conclusions (regarding causal relation) will this observed variation permit?

(i) Causes: Police officers/1,000 people
   1945, 11; 1955, 12; 1965, 14; 1975, 12; 1985, 10
   Effects: Crime rates/1,000 residents, all crimes
   1945, 23; 1955, 31; 1965, 41; 1975, 52; 1985, 71

(ii) Causes:
   Sex: 50% males, 50% females
   Age: 20% 14, 20% 15, 20% 16, 20% 17, 20% 18
   Residence: 100% middle class neighbourhoods
   Parents' income: 10% at poverty level or below
   40% moderately above poverty level
   40% high income
   10% very high income
   Effects:
   Rate of truancy 60% never, 30% twice a year, 7% monthly, 3% weekly
   Property crimes committed last year
   70% none, 20% 1-2, 6% 3-5, 4% over 6
   Victimless crimes (drug possession, under age sex, etc.)
   30% none, 40% 1-2, 20% 3-5, 10% 6 or more

(iii) Causes: Population growth rates:
   Decline   10% of countries
   No growth   15% of countries

0-2% increase	50% of countries
Above 2% increase	25% of countries
First/second/third world:	
First World	20% of countries
Second World	25% of countries
Third World	55% of countries
Effect: Calorie consumption	
Undernourished	15% of countries
Badly nourished	20% of countries
Adequately nourished	40% of countries
Well nourished	15% of countries
Overnourished	10% of countries
(iv) Causes: Population density	
0-5 persons/sq km	5% of countries
5-50 persons/sq km	50% of countries
51-200 persons/sq km	30% of countries
201+ persons/sq km	15% of countries
Effects: War between countries	
War	0% of countries
No war	100% of countries
(v) Causes: belief in supreme being	
Strong believer	15% respondents
Believer	40% respondents
Undecided	20% respondents
Disbeliever	25% respondents
Effects: Anti- or Pro-choice on abortion	
Anti-choice	17% respondents
Undecided	13% respondents
Pro-choice	70% respondents
(vi) Causes: Dominant religion	
Christian	95% of countries
Non-Christian	5% of countries
Effects: Mode of parliamentary election	
Democratic	40% of countries
Non-democratic	60% of countries

7. (a) In researching the following causal connections, it is decided to employ a cause strategy: observable variation is required in the causes below. Describe how you would sample cases or manipulate these cases or their behaviour in order to observe variation in cause

as a means of determining if the cause has an influence on the effect.

Possible cause	*Effect of interest*
Fat as percentage of total calories	Percentage over/under normal weight
Belief in god	Pro-choice re abortion
Driver training score	Number of traffic tickets
Exposure to sex education course in jr. high school	Information about AIDS
Native/non-native	Native attitudes toward non-natives and vice versa
Exposure to privatization/ socialization propa- ganda	Pro/anti attitudes toward public enterprise and private utilities
Exposure to pornography	Attitudes toward sexual violence
Married couples with high or low stress	Ability to conceive
Presence or absence of safe homes	Official reports of abuse

(b) What minimum range of variation in the cause is needed to inves-tigate causal connections with the effect? What ranges of variation would more adequately evaluate the hypotheses?

(c) What thresholds do you think might be involved in the causal con-nections above? In other words, do you think there are minimum levels of the cause below which it would be unlikely to influence the effect? Attempt to specify what this minimum level might be.

CHAPTER 7

Sampling Design

CHAPTER CONTENTS

7.1 WHAT ARE SAMPLES?

Samples are sets of cases/time periods that are selected for special attention in a research project. The special attention given to samples is that they are measured, and these measurements are the object of data analysis. Data analysis produces findings that are statements about the relations between causes and effects *for the sample of cases/time periods*.

The cases/time periods that are sampled may range from individual human beings at a single point in time to the entire globe over hundreds of years, and anything in between.

EXAMPLE: McKay (1988) in a study of the development of class conflict selected the coalfields *region* of Nova Scotia in the period 1872-76.

EXAMPLE: Sorokin (1957) examined theories of changes in revolution and internal disturbances, using a sample of civilizations and regions. He selected Europe from 525 to 1925, and ancient Greece from 600 to 126 B.C.

EXAMPLE: In a study of crime, age, and unemployment, Glaser and Rice (1959) used two samples. The first sample consisted of a *nation*, the United States, from 1932 to 1950. The second sample consisted of the cities of Chicago, Cincinnati, and Boston from 1935 to 1956.

EXAMPLE: Pammett (1987) in a study of class voting and class consciousness in Canada used 2,744 *individual* voters in Canada in 1979.

EXAMPLE: In a study of the origin of Canadian criminal law, Macleod's (1978) sample was an *institution*, the Parliament of Canada from 1982 to 1902.

EXAMPLE: Russell's (1984) study of rape and sexual abuse used a sample of randomly selected adult female *individual* residents of San Francisco in the summer of 1978.

EXAMPLE: Ramu (1984) studied voluntary childlessness, using a sample of married *couples* in Winnipeg in the mid-1970s. Half the couples were voluntarily childless. The other half were a matching sample of couples with children.

EXAMPLE: A study of how to reduce anxiety in children (Schreier and others, 1983) going into surgery used a sample of fifteen *mothers and their children* who elected for tonsillo-adenoidectomy in July 1980 in Johannesburg, South Africa.

EXAMPLE: In a study of violence, Torrance (1986) sampled *episodes* of public violence in Canada for the period 1867 to 1982.

EXAMPLE: In studying the development of science, Kuhn (1970) sampled the *disciplines* of chemistry, astronomy, physics, geology, and mathematics in Europe over a period spanning classical Greece to the present.

EXAMPLE: To study the relationship between arms races and wars, Wallace (1979) sampled *episodes* of serious disputes between pairs of nations over the entire globe between 1815 and 1965.

The notion of a sample of cases/time periods is usually linked to the notion of a population or universe—the entire set of cases/time periods from which a project sample was chosen. It should be understood that populations of cases/time periods are extraordinarily difficult to define and describe, even within clear geographical boundaries and the immediate historical period. (Try, for example, to define and describe the population of "Canadians" at this moment in history.) Outside such boundaries, it may become impossible to specify what should and should not be counted as part of the population. This is the nature of all populations, and it means that the relationship of samples to populations is never clear.

However, much social science research is designed to produce information useful for short- to medium-run application in a specified social, cultural, or geographic setting. When this is the case, it may be justifiable to define a population by including only the cases or time periods within specific time and space boundaries. We will see later that this type of definition is related to a strategy for controlling sample bias.

7.2 WHY ARE SAMPLES IMPORTANT?

Samples are necessary for several reasons. First, without samples, no findings about causal relationships can be reported. The use of a sample of cases or time periods is the distinguishing feature of empirical research.

Second, samples are important because they are the things that are subject to repetition (replication, triangulation, extension) studies. This means that a clear description of the cases/time periods selected for the project is essential. Without it, repetition studies of any sort are impossible.

Third, samples may be biased[1] and consequently produce findings

---

[1]The student should be aware of other ways of discussing sample bias. One common way is to use the term generalization, and be concerned with the generalizability of the findings from one sample to a population, or from one

about causal relationships that will mislead in policy or practice applications. The conclusions of all research are based on samples, rather than entire populations, and consequently on partial rather than complete information. This makes assessment of the presence of sample biases a necessary part of social research.

Note that sample bias is defined in relation to the possible applications of a research finding. The population from which a sample is chosen ought to be the set of cases that are relevent to the application of the project findings.

7.3 WHAT ARE THE STEPS IN SAMPLE DESIGN?

The first step in sample design is to determine the implications of the variation design for the sample design. The next step is to find and identify the cases/time periods that might possibly form part of the project sample. The third step is to choose the cases/time periods that will constitute the sample. The final step is planning the assessment of sample bias.

a. Determine the implications of the variation design

From the point of view of designing a sample, the variation design is only a way of planning some of the features of the sample design. The variation design is a set of instructions for what kind of characteristics the project sample requires.

When a variation plan specifies that variation is to be designed into a cause or effect, this means that cases/time periods must be sampled in such a way that this variation is observable and measurable on the cases or time periods selected. Often this means that subsamples of cases with each required value have to be chosen separately.

---

sample in one time and place to samples from other times and places. In the psychological experimental literature, discussions of sampling questions often use the term "external validity" when the researchers are concerned with the accuracy of experimental findings outside the laboratory for cases or time periods other than those included in the experiment.

EXAMPLE: Ramu (1984) studied determinants of voluntary childlessness in Winnipeg in the mid-1970s. In order to end up with a sample that included variation in voluntary childlessness, Ramu had to sample couples who were voluntarily childless separately from couples who were parents.

EXAMPLE: Marchak (1973) studied the influence of unions on male/female wage differences among white-collar workers. The design required samples of union workplaces and non-union workplaces. She first sampled union workplaces (of which there were few). Upon gaining their co-operation, she sampled non-union workplaces from the same region and type of industry.

EXAMPLE: A study of the influence of the Canadian Young Offenders Act (YOA) on juvenile crime, sentencing, and incarceration required a sample of time before and after the YOA replaced the Juvenile Delinquency Act. Samples of time periods before the YOA were selected separately from time periods after.

EXAMPLE: In a study of response to changes in medical record keeping, Hetherington (1982) sampled mental health regions. Three regions participated in the research, two as experimental groups and one as a control.

"Selection of these three groups was not random, but rather took advantage of the opportunity for a natural experiment." The first region was selected because of its use of the new problem-oriented system; the second region was selected because of its willingness to introduce the system. The third (control) region "was selected to resemble the other two as closely as possible in size and type of patients seen, and to afford data on a group whose use of the source-oriented record system was believed to be acceptable."

If the variation design calls for the sample contingent strategy, no subsampling is necessary. Once a set of cases/time periods is found, cases are chosen from the set. The variation strategy may have an effect here, however, by excluding some subset of the cases or time periods because they don't have a required constant value.

EXAMPLE: Pammett's (1987) study of "class voting and class consciousness in Canada" could use only *voters*. This means that immigrants, visa workers, foreign students, people in prisons or mental institutions, and people under eighteen years of age had to be excluded because they are not entitled to vote. If the study had been carried out before the First World War, women would have had to be excluded also.

EXAMPLE: Russell's (1984) study of rape and sexual abuse required that all respondents be female. All males had to be excluded from the set of individuals selected.

EXAMPLE: To study the relationship between arms races and wars, Wallace sampled *episodes* of serious disputes between pairs of nations over the entire globe between 1815 and 1965. His variation strategy required that all disputes be between great powers. He selected *all* dispute episodes except those between nations not meeting his definition of a great power.

b. Locating and identifying cases/time periods

Locating and identifying cases/time periods is the design step where the anticipated policy and practice application of the research comes into play. Depending upon what types are required, there may be a surfeit or a shortage of appropriate cases/time periods.

EXAMPLE: Where civilizations are the type of case needed, some definitions recognize fewer than twenty, most of them existing before the present era. All of these might be identified and located in some abstract sense but be unavailable for measurement.

EXAMPLE: If the disposition of party campaign funds is the expected policy or practice application of voter preference studies, there are in most constituencies many people eligible to vote.

EXAMPLE: Where the expected policy or practice application of a study of the effectiveness of a policy calling for the police to charge the perpetrators in wife abuse incidents, the amount of time after the policy change is limited to the time between the policy change and the time the study is undertaken.

c. Selection of cases/time periods

The selection of the cases/time periods that will constitute the actual project sample is governed by a number of obvious considerations. The first is of course availability of the cases/time periods for measurement, and the second is the money, time, and labour involved in the obtaining access to and measurements of those selected. Third is the minimum and maximum size of sample that will meet the requirements of variation and data analysis design. Finally, there is the question whether or not to use random probability selection.

d. Planning an assessment of sample bias

When policy or practice applications of findings based on biased samples are attempted, they are likely to be ineffective, inappropriate, or counterproductive. Assessment of sample bias is therefore an important part of sample design. The assessment is ordinarily based on repetition. This assessment may be supplemented with an assessment based on a comparison of samples and census information.

7.4 HOW ARE SAMPLE DESIGNS CHOSEN?

The sampling design is determined by the common sense criteria outlined below.

a. Availability of cases/time periods

Perhaps the most basic determinant of sampling design is the number of cases or time periods available for inclusion in the sample. The fewer there are, the more the researcher has to make do with what is available.

If the goal of a research project is to evaluate the effectiveness of recent changes in policy, practice, personnel, administration, party in power, and leadership, then the amount of time since the change occurred puts obvious limits on the time periods available for sampling. When the findings are to be applied in, for example, a particular country, province, or organization, cases other than the target case are of limited relevance because of unique characteristics of each unit.

EXAMPLE: It can be argued that a study to evaluate how the introduction of a freedom-of-information law in Canada has increased public access to government information should be restricted to examining the Canadian case. Freedom-of-information laws have been introduced in other places—the United States and Europe for example—and if these nations are considered relevant cases the available cases/time periods are expanded considerably. However, the federal system, party system, and extent of domination by multinational corporations are unique to Canada and make the argument for treating other states as possible cases less than compelling.

b. Minimum size requirements

The minimum number of cases/time periods that permit conclusions to be drawn on the accuracy of causal relationships is two. And two cases will do only when all causes save one are controlled because they all have the same value. In other words, for most social science research projects, the minimum sample size is larger than two. How much larger than two cases or time periods will suffice depends upon the variation design and the data requirements of the data analysis design.

EXAMPLE: Kopinak (1985) investigated women in municipal politics in London, Ontario. There were elections for school boards, public utilities boards, city council, board of control, and mayor, and both men and women candidates. The variation design minimum would be two (sexes) times six (types of municipal political offices), or twelve cases.

c. Cost per case/time period

There are two main categories of cost associated with each case or time period chosen for the sample. The first of these is the cost of finding the case or information about the case. When sampled individuals are to be interviewed personally, significant costs may be involved in finding and contacting them and setting up an interview.

The second category of cost is the amount of measurement planned for each case/time period. When the cases are political units, it is relatively inexpensive to find the cases, but the information necessary for making measurements may require extensive research in libraries or archives. When cost per case/time period is very high, very small samples are usual.

EXAMPLE: The Research Working Group of the Fernand Braudel Center (Hopkins and Wallerstein, 1987) examined the incorporation of regions or zones into the European-centered capitalist system. They chose three zones; "the Caribbean in the late seventeenth century, the Ottoman Empire in the late eighteenth and early nineteenth centuries, and southern Africa in the late nineteen and early twentieth centuries." Separate case studies were carried out for each zone because incorporation was considered an involved process that took 50 to 75 years.

d. Reasoned vs random selection

Reasoned selection means that the researcher chooses cases on the basis of variation design considerations or other relevent characteristics such as cost or ease of access. When reasoned selection is used, the reasons should be explicit and defensible. If the number of cases/time periods is only somewhat larger than can be included, reasoned selection is preferred

Ideally, the researcher should be able to demonstrate that the selected cases are not a biased sample.

Random selection of sample cases is ordinarily used when (1) the number of cases available is much larger than the project can manage, and (2) when statistical significance tests are planned for the data analysis.

Statistical significance tests are designed to inform researchers about the probability that certain results may occur by chance. In random sampling, a chance process is used to select or reject particular cases for the sample. Note that where reasoned selection is employed, chance processes are not used, and consequently statistical significance tests become useless.

It should be emphasized that, whereas random selection is often used to choose cases, it is rarely used when selecting time periods. One would be hard pressed to find any studies that randomly sample the points in time that measurements are taken. Ordinarily, every point in time at which measurements have been taken are included. Frequent measurements may be averaged, but rarely would they be randomly sampled.

EXAMPLE: In a study of unemployment as a cause of crime in Canada after the Second World War, measurements of crime rate were available only on an annual basis. Unemployment rates, however, which were derived from the labour force survey, were available by the month. Since the data analysis design called for correlating the two rates, the monthly unemployment rates for each year included were averaged (summed and divided by 12). In the data analysis the annual average unemployment rates were correlated with the annual crime rates.

What sample bias (if any) would be introduced if the monthly unemployment rates were sampled randomly?

The simplest random selection plan is usually called a simple random sample (SRS). A random selection device is applied to a list of the cases to be selected. The cases selected compose the sample.

Random selection devices

Any device that can be shown to generate a random series of numbers that can be used to select units from a population list is a random selection device. Such devices would include dice, coins, random number generators, and so on. One of the easiest to use is a list of random digits, produced by a computer, such as those in Table 7.1. These numbers are supposedly generated randomly and therefore can be used to choose the cases that should appear in the sample.

EXAMPLE:

Table 7.1
Computer Generated Random Numbers

Obs	X1	X2	X3	X4	X5	X6	X7
1	225859	556412	206003	373145	519437	403486	284306
2	220269	433593	505155	298250	326873	628584	660282
3	388092	284263	976397	267196	315669	427177	959690
4	247008	233593	254414	323039	394212	635430	713481
5	984967	651479	390612	128566	222868	135792	649003
6	927168	666739	188797	463136	369669	504317	059270
7	045032	227435	482275	110005	305655	667071	295134
8	975188	425065	242294	299986	707556	687019	181319
9	462946	614298	837604	145784	664802	648951	944931
10	201054	045783	423894	630053	815872	463420	311699
11	172195	883349	109691	623972	204784	550313	231951
12	769968	890109	593019	301219	572829	899601	616054
13	463060	461827	886757	831843	821530	765005	814717
14	036013	875848	813971	776547	654010	933770	285702
15	273816	788665	924211	143899	276857	275018	599386
16	300321	115514	669264	305538	013743	348677	670082
17	394985	329977	910231	056297	760012	410196	103356
18	932195	744955	492498	492408	536114	185853	952466
19	126811	327371	913522	746234	914026	000129	574576
20	738497	062976	210373	006559	591365	883395	623654
21	047886	608979	128989	946390	858922	344001	453879
22	507342	460236	269911	084126	740566	541145	732946
23	600622	659989	077622	257274	998439	553165	389903
24	336354	436178	784442	136268	775832	975298	486303
25	991607	811626	103675	919756	334690	564894	297724
26	198953	171279	552059	433890	477496	167019	659518
27	806588	177923	798920	718030	797129	351179	942742
28	077865	079685	091277	775058	757282	482967	691755
29	530015	599975	930272	677690	024609	855260	664758
30	646979	257373	031713	148207	288680	743957	036279
31	120013	958561	182120	645414	097740	878690	714298
32	543024	742886	155851	221034	961437	779036	165689
33	910306	559408	548427	673579	954477	682363	673032
34	345460	860231	515837	305561	928803	059995	175402
35	710806	382085	545340	919916	185171	282567	101597

36	754149	213975	432879	778793	825929	927482	196899
37	504306	025295	083156	409829	497522	360638	658344
38	047854	373673	628394	808305	363721	562223	655986
39	358168	228389	760629	090659	062740	258234	653323
40	177871	101093	820401	640120	259487	715065	969233
41	832468	958463	368942	236415	412673	084367	501999
42	685969	842094	004841	713584	482583	958024	418947
43	247773	931210	315879	753697	996304	397459	142968
44	842802	380082	837928	694075	105707	893131	401835
45	571249	286785	901185	059147	741636	836415	465643
46	608227	303496	477459	250444	828672	752352	606104
47	378035	366018	735559	385861	207514	110568	052679
48	033289	764360	437547	807420	127581	201474	575440
49	777732	408962	461624	448650	066643	976874	929515
50	785595	884752	928052	313076	641315	296650	818227

EXAMPLE: Selecting samples using a table of random numbers

Suppose we want to select a sample of five names from the following list numbered from 1 to 25.

1. Leslie, M.   2. Letvak, H.M.   3. Levine, N.   4. Phimister, J.   5. Pidsadny, L.Y.   6. Pilat, E.J. Dr.   7. Pilon, P.   8. Quinn, J.A.   9. Racano, S.T.   10. Radu, H.   11. Rasmussen, J.E.   12. Rattray, M.   13. Rea, P.   14. Sanatonio, B.   15. Sandulak, R.   16. Santucci, J.   17. Sawchuk, M.   18. Schnerch, R.   19. Seal, W.K.   20. Seaman, K.   21. Shewchuk, A.M.   22. Tidquist, H.M.   23. Trautman, W.   24. Unwin, R.   25. Vilar, J.

We enter the table of random numbers at any point and proceed in any direction to read pairs of numbers until five are found with any value between 1 and 25 inclusive. If we start at the top of the first column and work down, the first random number is 22, which is chosen. The next number is also 22, so we ignore it. The third number, 38, is too large, but the fourth, 24, is chosen. The random numbers in rows 5 and 6 are too large and are ignored, but the 7th number 04 is chosen. Rows 10 and 11 have suitably sized random numbers, so they are included. Our random sample then would consist of the above individuals with numbers 22, 24, 4, 20, and 17: Tidquist, Unwin, Phimister, Seaman, and Sawchuk.

If we had started in the same place but moved sideways rather than down the columns of numbers, our samples would consist of those names corresponding to the numbers 22, 12, 20, 3, and 6.

If there were a large number of units in the population, say 1,200, then the same procedure for choosing random numbers would be used, but more columns of figures would have to be observed. Instead of pairs of numbers we would observe quadruples of numbers and select values between 1 and 1,200 inclusive. Proceeding down the first column again, we would choose the random number 0450 (row 7), 0360 (row 14), 0478 (row 21), and so on. The other quadruples of numbers in rows 1 to 21 are all larger than 1,200 and so would be ignored.

For some case selection problems, simple random samples may be expensive or ineffective. They may be expensive because they require a complete list of the cases to be selected. To avoid this expense, researchers may sample clusters of cases first. It is often possible to obtain complete lists of clusters of cases and then take the sample in two stages. After a cluster sample (a simple random sample of clusters) is selected, a simple random sample of cases is selected from each cluster.

EXAMPLE: Accurate up-to-date lists of the residents of a city, province, or country are ordinarily very difficult to obtain. On the other hand, maps of city blocks are relatively cheap and accurate. To obtain a sample of city residents, one samples city blocks randomly in the first stage. In the second stage, each block is treated as a population, and one or more residences from each block would be selected randomly.

EXAMPLE: Grayson (1983) sampled novels by members of the Canadian "literary elite" to study the Canadian novel as a vehicle for male hegemony. The sampling process had two stages. Authors were sampled first, and then one novel by each was selected.

EXAMPLE: If a representative sample of school children is desired, a two-stage sampling plan might treat schools as clusters of children. In the first stage of the sampling plan, schools are selected; in the second stage, students at the selected schools are sampled. The information costs of the first stage—obtaining a list of schools—would be minimal. In the second stage, information costs are reduced to that of obtaining complete lists of students only for those schools selected in the first stage.

More than two stages of clustering are possible. If schools are clusters of school children, cities and towns are clusters of schools. A three-stage sampling plan can then select cities and towns in stage one, schools from these cities and towns in stage two, and children from these schools in stage three.

When simple random samples are small, they may be ineffective because types of cases rare in the population are unlikely to appear in the sample at all. This problem is solved by stratifying the population before selecting the sample.

A stratum is any subgroup of a population of cases that have the same value (or range of values) on a variable. Populations are stratified by grouping cases according to their values on a variable. Cases are then sampled randomly from each stratum to produce a *stratified sample*.

EXAMPLE: A population grouped by sex has two strata—male and female. When samples are selected from each stratum the product is a (sex) stratified sample.

When a population is grouped by more than one variable simultaneously, the result is multiple stratification.

EXAMPLE: Suppose we have a population of the twenty-five persons listed in Table 7.2. Using names, we can stratify by sex categories. Using occupation information, we can classify cases by occupation categories. Using sex and occupation categories simultaneously, we can categorize the population into occupation and sex categories. With these groups of cases, samples may be selected from each stratum. Note that the relatively small proportions of white-collar male and blue-collar females would appear in the sample according to the proportion of each in the population.

Table 7.2
Population Listing

---

1. Jane Addams, secretary
2. Jane Buckner, housewife
3. Allan Cairns, carpenter
4. Bill Clairmont, sociologist
5. John Downs, labourer
6. Evelyn Everett, nurse
7. June Fogarty, policewoman
8. Linda Gourd, teacher
9. Paul Husser, teacher
10. Donald Juno, programmer
11. Fay Kester, programmer
12. Mike Dorner, electrician
13. Mark Muskovic, manager
14. Jenny Nivic, cook
15. Jan Nester, pharmacist
16. John Novac, gardener
17. Bev Newton, waitress
18. Jack Owen, taxi driver
19. Rhonda Pear, sewing mach. oper.
20. Ray Rogoz, electrician
21. Reena Roman, key punch operator

22. Frank Soge, day-care worker
23. Marcel Touichot, labourer
24. Gina Sadowski, sales clerk
25. Eric Viz, janitor

| | Sex Stratum | |
Occupation Stratum	Male	Female
White collar	4, 9, 10, 13 22	1, 2, 6, 8, 11 15, 21, 24
Blue collar	3, 5, 12, 16, 18 20, 23, 25	7, 14, 17, 19

Stratification can be combined with clustering, either or both being done in each of several stages.

EXAMPLE: If a sample of school children is needed, towns (as clusters of schools) could be stratified by size, and schools (as clusters of children) could be stratified by size and public or private. Finally children could be stratified by grade and sex.

The most expensive operation here would be stratifying the school children, but that has to be done only for selected schools rather than for all children. Because there are relatively few towns and schools, it would be less expensive to stratify them. Together, clustering and stratification can produce representative samples at lower costs than non-stratified single-stage designs.

7.5 WHAT CAN GO WRONG IN SAMPLING?

There are several things that can go wrong in the sampling process. The cases selected for inclusion might not be found. Or they might be found but might not be measured. Or the cases that can be found and measured will not meet variation design requirements or data analysis requirements. Or the use of random selection produces unrepresentative samples. If any of the above occur, the sample may be biased.

EXAMPLE: Chalmers and Smith's follow-up study (1987) of former residents of a Regina shelter for battered women interviewed 105 of the 709 women who had used the house between 1976 and 1982. The researchers did not describe their sampling procedure other than to say that most were urban women. They suspect that their sample may be biased: "No claim is made that these 105 women are representative of the 709 or of the battered women generally."

EXAMPLE: Querido sampled 2,200 patients admitted to an Amsterdam hospital in order to investigate the relationship between stress and the patients' recovery. Even with a sample of this size, Querido says, "There are many reasons for limiting these conclusions to the present sample, but it cannot be denied that something useful may be abstracted from this sample and placed within the frame of reference of more general medical problems." (1959:48)

EXAMPLE: Russell (1984) surveyed 930 randomly selected San Francisco women about their experiences of rape and sexual abuse. Nineteen % of the respondents refused to be interviewed when they learned the subject was rape. If men as well as women who declined to give a list of household members is included, the refusal rate is 36%. If households (1) where no one was ever home, (2) were physically inaccessible, and (3) where the interviewer was prevented by circumstances or husbands from completing an interview are included, the refusal rate is 50%. Russell devotes several pages to discussing the possible sample bias that the refusals may have introduced into her data.

EXAMPLE: Schreier and Kaplan, after studying anxiety reduction in fifteen mothers and their pre-operative children, state, "it is apparent that generalization cannot be made on the basis of such a small sample. It is therefore concluded that a similar research project should be undertaken with a larger sample in order to ascertain whether some of the tentative findings here could perhaps be substantiated." (1983:147).

7.6 HOW CAN SAMPLE BIAS BE ASSESSED?

Ineffective, unsuitable, or counterproductive policy or practice applications are very likely when the applications are based on findings from biased samples. The basis for judging sample bias is the anticipated application of the findings.

The principal method for assessing sampling bias is repetition. The findings based on one sample are compared to the findings based on other samples. Similarities and differences in findings and sample characteristics lead to judgements of sample bias or otherwise. Table 7.3 displays the possible judgements when two studies are compared.

Where more than two studies are compared, the weight of evidence principle becomes operative. In row three, for example, if two studies with

Table 7.3

Sample Bias Judgements from Comparison of Two Studies

Characteristics of Samples	Findings	Judgement
1. Same	Same	Samples are unbiased
2. Different	Same	Samples are unbiased
3. Different	Different	Samples may be biased
4. Same	Different	Samples may be biased

different samples have the same findings but a third study does not, the third study would be judged to have a biased sample. Of course, this judgement might change as more repetition studies are completed.

The repetition method of assessing sample bias may be supplemented with a procedure based on how well a sample represents a precisely defined population. This method assesses sample bias in terms of the similarity or dissimilarity of the sample and the population it was drawn from. It requires recent census-type information. Census-type information is information based on a complete enumeration of the population of cases from which the sample will be drawn. Government statistics bureaus are a usual source of census information, but any complete enumeration of members, businesses, churches or unions, for example, can be considered as census-type information.

This supplemental method of assessing sample bias compares the characteristics of the sample to the characteristics of the population enumerated in the census; if they are similar the sample is said to be unbiased. If they are different, biases are identified.

Table 7.4

Sample Bias Judgements from Comparison of Sample and Population

Characteristics of Population and Sample	Judgement
1. Same	Sample is unbiased
2. Different	Sample is biased

a. Repetition-based sample assessment

There are only two simple steps in sample bias assessment based on repetition studies. The first is to find a set of repetition studies—investigations of the same cause and effect relationships. The bibliography and review of literature carried out in the theoretical or policy analysis section of the project will provide an initial list of studies for the first step. The second step is noting (1) the findings and (2) the sample characteristics of each study and organizing them to facilitate comparison.

EXAMPLE: Walters, in a study of occupational health and safety legislation, selects Ontario as a sample and examines the events surrounding the introduction of legislation in 1977-78. Assessing her sample by means of repetition studies, she states that "there is evidence to suggest that conditions similar to those identified in this paper prevailed in both Britain and the U.S. prior to the introduction of occupational health and safety legislation" (Walters, 1983:430). She cites two repetition studies.

EXAMPLE: In the study of parents' behaviour when they were anticipating the death of their child (Friedman and others, 1963), it was found that friends and relatives provided offers of service and sympathetic, supportive listening. They cite another study with similar findings. They found also that the primary emotional support came from other parents whose children were dying. They cite one other study with similar conclusions. Only the findings were compared—there are no descriptions of the sample characteristics of the repetition studies.

b. Census-based sample assessment

The first step in census-based assessment of sample bias is to obtain the census information. The next is to find the characteristics of the population covered in the census. Once the sample is drawn, the population and sample characteristics are compared.

Note that if these comparisons are to be effective, indicators used to measure the sample must be identical or equivalent to those used in the census. The measurement design must include plans to facilitate census-based sample assessment.

How recent the census data has to be depends upon the kinds of sample characteristics the researcher is planning to use in the bias assessment. The more quickly that characteristics change, the more recent the census information must be to provide an effective bias assessment.

EXAMPLE: Sex distribution, for example, is usually about 50% females, 50% males, and changes relatively slowly in large units such as provinces or cities. In these settings, five-year-old census data is likely to serve as an effective base for assessing sample bias for the distribution of sex. In frontier communities and mining towns, on the other hand, where the sex distribution may change rapidly with economic development or crisis and be quite imbalanced, five-year-old data could be wildly inaccurate.

EXAMPLE: Marital status, unlike sex, has been changing relatively quickly in the present decade (1980s), and separated and divorced status is increasing. If the census data is five years old, then, it is not very useful as a base for assessing sample bias in marital status.

EXAMPLE: Table 7.5 illustrates a simple representativeness assessment. The information about the population was taken from two-year-old census data. The researchers estimated that with rising wages over the two-year period, 10% error (difference between sample and population) for the income data would be acceptable. In the illustration, the sample income data are within the 10% margin.

Table 7.5

Income $000	Sample %	Population %	Error (S%-P%)
0-3	3	5	-2
4-6	4	5	-1
7-9	20	15	5
10-12	22	20	2
13-15	10	15	-5
16-18	10	10	0
19-21	1	5	-4
22-24	2	5	-3
25-27	3	1	2
28-30	7	1	6
31-40	10	1	9
41-50	5	1	4
51-75	3	1	2

EXAMPLE: Grayson sampled novels by members of the Canadian "literary elite" to study the Canadian novel as a vehicle for male hegemony. The sampling process had two stages. Authors were sampled first, and then one novel by each was selected.

Assessing the sample for possible bias, Grayson compares the percentage of female novelists in the Writers' Union of Canada to the percentage of contemporary female novelists that show up in his sample. The percentages are approximately equal. "Consequently, there are grounds for believing the sample to be fairly representative of the works of individuals who have been defined as the English Canadian literary elite." (Grayson, 1983:4)

EXAMPLE: To assess the adequacy of her 1978 random sample of 930 San Francisco women who completed an interview on rape and sexual abuse, Russell (1984) compared the characteristics of the sample to the characteristics of all women residents according to the census of 1980. Table 7.6 is adapted from Russell's tables.

Table 7.6
Comparison of Marital Status of Respondents in Russell's Sample
with 1980 Census Data for San Francisco

Marital Status	1980 Census	Russell Sample	Difference
Single	33.0	31.0	2.0
Married	38.0	39.0	−1.0
Separated	3.0	4.0	−1.0
Widowed	15.0	12.0	3.0
Divorced	11.0	14.0	−3.0
Ethnicity			
White	57.2	67.4	−10.2
Latin	10.8	7.1	3.7
Black	10.8	9.6	1.2
Asian	20.1	13.1	7.0
Other	1.1	2.7	−1.6

In marital status, the sample is very similar to the census, but for ethnicity white is over-represented and Asian under-represented to such an extent that bias may be suspected. Russell argues that the under-representation of Asians is not as large as it appears. (1) Asians had been flowing into the city rapidly, so that the 1980 census information would overstate the proportion of Asians in 1978, when the sample was drawn. (2) The study accepted only English- and Spanish-speaking women, and a significant number of Asians spoke neither survey language. Russell claims that her sample is closely representative of English-speaking Asian women.

c. Repetition-based vs census-based assessment of sample bias

Repetition-based assessment requires repetition studies, while census-based assessment requires census-type information.

Repetition-based assessment places fewer constraints on the measurement phase than census-based assessment. Since the value of comparing the sample with the census depends on having identical categories, the project measurement must duplicate all the census measurements employed in the assessment. Since, in contrast, repetition-based assessment focuses on the relationships between causes and effects, the measurements here need only be similar rather than identical.

Repetition-based assessments of sample bias is direct: the emphasis is on the findings that describe the relationship between causes and effect. Census-based assessment is indirect: the emphasis is on sets of simple characteristics of the sample and population, but not on the relationship between causes and effect.

Probably the best advice is this: if both repetition studies and recent census data are available, supplement repetition-based assessment with census-based assessment. At some point the amount of time and money it takes to obtain census-type information becomes a consideration. (When neither repetition studies nor census-type information is available, describe your sample in sufficient detail to permit the sample bias to be assessed in the future.)

7.7 SUMMARY

Samples are sets of cases or time periods selected for special attention in a research project. Sample cases or time periods are important because the conclusions of an investigation are statements about the relationships observed between the causes and effect measured on the sample.

The variation design sets the boundaries for the sample design. Given the requirements of the variation design, sample design consists of finding and identifying suitable cases or time periods, choosing some of those cases or time periods, and planning the sample bias assessment.

Sample designs are selected on the basis of availability of cases or time periods, minimum size requirements, and cost. Random selection of cases is preferred when the number of potential cases is large in relation to the desired sample size.

Since the project's findings are a description of the sample, sample bias will make the findings less useful. Sample bias is assessed directly by comparing findings from repetition studies, or indirectly by comparing measured characteristics of the sample to measured characteristics of the census.

7.8 EXERCISES

1. Why do some pregnant teenage women have abortions whereas others complete their pregnancies? One study found that age was a cause: the older the woman, the higher the rate of carrying to term. A second study found little relationship with age.
   (a) Why would you suspect that sample bias produced the differences?
   (b) If these differences were produced by sample biases, what features of the sample would you investigate?
   (c) The variation design requires observed variation in the age of pregnant teenagers. How would you find pregnant teenagers, and how would you select cases to guarantee variation in their ages?

2. One study of police investigations of serious crimes found that when the victims were natives, less time and resources were devoted to the investigations than when non-natives were victims, and the investigations were less successful. A second study found no such differences.
   (a) Why would you suspect that sample bias produced the differences?
   (b) If these different findings were due partly to sample biases, what features of the sample would you investigate?
   (c) If you were to design a repetition study, how would you select cases, how would you guarantee that the crimes were serious, and how would you guarantee that victims consisted of roughly equal numbers of native and non-natives?

3. One study of university social science researchers found that women thought that threats to academic freedom were more serious than men. A second study found no difference among the sexes.
   (a) Why would you suspect that sample bias produced the differences?
   (b) If these different findings were due partly to sample biases, what features of the sample would you investigate?

(c) The variation design requires sex variation among academics. How would you find academics, and how would you select cases to guarantee variation in their sex?

4. (a) In chapter 6, exercises 1, 2, 3, 4, and 5 specified variation designs or required the description of variation designs. Using the materials in the questions or your answer to the questions, determine a sampling plan for these variation designs.

i) Specify how and where you could obtain information that would allow you to locate and identify possible sample cases.

ii) Specify how sample cases would be selected for inclusion in the sample.

iii) For which of these samples do you think would it be possible to carry out a census-based assessment?

iv) Suppose that no studies could be found for a repetition-based assessment. In order to make it possible for future researchers to do sample assessments, you decide to describe your sample in detail. What characteristics of the sample would you include in this full description?

5. In chapter 6, exercise 6, samples were described and the amount of variation in the sample was the focus. Now think about these same samples as samples and consider how you would assess the sample bias. To what other set of cases would you compare those listed in order to do a census-based assessment?

6. Describe the populations from which the samples in the examples in section 7.1 were drawn.

7. In exercise 6 above, you attempted to describe the populations from which the samples in the examples in section 7.1 were drawn. Now try to describe the variation designs that guided the sampling plan.

8. From the information in the above questions (or your answers to them), choose several sample plans with some variety in the types of cases involved.

(a) Estimate how much time and money it would cost to find one sampled case or time period (or find the information about that case or time period).

(b) What is the *minimum* sample size that would permit some conclusion about the accuracy of the hypotheses under investigation? How much would this sample cost?

(c) What sample size would provide significantly more confidence in the conclusions of the study? How much would this sample cost?

9. (a) How would you demonstrate or prove that
    i) a set of random numbers, or
    ii) a device purported to be a random number generator is really random?
(b) Apply your demonstration method to the list of computer-generated random numbers. What conclusions do you come to?
(c) Use a coin (heads = include, tails = exclude) or a die (1 – 3 = include, 4 – 6 = exclude) to select sample cases from a list. Record the results of 25, 50, and 100 trial tosses. Does the evidence from your trial data convince you that the device is fair, and therefore can be relied on to produce random samples?

10. Below are several sets of comparisons of sample characteristics and census-type information.
(a) When the samples are compared to the census information, would you judge them to be representative or unrepresentative of each characteristic?
(b) Is there a pattern in the unrepresentative characteristics, or do they appear to be random?
(c) If a sample that matched the census-type information exactly were desired, how would you modify or expand the sample?

	Census-type Information Percentage	Sample Percentage	Number of cases in sample
(i) *Sex*			*88*
Males	37	30	
Females	63	70	
(ii) *Class*			*240*
Working class	75	65	
Middle class	20	25	
Upper class	5	10	
(iii) *Age*			*312*
15-19 years	14	7	
20-24	15	10	
25-29	15	20	
30-34	25	28	
45-64	12	20	
65+	19		
(iv) *Community population*			*45*
1 000-9 000	33	21	
10 000-99 000	61	73	
100 000 +	6	6	

	Census-type Information Percentage	15 Sample Percentage	Number of cases in sample
(v) *National economies*			*30*
Low income	33	41	
Middle income	28	33	
Upper-middle income	20	23	
High income oil export	3	0	
Industrial market	16	3	

CHAPTER 8

Measurement Design

CHAPTER CONTENTS

8.1 WHAT IS MEASUREMENT?

Measurement is a process we all use virtually all the time in all our activities. It consists of applying an indicator to an object or event and noting the values on the indicator.

EXAMPLE: When someone asks, "How are you?" they are requesting that you measure your well-being and give a report. No indicators are specified—you are being invited to apply and report on whatever indicators you choose. Ordinarily people choose from tired/not tired, sick/not sick, hungry/not hungry, excited/not excited, fine/not fine, and a few other indicators of feeling. Your reply represents the value you have read from the indicators you apply to yourself.

EXAMPLE: Most conversations can be seen as exchanges of reports of measurement processes. Even listening and understanding (or being puzzled) by what someone says involves measurement. The listener (1) hears a vocalization, (2) classifies it as a word, (3) connects it with the other classified words, (4) takes a reading of the message, (5) notes its import, and (6) formulates a reply which will report other measurements. All this measuring goes on much faster than it can be told.

EXAMPLE: Descriptions of the weather are produced by applying an indicator with categories like beautiful, nice, *OK*, not so good, bad, miserable, terrible, and so on to observations of the general outdoor environment. This indicator is a kind of summary indicator that could be broken down into a number of indicators used to describe all aspects of the weather: a temperature indicator, a cloudiness indicator, a windiness indicator, a humidity indicator, and so on.

For social scientific purposes, an indicator is an observable and recordable variable that will serve as a measure of a theoretical cause or effect. A measurement is a record of the value observed when an indicator is applied to a sampled case or time period.

EXAMPLE: Harvey and Kalwa (1983) measured the educational achievement of university graduates as one of the causes of differences in their success after graduation. To measure educational achievement, grade-point average was used as an indicator.

EXAMPLE: To measure the male hegemony content in novels, Grayson (1983) classified each novel's attitude to women's subordination as accepting, questioning, rejecting, or ambiguous. The classification is an indicator based upon a common-sense reading and interpretation of the novel.

EXAMPLE: Gerber investigated communal and individualistic values as causes of rates of off-reserve residence for Indians in Canada. The type of case was a reserve. The cause was measured with a Prairie location or other location indicator. Gerber says, "Most Prairie bands were established on a communal basis, whereas those in the other provinces were set up with more individual control of land and other assets." (1984:147)

The effect variable—the rate of off-reserve residence—refers "only to those band members who have resided away from the reserve for more than one year, indicating some sort of commitment to off-reserve life." (1984:146). Gerber says this indicator of out-migration is crude, but short-term or seasonal movement has no influence on it.

EXAMPLE: An investigation of the relationship of stress to post-hospitalization recovery required the measurement of stress at the point of hospital admission. The indicator for stress was a team decision regarding the patient's previous history, behaviour in former difficulties, attitudes toward actual problems, and subjective expressions. "A decision did not rest upon the question whether stress was adjudged to be present but upon the question whether the patient was hampered by his problems. When it was decided that the patient was not able to handle his problems and was hampered or burdened by them, the team used the expression *distress*. When problems were mentioned by the patient but the team judged that he was able to manage them, the expression *stress* was used. In this article, therefore, 'distress' refers to social and/or psychic tensions too heavy for the patient to bear, while 'stress' refers to tensions which are satisfactorily integrated in the patient's life pattern. The term 'somatic' means that no distress could be found or that the somatic illness was so serious that it dominated the entire picture. The type of 'distress' was classified as follows: psychic only; psychosomatic; somatic with psychic parallel problems; somatic with social parallel problems; somatic with psychic and social problems." (Querido, 1969:34)

To measure post-hospitalization recovery, Querido uses a satisfactory or unsatisfactory indicator. He states, "There was some difficulty in formulating the follow-up assessment. The term 'cured' could not be used, because it required a distinction to be made between anatomical, physiological, and functional cure, and between objective and subjective cure. For some time the term 'benefit' was used, but this was finally rejected because it seemed to imply a too direct causal relationship between hospital admission and the later condition of the patient. Finally the neutral terms 'satisfactory' and 'unsatisfactory' were chosen, and these are used in the rest of this paper. Cases were assessed as 'satisfactory' when the patient was (a) free from any complaint; (b) suffering from typical residual complaints (pain in scar, etc.) only; (c) free from any complaint for a time but now showing sharply-defined symptoms which could not possibly be related to the illness for which he had been admitted to hospital.

"The term 'unsatisfactory' was used for all other cases, in which the patient was: (a) free from complaints for some time but now experiencing a return of the former symptoms; (b) suffering from complaints equal to or worse than those experienced before admission; (c) slightly improved but substantially unchanged; (d) suffering from a recurrence, with or without a complaint-free period" (1969:35).

The last example above details the observations involved in arriving at a recorded value of (1) stress (the cause) and (2) recovery (the effect) for each patient sampled. An indicator consists of all the observations used to arrive at a recorded value. The amount of detail appearing in Querido's article is used only where the indicators are not in common use.

8.2 WHY IS MEASUREMENT IMPORTANT?

Measurement is important because no research findings are possible without it. Research findings are constructed out of measurements. Measurements are the raw materials of data analysis, which in its simplest terms is the organization and display of sets of measurements.

EXAMPLE: The finding that women are paid lower average wages than men is no more and no less than a description of the pattern that emerges when a set of measurements of wages and sex is organized and displayed in a way that makes the pattern of interconnections apparent.

The sex measurements are used to group the wage measurements, and then some mathematical operations are used to average the wage measurements. The finding that women's wages are lower than men's is nothing but a description of the pattern observable in a set of measurements when they are arranged, displayed, and summarized. Obviously, without the measurements there is no material to produce the findings.

EXAMPLE: After measuring the acceptance or rejection of the subordination of women in Canadian novels from 1800 to the present, Grayson (1983) finds there has been little change in the acceptance of subordination. This finding reports a summary of the arrangement and display of measures of time of publication and the acceptance or rejection content of novels.

EXAMPLE: Wallace (1979) finds that arms races cause wars. This finding is based on the arrangement and display of measurements of war/no war and arms race/no arms race.

8.3 WHAT ARE THE STEPS IN MEASUREMENT DESIGN?

There are two steps in measurement design. The first is choosing indicators; the second is planning the control of measurement error.

a. Choosing indicators

While apparently simple, the choice of indicators can be demanding.

1. Within each alternative theory, the effect cannot be chosen without regard to the choice of indicator for the cause; indicators for one cause must be chosen in the light of choices for other causes; the indicator chosen must be consistent with the theory under investigation, including those aspects of the theory not under direct investigation.
2. Between alternative theories: indicator choices must be consistent with the theoretical differences between the theories.
3. The whole design must be practical: ways must be found to apply each indicator to each sampled case; records of indicator readings must be kept; if an effect is to be measured some time after the causes were measured, records must be kept in such a way that earlier and later measurements can be related, and so on.

Indicators can be defined as observable and recordable phenomena that will serve as measures of a cause or effect. Indicators are themselves variables, but not necessarily theoretical ones.

Indicators have to be selected because, ordinarily, the cause and effect terms that appear in theories and hypotheses may be measured by any of a whole set of indicators.

EXAMPLE: The sex of an individual could be measured by the following indicators: presence or absence of facial makeup, voice differences, height and weight differences, physiological characteristics, anatomical characteristics, chromosomal differences, self-description, and so on. Each of these is an observable and recordable variable.

EXAMPLE: The presence or absence of war between two nations could be indicated by some or all of the following observable and recordable indicators: destructive activities by agents or citizens of one nation toward another, mobilization of institutionalized armed forces, border incidents by citizens or guerillas, assassination attempts on the political or military leaders, pitched battles, formal declarations of war, number of military battle deaths, number of civilian casualties, and so on.

EXAMPLE: In the study of the effects of stress at admission to a hospital and subsequent recovery, stress was measured in a clinical setting by a team of clinicians. Possible indicators of stress in this setting are numerous. Patients could be queried about their attitudes and behaviour. Case histories could be used. Clinicians could observe the patients' behaviour and take various anatomical and physiological measurements.

Querido (1969) settled upon a team decision indicator for stress; it is based upon the patient's (1) previous history, (2) former behaviour, (3) attitudes toward problems, and (4) subjective expressions. But the decision rested, not upon whether stress was present, but on whether patients were hampered by their problems.

For most theoretical causes and effects there will be a variety of observable and recordable indicators that can serve as measurements. Different indicators often have different observing and recording costs. They often have different possibilities of error as well.

EXAMPLE: In any face-to-face situation, the measurement of sex by self-description, makeup, voice, height, and weight indicators is easy to observe and record. Physiological, anatomical, and especially chromosomal indicators are much more difficult and expensive to observe and record.

In this case, the more expensive indicators are also much less subject to error than the inexpensive ones. It is no accident that in international sports events where competition is divided according to sex (the Olympics, for example), chomosomal indicators are the only accepted measurement of sex. It is the only indicator that cannot be changed by the competitor, either by him- or herself or with the help of makeup artists, plastic surgeons, sex-change surgeons, and so on.

When more than one indicator is chosen for a theoretical cause or effect, some plan for combining the indicators becomes part of the measurement design.

EXAMPLE: In a study of the effects of war on birth rates in developing countries, it is important that the dates of the beginning and ending of war be fairly accurate. Suppose the indicators chosen were (1) formal declaration of onset and cessation of war, (2) at least 1,000 deaths in battle, and (3) some amount of property destruction. The researcher will have to plan how the indicators will be combined, because it is possible that declarations are made but there are no military deaths or destruction of property. The reverse is also possible; that is, military deaths occur, but no formal declarations of war are issued. Or extensive property destruction takes place but without enough military deaths and without formal declarations.

EXAMPLE: To appreciate the problems of measuring the presence or absence of war, use these indicators to determine if South Africa is currently at war with Mozambique, Angola, and Namibia. If these indicators don't work, which ones would you choose?

EXAMPLE: In a study of social class as a cause of psychiatric disorder, Hollingshead and Redlich (1953) measured individual social class with three "scaled factors": area of residence, occupation, and education. Each person's address, occupation, and completed years in school were assigned a scale score, and then these were multiplied by a "factor weight." "The factor weights are as follows: ecological area of residence, 5; occupation, 8; and education, 6. The three factor scores are summed, and the resultant score is taken as an index of this individual's position in the community's social class system."

   Hollingshead and Redlich call their indicators "factors." They combine the three indicators as described to produce a single composite indicator of social class. They group this indicator into five major social classes. In their data analysis they examine the relationship between this single combination indicator and an indicator of psychiatric disorder (Hollingshead and Redlich, 1953).

EXAMPLE: To measure "institutional completeness" as a cause of off-reserve migration of Indians in Canada, Gerber (1984) used an index of eleven administrative, education, and economic activities on the reserve. Each of the eleven items is a separate indicator. Gerber combined them by addition—she simply counted the number of index activities existing on each reserve.

EXAMPLE: In his study of stress and recovery from hospitalization, Querido (1959) used the judgements of a team of clinicians about each patient as an indicator of stress. The clinicians' judgements were combined on the basis of consensus. If there was disagreement, the case was reviewed until a consensus was obtained.

b. Planning control of measurement error

Where qualitative indicators are used, measurement error consists of classifying a case/time period in a wrong category. When quantitative indicators are used, measurement error consists of underestimating or overestimating the value of the case/time period on the indicator. Quantitative errors can be large, medium, or small. Measurement error is controlled by applying replication and triangulation to those measurements where error is suspected.

When large numbers of cases/time periods are measured, two types of measurement error—random and systematic—can be distinguished on the basis of patterns of error. When all kinds of misobservation or misrecording appear equally, the error is random; when one kind appears much more frequently or exclusively, the error is systematic. Controlling random error requires replication, while controlling systematic error requires triangulation.

It should be understood that measurement accuracy cannot be known in the short run. In-project replication and triangulation do, however, produce information useful for judging accuracy.

In the long run, deciding the accuracy of measurements in one project requires replication and triangulation by other projects, as well as successful sustained practical application of the findings.

EXAMPLE: More confidence can be placed in a project that found that affirmative action programs would correct wage discrimination against women when those findings are replicated in different times and places. The confidence would be greater if several different measures of discrimination and affirmative action had been employed (triangulation). However, only after sustained operation of affirmative action programs actually resulted in the diminution and final disappearance of wage differences between men and women could anyone be fully confident in the accuracy of the measurements.

8.4 HOW ARE MEASUREMENT DESIGNS CHOSEN?

Measurement designs are chosen on the basis of a few simple considerations. The first is the decisions already made about variation and sample design—the type of case chosen and the time periods selected. A second is the cost and availability of indicators. A third is the amount of precision necessary. The final considerations are the nature of the causes and effects to be measured and the coherence of the entire measurement design.

a. Variation and sample design choices

Type of case selections

In the variation design of a project, basic choices have been made regarding the type of case to be measured. In the sampling design, decisions have been made regarding how a sample of cases is to be located and measured. These choices place limits on the indicators that might be chosen for measurement purposes.

EXAMPLE: If the variation and sampling phase designs specify (1) nations or other large collective units as the type of case, and (2) the causes and effects investigated are collective rather than individual, then the choice of indicators is effectively restricted to a question of what can be found in libraries and archives.

Gerber (1984) studied the causes of rates of off-reserve residence of Canadian Indians. The case was the reserve community. Some of the causes she examined were regional location, urban proximity, band size, linguistic acculturation, male/female ratio and fertility. The indicators for the measurements were those available from the Department of Indian Affairs records, surveys of reserves, the Indian census, and the Government of Canada official atlas of reserves and settlements.

Time period selection

The further in the past the sampled cases or time periods are, the more one must rely on libraries and archives as sources of records and documents for indicators. Usually this will seriously limit the choice of indicators. Indicators that demand information not contained in a document obviously cannot be employed in the project. And if the persons who prepared the documents originally are no longer living, there is no help save further documentary research.

In opposite fashion, the more recent the time periods selected in the measurement design, the more the researcher is restricted to indicators based on direct observation and interviews. Indicators that require the completion of bureaucratic work—large-scale surveys, censuses, annual reports, and so on—are ordinarily months and even years out of date.

b. Cost and availability of indicators

Indicators are often chosen because others are not available, or if they are available, cost too much.

EXAMPLE: Harvey and Kalwa studied academic achievement vs labour market conditions as causes of variation in the job status of university graduates. Their indicators of academic achievement were obtained from a series of surveys of students who reported their grade-point averages. However, since labour market condition is not an individual characteristic, it could not be obtained by the same survey.

The measure they used was the unadjusted overall unemployment rate for Ontario, averaged over a four-year period beginning with the respondent's year of graduation. They chose it because "the general unemployment rate is the only labour market index readily available for the period (1960-76) to which [their] data pertain." Earlier studies had used specialized measures of the labour market such as the ratio of graduates to job openings, the ratio of the salaries of graduate to overall mean salaries, or the proportion of graduates employed in low-paying or "non-highly-qualified" jobs. Because the general unemployment index is not "specialized," it will measure more than just the labour market conditions faced by university graduates: "This variable will reflect the interaction of supply and demand in the labour market as well as the overall state of aggregate economic activity." (All quotations: Harvey and Kalwa, 1983:443- 4).

c. How much precision is necessary?

First of all it is useful to distinguish precision from accuracy. Precision of measurement can be defined in terms of the number of distinct points or categories that an indicator will distinguish. The measurement of the size of microbes, for example, requires high precision at the level of micrometres. Ordinary household rulers have a lower level of precision of millimetres, centimetres, or sixteenths, of an inch.

Accuracy can be defined as the precision necessary to make the distinctions required. Cooks, for example, know that imprecise measurements of amounts of ingredients are accurate enough to produce tasty meals. If a pinch of salt is called for, it means that half a teaspoon is too much and a couple of grains will be too little. A pinch could be specified more precisely in terms of sixteenths of a teaspoon or hundredths of a gram, but the increased precision would make no difference to the taste of the dish.

The amount of precision necessary is the amount that will provide accurate conclusions about the policy or practice issues that led to the research. This will vary with the goals of the project and even for different causes and effects to be measured. Informed common sense is needed to choose a suitable and practical level of precision.

EXAMPLE: In a project to estimate the sex wage gap, full-time male and female workers in the same jobs were compared. Annual wage differences were found to be about $6,000. This finding involved some measurement error because the wages were rounded to the nearest dollar. Common sense would suggest that the magnitude of the rounding error (in dimes and cents) is trivial in relation to the magnitude (thousands of dollars) of the differences discovered. Even though it would be possible to redo the measurement to remove the error completely, common sense suggests that such work would be a waste of time and money.

Notice in the above example that the project would have to be completed before the importance of the measurement error to the findings could be determined. If the findings had been different, say less than $100 annually, the magnitude of the rounding error on wages becomes relatively more important. In general, the impact of a given magnitude and amount of measurement error is relative to the magnitude of causal influence on the effect. The smaller the causal influence, the more important are small amounts of measurement error.

EXAMPLE: If someone planning to venture outdoors asks the temperature, an accurate measure for the purpose would use the categories "hot" (remove extra clothing), "warm" (no clothing implications), "cool" (perhaps add clothing), "cold" (definately add extra clothing). A precise reading of a thermometer to, say, the third decimal point of a degree may be precise, but the precision contributes nothing to the accuracy of clothing choices.

d. Nature of the causes and effects

Some causes and effects are easier to measure than others. Those that are public, undebatable, non-sensitive, and unambiguous are easier to measure than those that are private, debatable, sensitive, and ambiguous.

Some examples of causes and effects that are at the extremes are given in Table 8.1 below.

Table 8.1

Public	Private
Sex	Sexuality
Citizenship	Feelings
Family membership	Emotions
Undebatable	Debatable
Marital status	Value of labour
Terms of contracts	Custody disputes
Non-sensitive	Sensitive
Occupation	Criminal record
Size of national population	Ethnic and race relations
Unambiguous	Ambiguous
Marital status	Responsibility for a marriage failure
Which team won	Which team is the better

When a variable is placed on each dimension, some of the important features of the variable have been made explicit for measurement purposes.

EXAMPLE: A person's sex, for example, is ordinarily public, undebatable, non-sensitive, and unambiguous. In contrast, sexuality is ordinarily private, debatable, sensitive, and ambiguous. Custody disputes are public, debatable, sensitive, and ambiguous.

EXAMPLE: For small businesses, corporations, and trade unions income is, in most senses, public and undebatable. However, since many organization activities hinge on income (taxes, for example) it tends to be very sensitive.

Given an organization of any size, income tends also to be something that requires a fair amount of effort (bookkeeping) to calculate, and so may be ambiguous, especially when copious records have not been kept. When important decisions like unionization or renegotiation of collective agreements are approaching, the profits (a form of income) may become ambiguous to all but senior management because collective bargaining outcomes are very sensitive to information about profits.

Ordinarily, the more sensitive the information, the more costly and difficult it is to obtain.

e. Amount of previous experience with indicators and pretesting

If indicators for the causes and effects to be measured have previously been used successfully, they are to be preferred over other indicators. In other words, when an earlier measurement design can be replicated either wholly or partially it should be, *provided it serves the goals of the research*.

There are many indicators that have been used to measure any number of causes and effects. Government bureaus conduct the census and continual surveys of business, labour, agriculture, and consumers. They have developed standard measures of many individual and aggregate phenomena and regularly publish assessments of the accuracy of the measures.

In addition, regular academic research reports ordinarily contain enough detail to permit indicators to be duplicated. (In psychology and education, standardized questionnaire and interview forms are even copyrighted.) Whenever existing indicators are suitable, they should be used, but only after reviewing the literature in which they are used and any available supplementary information on their accuracy.

Pretesting a measurement design is a means of gaining some experience with how the indicator works before applying it to a large sample of cases or time periods. It is also a small-scale form of replication.

When individuals are to be asked a large number of questions, pretesting consists of interviewing a small sample of respondents using the planned measurement design. Respondents are also asked whether they could understand the questions, whether the wording should be changed, and so on. Modifications are incorporated on the basis of the pretest information.

In other designs, the pretest usually amounts to examining very carefully the measurement of the first few cases or time periods sampled.

8.5 WHAT CAN GO WRONG IN MEASUREMENT?

Once the indicators have been selected, measurement consists of applying each indicator to each case or time period. The researcher observes the value and records it (for later data analysis). Two things can go wrong here. An indicator may be observed incorrectly, or recorded incorrectly (or both).

For quantitative indicators, each recorded observation is either correct or incorrect, but errors may be (1) above or below the correct value, and (2) large, medium, or small.

EXAMPLE: When the reading on an ordinary bathroom scale is taken as an indicator of your weight, it may be too high (your weight is overstated) or too low (your weight is understated). The size of the error may be large (5-10 kg) or small (1-100 gm).

EXAMPLE: Annual income taxes paid is often used as an indicator of an individual's income—the higher the taxes, the higher the income. However, the taxes paid may understate or overstate the income, and the overstatement or understatement may range from very small to very large. The taxes paid indicator usually overstates wage earners' real incomes and understates managers' and owners' real incomes.

Each recorded observation of a qualitative indicator is either correct or incorrect for two-valued indicators like sex. When many categories are involved, however, errors can be thought of as larger or smaller.

EXAMPLE: The name of an occupation is a name for a set of work activities that is a source of income. Occupations can be distinguished qualitatively from each other. One indicator of occupation is individual self-report. Self-reports are either correct or incorrect descriptions of an individual's occupation. Errors can occur when occupations are grouped into qualitatively similar types. The self-report may be very similar or very dissimilar to an actual occupation.

When measurements are taken on many cases or time periods, the notions of random and systematic measurement error are useful. The terms refer to patterns in the errors. If a sales clerk or bank teller sometimes gives too little change, and sometimes too much, the pattern of error is random. If she or he always gives too little change (or too much), the pattern is systematic. The size of the errors may be small or large, and may occur frequently or infrequently.

Of course both random and systematic patterns may exist at the same time. If small errors are random and frequent, but the large ones systematic and infrequent (or vice versa), the two patterns could be distinguished.

When all kinds and magnitudes of misobservation or misrecording occur equally, the error is random; when one kind occurs much more often or exclusively, the error is systematic.

EXAMPLE: To measure communal vs individualistic values on Indian reserves, Gerber (1984) uses Prairie location vs location elsewhere as the indicator. She appears to suspect some random error when she says, "There is no guarantee that Prairie bands are more communal in their values" (1984:147). This implies that some non-Prairie reserves might have communal values, while some Prairie bands have individualistic values.

EXAMPLE: As an indicator of crime rates, crimes reported to the police contains systematic error: it always understates the amount of crime. The amount of understatement varies with the type of crime. About "twice as many crimes as are reported to police" were reported in a Canada-wide victimization survey, but for property crimes, about two-thirds of the unreported crimes were "too minor to warrant criminal justice system intervention." For crimes of violence, however, even serious crime went unreported "because the perceived danger or costs of reporting outweighed the advantages" (Evans and others, 1982).

EXAMPLE: Rosenhan (1973) and eight associates without any history of mental illness presented themselves for admission to psychiatric institutions, changing only their names and occupational histories, and reporting no symptoms save voices that mumbled "hollow" or "empty." None of the pseudo-patients were diagnosed as sane, and all but one were diagnosed as suffering from schizophrenia.

Later Rosenhan informed several mental hospitals that as a test of the diagnostic accuracy of the hospital staff, bogus patients—ones without any symptoms of mental illness—would attempt to be admitted. No bogus patients were sent by the researchers, but all the hospitals identified a large number of "pseudo-patients."

If the indicators selected have an artificial relationship to the theoretical variables, the result is a combination of systematic error and random error in some unknown mix.

EXAMPLE: Abrams (1982) investigated whether children prepared for surgery with a media presentation coped better than children without the preparation. Checklists of resistance behaviours completed by hospital staff were used as indicators of effective coping.

Abrams found that prepared children coped better than the non-prepared. But she also concludes that new indicators that "more accurately reflect the dynamics of real life" are required. She notes that children's resistance behaviour may be caused by many things besides their ability to cope with the hospital experience.

A form of systematic measurement error called "dependent measurement" can result when the same case is observed over several time periods or by several observers. When knowledge about an earlier measurement influences a later measurement, or when one observer's judgement influences another's, the later measurements are dependent upon the earlier.

EXAMPLE: In criminal investigations, standard procedure calls for the private questioning of different witnesses without permitting communication between witnesses. This procedure is usually replicated in criminal trials where the witnesses are not permitted to hear the testimony of those who precede them. This procedure is designed to prevent the observations of one witness from influencing others.

EXAMPLE: To investigate their ability to distinguish the sane from the insane, a group of mental health professionals were shown videotaped interviews of persons to be diagnosed. The persons interviewed were actors who had memorized scripts developed by the research team to represent people with and without psychiatric symptoms. When the video was presented without comment, the diagnoses varied considerably. When another professional's diagnosis was given before the video, a very high percentage of the diagnoses matched it.

EXAMPLE: Querido (1959) used a team assessment (by a physician, social worker, and psychiatrist) of hospital patients as an indicator of stress. To "prevent the judgement of the team being distorted by the domination of any one member," the work of the team was observed by a psychologist, who observed how the judgements about stress were formed.

The most serious form of dependent measurement occurs when measurement of the effect is dependent upon measurement of a cause or vice versa. When this occurs the measurement process is building in, or producing, a relationship between a cause and effect rather than uncovering it. Rather than being the means by which relationships between variables are made observable, measurement becomes the process by which observed relationships are generated. And, because findings are constructed out of the measurements, the data analysis phase of the research project will produce bogus findings that are only indirect descriptions of dependent measurement. One way of controlling dependent measurement in medical, psychiatric, and psychological research is through "blind" design.

In "single blind" studies, patients do not know what remedy they are getting. The method was invented to solve the problem of the "placebo effect," in which patients improve even if they are given a treatment known to have no beneficial effects.

In "double blind" studies, neither patients nor physicians know who is getting the remedy and who is getting the placebo. This method was devised to solve another problem. Physicians, knowingly or unknowingly, might also bias the study by encouraging those with the remedy and discouraging those without. The problem being addressed is a dependent measurement of the cause (the remedy) and the effect (getting well). The double blind design is a strategy to prevent dependent measurement.

a. What difference does measurement error make?

The influence of random error by itself is fairly easy to specify. It (1) always increases the observed variation, (2) doesn't change the mean (of qualitative indicators), and (3) always reduces the strength of the relationship between a cause and an effect.

The influence of systematic error is another matter. It may (1) increase or decrease observed variation, (2) change the mean of quantitative indicators upward or downward, (3) produce misestimates of the direction of a causal relationship, and (4) produce over- or underestimates of the strength.

How much random error or measurement error will make a difference to any particular research findings? Since findings are constructed out of measurements, any error in the measurements will necessarily appear in the findings. An ordinary amount of random error, however, is tolerated because it is unlikely to produce misdescriptions of the direction of causal relationships—the most important kind of accuracy for policy application. Getting the direction right will prevent counterproductive policy application.

But to be effective, policy and practice has to be more than not counterproductive. It requires that the strength of a causal relationship be accurate as well as the direction. We have to know if a given change in a cause will bring a small, moderate, or large change in the effect. Small amounts of measurement error can be tolerated as long as they do not get the magnitude of the strength of a relationship wrong—if a given change in a cause brings about a *moderate* change in the effect, it should not be incorrectly described as *small* or *large*.

In short, while 100% accuracy in social science research measurement is desirable, small amounts of error are tolerated. What is tolerable is that amount of measurement error that (1) gets the direction right and (2) the strength roughly correct. Anything more is too much. What this adds up to is an attempt in social science to avoid *systematic* measurement error. Ordinary care will prevent random error from having enormous effects, and the effects are known as discussed above. The same is not the case with systematic error, and its effects depend entirely on the nature of the error.

A useful analogy here is the amount of accuracy that the criminal justice system attempts to achieve. Determining guilt or innocence is similar to determining the *direction* of a causal relationship, and determining the degree of guilt is similar to determining *strength*. Trials are reviews of evidence for the purpose of getting the *direction* right, that is, deciding whether or not the accused is guilty. Juries are enjoined to come to a guilty verdict only if that decision can be made without a *reasonable doubt*. The consequences of a guilty decision are so serious for an accused person that if the jury is not sure, it is instructed to bring in a not guilty verdict.

The question of *strength* of relationship—"how guilty" is the accused, was premeditation, malice, deliberate destructiveness involved or not—is left open to common sense determination in that possible errors here are not specifically directed against. A jury can bring in a guilty verdict but recommend, according to its assessment of the degree of guilt, that the punishment be harsh, moderate, or light or that there be no penalty at all.

Systematic measurement error especially can lead to findings that describe the relationship between causes and an effect incorrectly. When real causal relationships do not correspond to the scientific picture of them, a policy or practice based on the findings will be ineffective or counterproductive.

EXAMPLE: According to some critics of the medical profession, doctors' measurement of the need for medical intervention is systematically in error, because of the doctor's self-interest: "Doctors almost always get more reward and recognition for intervening than for not intervening. They're trained to intervene and do something rather than observe, wait, and take the chance the patient will get better all by himself or go to another doctor." (Mendelsohn, 1979:12) The results are as expected: "As a patient, once you submit to a physical examination, your doctor might interpret minor abnormalities—real or bogus—as pre-conditions of some serious illness, requiring, of course, serious pre-intervention. A minor fluctuation on a blood sugar test might be interpreted as pre-diabetes, and you'll get some medicine to take home" (Mendelsohn, 1979:12) This over-medication is seriously counterproductive. "Not only are these people duped into paying for something which has no effectivenesss against their problem, but they're set up for the hazards of side effects and the risks of deadlier infections.

"The doctor, once the agent of cure, has become the agent of disease." (Mendelsohn, 1979:24)

EXAMPLE: Critics of Freudian psychoanalysis see the entire profession based on a long-term continuation of Freud's early systematic mismeas-urement of real memories as fantasies. "Between 1897 and 1903, Freud came to believe that the case of his early patient Emma Echstein was typical: most (though not all) of his women patients had deceived them-selves and him. Their memories of seduction were nothing more than fantasies, or memories of fantasies—they were products of the Oedipus complex, part of normal childhood sexuality." (Masson, 1985:189) Critics argue that psychoanalysis would not have emerged if Freud had retained his earlier belief that the memories of his patients were real, not fantasies.

The result is, again, seriously counterproductive. "Many (probably most) of their patients had violent and unhappy childhoods, not because of some defect in their character, but because of something terrible that had been done to them by their parents. If this etiological formula is true, and if it is further true that such events form the core of every serious neurosis, then it would be impossible to achieve a successful cure of a neurosis if this central event were ignored. But whether it is openly stated or merely accepted as a hidden theoretical premise, the analyst who sees such a patient is trained to believe that her memories are fantasies. As such, the analyst, no matter how benevolent otherwise, does violence to the inner life of his patient and is in covert collusion with what made her ill in the first place." (Masson, 1985:191)

8.6 HOW CAN MEASUREMENT ACCURACY BE ASSESSED AND CONTROLLED?

a. Determining measurement accuracy in a project

In the short run, information useful for judging measurement accuracy can be produced by replication and triangulation within the project. In-project replication and triangulation are similar to the cross-project versions of these techniques. In-project measurement triangulation, like the cross-project version, uses alternative measures. The same cause and effect is measured on the same case with a different indicator.

EXAMPLE: A study of voluntary donations surveyed respondents on the amount of their donations to several charitable organizations. The organizations supplied records of donations, which were compared to respondents' reports.

In-project measurement replication involves measuring the same variable, on the same case, in the same way, more than once. This may also be described as taking two or more readings of the same indicator on the same case. When the replication measurements are taken on living, changing individuals, groups, or social relationship, the readings should be taken simultaneously or very close together in time. When documents are to be read more than once, it is only important that identical documents be used in each reading.

EXAMPLE: Hertler (1983) examined the relationship between social class and symptoms of schizophrenia for a sample of male former psychiatric patients. Hertler measured both social class and symptoms using indicators based on information in patients' case files. After being trained, a co-worker applied the same indicators to the same files independently and without knowing Hertler's measurements. Cases were discarded when Hertler and his co-worker's measurements disagreed and neither could convince the other that his reading was correct.

Note that in-project replication is a logical response to the problem of random measurement error. Random error in measurements is the result of the influence of many small factors on the measurement process which cause an overstatement here, an understatement there, a misstatement now, an opposite misstatement later. Included in these factors are all of the conditions under which the observation and recording take place: light, heat, noise, tension, general working conditions, fatigue, anxiety, acuteness of hearing and sight sensitivity, and so on. In short, any factor in the setting, the observer, or the thing observed that can have an effect on the human ability to observe, record the observations, and process the records, may produce random error.

If the randomness of the error is caused by a multiplicity of small causes that pull now in one direction and now in another, then the logical general strategy for its control is *replication*: repetition of the measurement process and combination of the results. The idea is to use random error against itself, so to speak. The amount of random error in a replication or repetition will be about the same amount as initially, but it is likely to be opposite in direction. The error in the second will cancel out the error in the first, and the average of the two measurements should have less random error than either of them alone. Averaging in more repetitions should diminish the random error even further.

Obviously, in-project replication will work only for random error. If the same mistakes were to be repeated (or made worse), then no improvement in accuracy would be achieved by the repetition. But note that in-project triangulation is a logical response to systematic error.

Systematic error occurs when one kind of misobservation or misrecording appears much more often or to the entire exclusion of other kinds of mismeasurement. The pattern suggests the persistent operation of a biasing factor that is stronger than other factors that could produce the opposite kinds of mismeasurement. Until the biasing factors are understood, replication (repetition and combination) will not diminish systematic error and might even increase it.

Logically, the general strategy for controlling systematic error is in-project triangulation: measurement of the same cause and effect with two or more indicators. If the measurement error is systematic, some indicators should give systematically higher or lower values than others. Each indicator can be used separately in the data analysis phase. (If the different indicators result in different estimates of the strength of causal influence, the difference between smallest and largest gives the range of possible error in the strength of the causal relationship.)

b. How much in-project replication and triangulation?

Since the measurement of each cause and effect may contain errors, should every indicator be replicated and triangulated? Common sense says no—most attention should be given to those causes and effects most likely to be inaccurately measured. And the more serious the error, the greater the attention.

EXAMPLE: In a study of sex discrimination vs education and experience as a determinant of wages, the measurement of sex and education is the least likely to be inaccurate. The measurement of wages and experience is more likely to be inaccurate. Replication and triangulation should therefore concentrate on wages and experience.

EXAMPLE: Ramu (1984) investigated voluntary childlessness as (1) an effect of social class, education, family experiences, working mothers, and the like and (2) a cause of marital satisfaction. Given the central role of voluntary childlessness in the project as both effect and cause, he is most concerned with the accuracy of its measurement. One indicator he uses is the "declared intentions of the couple to remain permanently childless." He triangulated this with indicators of how the decision to remain childless was arrived at, and with birth control behaviour. Finally, he used replication: four years after the initial measurements the childless couples were contacted to determine if they (1) were still childless and (2) still intended to remain so.

EXAMPLE: Harvey and Kalwa (1983) investigated labour market vs sex and educational achievement as causes of job status among university graduates. They are most concerned with measurement error in job status because other researchers suggested that women on the whole are assigned to higher-status jobs than men. If this is the case, then findings in job status will understate the differences between men and women. While expressing the hope that the bias will be small (because all of their sample are university graduates who will be concentrated in higher-status jobs), they carry out separate analyses for men and women.

On the other hand, no replication or triangulation may be required at all. If only a small amount of random error is involved, it might be noted then ignored.

EXAMPLE: Gerber (1984) measured communal vs individualistic values using a Prairie location vs other location indicator. Gerber notes that although it is highly plausible, "There is no guarantee that Prairie bands are more communal in their values" (Gerber, 1984:147), and no replication or triangulation is attempted.

EXAMPLE: Grayson (1983) examined changes in the acceptance or rejection of the subordination of women in English Canadian novels before and after the turn of the century. Grayson is concerned with the accuracy of the measurement of ideology in the novels. He outlines the indicators and gives several examples of their use. He rejects replication by other readers because "it is possible to provide the reader with sufficient information...to determine whether or not the typification of ideologies or aspects of them are adequate" (1983:5).

EXAMPLE: To measure labour market conditions facing university graduates, Harvey and Kalwa use the general unemployment rate. They say, "Although the unemployment rate for younger or highly educated workers generally differs from the overall rate, the influence of age and education work in opposite directions" (Harvey and Kalwa, 1983:443-4). In other words, the general unemployment rate understates the rate for younger workers but overstates it for highly educated workers. If these two kinds of systematic error are more or less equal, they should cancel each other, and any error remaining should be small and random. Whatever the case, after noting the problem, Harvey and Kalwa attempt no replication or triangulation.

If much of the measurement is potentially inaccurate and the amount of replication or triangulation might be overwhelming, the researcher should concentrate on the error that is likely to be most damaging to the goals of the project.

EXAMPLE: An investigation of the relationship of stress to post-hospitalization recovery required the measurement of stress at the point of hospital admission and the measurement of the degree of recovery six months after discharge.

The indicator for stress was a team decision regarding the patient's previous history, behaviour in former difficulties, attitudes toward actual problems, and subjective expressions. The measurement work of the team was observed by a psychologist to "prevent the judgement of the team being distorted by the domination of any one member."

The indicator for recovery was a follow-up investigation by a physician who knew the contents of the clinical case history, but did not know the team's assessment of stress.

With this design Querido has attempted to guard against two forms of dependent measurement error: (1) the measurement of the effect (satisfactory or unsatisfactory recovery) being dependent upon knowledge of the value of the cause (no stress/stress/distress), and (2) the decisions of some members of the team becoming dependent on other members.

To determine how much replication or triangulation should be used, concentrate (1) on those causes or effects most likely to be measured inaccurately, and (2) on those inaccuracies that will be most damaging to the project.

EXAMPLE: Gerber (1984) investigated off-reserve residence of Indian bands as caused by the following causes: communal-individualistic values, urban proximity, band size, personal resource development, linguistic acculturation, earned income, quality of housing, male-female ratio, fertility and institutional completeness. Her measurement accuracy concerns focus on the indicator for institutional completeness because it seems to measure community development. The problem is the possibility of dependent measurement because community development could also be indicated by the other causes—quality housing, road access, income, and personal resource development.

EXAMPLE: Durkheim claimed that great social disturbances and great popular wars cause, at least temporarily, a stronger integration of society and thereby temporarily decrease the rate of suicide. One alternative theory postulated that political crises are a cause of suicide and therefore increase suicide rates.

Durkheim is seriously worried about the accuracy of the suicide measurements because of the problem of dependent measurement: changes in suicide rates during wars and domestic political crises may be due to faulty record keeping occasioned by the crises. An observed decline in suicide rates, in other words, might be due, not to changes in integration, but to a systematic undercounting of suicides during crises. Durkheim argues that (1) the changes are widespread, occurring for both winners and losers, (2) the effects persist for a time after the crisis, (3) the regions most involved in the disturbances show greater rate changes than those less involved, and (4) crises that do not "excite the passions" do not exhibit the pattern. Durkheim's argument, in short, is that the patterns of change are too large, consistent, and persistent to be attributed entirely to a systematic undercounting of suicides. Durkheim notes that the same patterns of change are found among (civilian) women as among enlisted men engaged in military activities in the field. While it might be difficult to keep track of suicides in an army in the field, it should be much easier for civilians.

As indicators of great social disturbances and wars, Durkheim examines historical events that involved entire nations. He is unconcerned with the accuracy of these measurements.

When it is possible to obtain error-free measurement of some causes or effects, there is no need to be concerned about measurement accuracy for that variable. One of the distinguishing features of laboratory experimental designs is the possibility of all but error-free measurement of a cause.

EXAMPLE: In an experiment on the effects of movies on prejudicial attitudes, the experimental groups are shown films that the control groups are prevented from viewing. With a little effort to (1) prevent some people from sleeping through the movies, and (2) to determine that no one in the control group had seen the movie elsewhere, this procedure guarantees that the measurement of the cause (exposure or non-exposure) is totally error-free. When lab researchers worry about accuracy of measurement, they are usually thinking about the indicators used to measure the *effect* of exposure.

EXAMPLE: In their investigation of social class as a cause of psychiatric disorders, Hollingshead and Redlich (1953) sampled the residents of an urban community but carried out a census (complete count) of all individuals receiving psychiatric care. Their design called for them to compare the social class of a random sample of residents with the social class of all psychiatric patients. One major concern is with the accuracy of the indicator for social class. Another was the inclusion of *all* psychiatric patients. They expressed little doubt about the accuracy of the types of psychiatric disorder or the types of treatment.

EXAMPLE: Not surprisingly, in studying arms races as a cause of war, Wallace is little concerned with the accuracy of the war/no war indicator. He has two misgivings, however, about the accuracy of the arms race indicator. First, the indicator must distinguish normal increases in arms expenditure from an arms race. Second, it must be sensitive only to competitive growth, "where both sides are increasing rapidly and simultaneously." He devises an index that uses ten successive years of data for each pair of countries.

8.7 AN ALTERNATIVE THEORY OF MEASUREMENT AND MEASUREMENT ERROR

Readers who have had some exposure to the theory of measurement and measurement error in psychology will have noted that the terms "reliability" and "validity" have not been used in the foregoing paragraphs at all. These two terms are central concepts in what might be called the rel/val theory of measurement favoured by some social scientists, particularly in psychology.

The rel/val theory has not been used in this chapter because (1) it is confused and confusing, (2) its procedures are unjustifiable, and (3) nothing can be stated using the terminology of rel/val theory that cannot be stated more clearly in terms of the concepts of random and systematic error.

If the procedures for assessing reliability are looked at closely, they can be seen to correspond almost exactly to those procedures described above for assessing random error. Definitions of reliability, on the other hand, are rarely stated in terms of the concept of random error. In their definition, Selltiz and others (1959:148), for example, state, "Independent but comparable measures of the same object (or attitude, or whatever) should give similar results (provided, of course, that there is no reason to believe that the object being measured has in fact changed between the two measurements)." Reliability is assessed in terms of the similarity of the independent measurements: the greater their similarity, the greater the reliability is said to be.

Some of the procedures for assessing validity correspond to those for assessing systematic error, but some do not. The most common definitions for validity contain statements similar to the following: "The matter of the validity of a measure concerns the question as to whether it, in fact, measures what it purports to measure" (Phillips, 1971:15). Different research problems have led to the definition of various subtypes of validity.

"Construct validity," perhaps the most important subtype, is assessed by comparing the relations observed between two scales to the expected relations between two scales. The expected relations between the scales are derived from theory or on a priori grounds.

"Content validity" is assessed by judging the degree to which a scale is representative of all the content to be measured.

"Concurrent validity" is assessed by determining the degree to which a scale distinguishes between those already known to differ on the attribute of interest.

"Predictive validity" is assessed by determining the extent to which values on one scale at an earlier point in time predict the values of a different scale at a later point in time.

"Discriminant validity" is assessed in terms of the degree to which a scale permits one variable to be distinguished from another, particularly when the variables are either conceptually simpler or more complex.

Both validity and reliability, then, are assessed by comparing sets of measurements. Reliability is assessed by comparing the measurements from the same scale at different points in time. Validity is assessed by comparing measurements from different scales. Depending upon the type of validity, the measurements may be taken at the same or different points in time.

There are two main problems with the rel/val theory of measurement and measurement error. One is that reliability is defined independently of the variable that a scale is designed to measure, and consequently independently of the validity of a scale. Perhaps the most common claim made by rel/val theorists is that reliability "is distinctly different from the question of validity: for we may have totally reliable information about an individual that is absolutely invalid for whatever purpose it was intended" (Phillips, 1971:15).

On the other hand, the opposite claim, that a scale may be valid but not reliable is never made. The logic behind this curious discourse is, according to Zeller and Carmines (1980:14), that "the difference between reliability and validity is entirely dependent upon systematic error. If a set of indicators contains no systematic error...then validity will equal reliability." Readers can judge for themselves if anything beyond confusion is gained by using the terms reliability and validity in this peculiar fashion.

Perhaps the most serious problem associated with rel/val theory is that procedures for assessing validity cannot be distinguished from the procedures for evaluating theories. In assessing construct validity, according to Selltiz (1959:159), the following questions should be asked: "What predictions would one make, on the basis of these sets of propositions, about the relationship to other variables of scores based on a measure of this construct? Are the measures obtained by using this instrument consistent with these predictions?"

The answers to the first question would postulate the strength and direction of the relationship between the scores for the variables. They would look, in other words, like theoretical statements. The answer to the second question would involve using data analysis to describe the relationship between the variables to see if the relationships correspond to the predictions. It would look, in other words, like the evaluation of a theory.

Now suppose we have taken up a research project to evaluate alternative theories and have measured some variables before examining the relationships between them. If the theory is accurate we expect a certain relationship between the variables. If our measurements are valid we expect the same relationship between these variables. If the measured variables correspond to our expectations, we conclude that (1) our measurements are valid and (2) one of our theories is correct. If the relationship between the measured variables does not correspond to theoretical statements and the "validity predictions," we conclude that (1) our measures are invalid and (2) at least one of our theories is inaccurate. The implication of all of this is that theories could never be evaluated independently of the validity of the measurement. Another way of putting the point is that the researcher would never have to concede that a theory was incorrect; she or he could always claim that the measurement was invalid.

Clearly something is wrong with definitions that lead to these kinds of procedures. Either validity will have to be redefined, or the evaluation of theory will have to be redefined. Procedures must allow researchers to distinguish between valid measurements and accurate theories and between invalid measurements and inaccurate theories. We must be able to demonstrate both that (1) a theory may appear to be accurate because of inaccurate measurement and that (2) accurate measurement shows a theory to be incorrect. Another problem may have occurred to the reader: if the researcher is attempting to evaluate alternative theories, which of these will be the source of the "validity predictions"? By definition, alternative theories will contain contradictory validity prediction statements. It should be clear, then, that the validity assessment procedures are based upon a conception of social science research that sees value in researching single theories rather than alternatives.

It is the conception of validity that is at fault. By failing to notice that validity testing involved procedures that are identical to theory evaluation procedures, advocates of these notions of validity have claimed that sociologists and other social scientists rarely investigate the validity of their measurements. But an examination of every research literature will show that virtually all the studies examine relationships between variables. Given that this is exactly what all the validating procedures call for, it is clear that the problem lies, not in the research practice of sociologists, but in the conceptions of the rel/val measurement theorists. It is not going too far to argue that these theorists advocate invalid methods for assessing measurement validity.

8.8 SUMMARY

Measurement consists in applying an indicator to a sampled case or time period and noting the value of the indicator. Indicators are observable and recordable variables that serve as measures of theoretical causes and effects. Measurement is important because research findings are constructed out of measurements.

The first step in measurement design is to choose indicators. Indicators are chosen on the basis of variation and sampling design considerations, availability and cost, estimates of required precision, the nature of the causes and effects, and the coherence of the entire design. The final product of the design must include at least one indicator for each cause and effect investigated. When more than one indicator is produced, plans for their combination are a critical part of the design.

The second part of measurement design is planning the control of error. Measurements may contain random error that can be controlled by using internal replication. Measurements may also contain the much more important systematic error, which is controlled by internal triangulation. A serious measurement error is one that can produce seriously inaccurate findings. Decisions about how much internal triangulation and replication to do are made by estimating where serious error is likely to occur.

8.9 EXERCISES

1. The claim that the greater the emancipation or equality of women, the lower the fertility rate is to be researched on a sample of countries, for 1980. The indicators for emancipation or equality of women considered were the following:
   (a) percentage of women in elementary school
   (b) percentage of women in high school
   (c) percentage of women in post-secondary education
   (d) percentage of women employed in non-domestic jobs
   (e) percentage of adult women not married
   (f) the right to vote
   (g) the right to initiate divorce
   (h) the right to own property
   (i) the right to abortion
      i) Would you add or delete any indicators?
      ii) What do you think is the single most accurate indicator for western industrialized countries? For Third World countries?
      iii) If the sample of countries will include First, Second, and Third World countries, is there a single most accurate indicator?
      iv) If it were decided to use a combination indicator, which items in the list would you choose, and how would you combine them?
      v) Suppose changes in emancipation or inequality in 1960, 1970, and 1980 were to be investigated as a cause of changes in

fertility. Would your answers to earlier parts of this question change? If so, describe how your decisions would change.

    vi) Design an indicator for fertility rates.

2. Vogel claims that huge increases in incarceration lead to prison uprisings. This suggests that the greater the overcrowding in prisons, the more prisoner unrest there is. The indicators considered for prisoner unrest were the following:

(a) rate of scuffles among prisoners

(b) rate of sabotage of work, meals, and recreation activities

(c) rate of restrictions of privileges

(d) rate of restrictions of visiting rights

(e) rate of general lockups (confinement to cells)

(f) rate of threats to guards

(g) rate of failed dispute resolution through prison channels

(h) rate of solitary confinement

(i) rate of prisoners rioting or number of prisoners involved

(j) rate of prisoners taking hostages or number of prisoners involved

    i) Would you add or delete any indicators?

    ii) What do you think is the single most accurate indicator?

    iii) If the sample of prisons includes small municipal jails and holding facilities, is there a single most accurate indicator?

    iv) If it were decided to use a combination indicator, which items in the list would you choose, and how would you combine them?

    v) Design an indicator to measure degree of overcrowding.

3. Vold's theory (see the exercises for chapter 3) suggests that changes in the relative power of an interest group should be followed by changes in law making, breaking, and enforcement. If this hypothesis is applied to natives as an interest group in a province or state for the past 90 years, an indicator for relative power and changes in relative power is required. The following possible indicators were considered:

(a) percentage of total population

(b) relative rate of unemployment

(c) relative rate of high school graduates

(d) relative rate of post-secondary education graduates

(e) relative rate of voting

(f) relative rate of representation in legislatures

(g) relative rate of representation in high political office

(h) relative number of businesses

    (i) relative number of service or interest organizations

    (j) relative alliances among organizations

    (k) relative rate of local control of local institutions

    (k) success or failure in land claims actions

    (l) success or failure in other negotiations

        i) Would you add or delete any indicators?

        ii) What do you think is the single most accurate indicator?

        iii) If the sample of time periods were to include only the past 20 years, would the list of possible indicators change?

        iv) Because the study must use indicators that provide accurate measurement over the entire ninety years, multiple indicators will likely be necessary. How would you combine a set of the above indicators so it will be as accurate for 1910 as for 1980?

        v) Design indicators for changes in law making, law breaking, and law enforcement.

4. You have a job in an infant and child care centre. The policy of the centre calls for children to be evaluated for hyperactivity. Upon this determination, instructional and therapy programs to control hyperactivity are instituted. Hyperactive children are commonly said to be "inattentive" and "unable to sit still."

    (a) Design a plan for accurately measuring the presence or absence of hyperactivity.

    (b) How would you guarantee that your indicator did not inaccurately classify children who were simply excited and excitable as hyperactive? Is there much likelihood of the reverse measurement error?

    (c) The usual treatment for hyperactivity is diet (for example, the Feingold diet) or drugs (amphetamines). Could these treatments be helpful for increasing the accuracy of your measurement of the presence of hyperactivity? Describe how they might be used or why they should not be.

5. (a) Select hypotheses from the theories listed in the exercises for chapter 3 (or use hypotheses of your own choosing). Specify the type of case to be sampled; then describe three possible indicators (observable and recordable variables) for each of the causes and effects in the hypotheses.

    (b) Where appropriate, specify a different type of case and describe three possible indicators for this kind of case.

    (c) Which are the most accurate indicators for evaluating the hypotheses? Which of your indicators is the most precise?

(d) Describe what systematic error might make each indicator less accurate.

(e) Estimate the cost of obtaining measurements; that is, estimate the cost of observing and recording the value of your indicators for one case. Which indicator is the most expensive? The least expensive? Are the more accurate indicators also the more expensive?

(f) Suppose you want to combine your indicators. How would you do it? Which combinations of indicators would improve the accuracy, and which would not? How would you evaluate whether combined indicators were more accurate than single indicators?

6. The data below is a set of exam scores assigned by two teaching assistants (TAs) to a random sample of papers from a larger set. Both graders were given similar training and kept uninformed of the grades assigned by the other TA. The purpose of the double grading was to assure that the TAs were assigning similar grades for similar work.

Student	TA#1	TA#2 Score	Measurement Error Score	Sex	Student's Ethnicity (TA1-TA2)
1	74.0	74.5	-0.5	M	ANGLO
2	71.5	72.0	-0.5	M	ANGLO
3	71.0	71.0	0.0	F	OTHER
4	68.0	68.0	0.0	M	ANGLO
5	66.5	66.0	0.5	F	ANGLO
6	65.0	65.0	0.0	F	OTHER
7	63.0	62.5	0.5	F	ANGLO
8	63.0	63.0	0.0	M	OTHER
9	62.5	62.0	0.5	M	ANGLO
10	60.0	60.0	0.0	F	OTHER

(1) On the basis of this sample, what percentage of papers would you expect the TAs to mark differently?

(2) On the basis of these results, would you review the grading instructions and the TAs' interpretation of them?

(3) Looking only at the kind of error and the size of the grades assigned, would you say the error was systematic or random?

(4) Does the sex or ethnicity of the student appear to have any connection to the measurement error? In other words, is there a sex or ethnic bias in either of the TAs' grading?

(5) Letter grades are to be assigned to the percentage scores as follows: F < 49.4; D = 49.5 to 59.4; C = 59.5 to 64.4; C+ = 64.6 to 69.4; B = 69.5 to 74.4; B+ = 74.5 to 79.4; What difference will this make to your answers to questions (1) and (2) above?

7. The observations below are the records of assessments of children in a daycare centre as possibly hyperactive. The observers, who were trained to recognize hyperactive children, observed the children in the same settings at the same time, but did not tell each other their judgements. The "hyper" classification indicates a strong likelihood that the child is hyperactive. "Excite" means that the child is judged to be excitable but probably not hyperactive. "Passive" means that the child, in the observer's judgement, is definitely not hyperactive. The child's size records represent judgements of the child's size in relation to the other children being played with in the room or playground at the time of observation.

Child	Observer #1	Observer #2	Child's Sex	Child's Size
1	hyper	hyper	female	big
2	hyper	excite	male	big
3	passive	excite	female	medium
4	passive	passive	male	medium
5	excite	hyper	female	small
6	excite	excite	male	medium
7	hyper	hyper	male	big
8	passive	passive	female	small
9	excite	excite	female	small
10	hyper	excite	male	medium
11	hyper	excite	female	small
12	hyper	hyper	female	big
13	hyper	passive	male	small
14	passive	passive	male	medium
15	passive	excite	female	medium
16	passive	hyper	male	big
17	excite	excite	male	big
18	excite	passive	male	small
19	excite	hyper	male	medium
20	passive	excite	female	big

(a) On the basis of this group of judgements, what percentage of children would you expect the observers to judge differently?

(b) On the basis of these results, what confidence would you have in the training of the observers?

(c) Looking only at the different judgements of observer #1 and #2, would you say the error is systematic or random?

(d) Does the sex or size of the child appear to have any connection to the measurement error? In other words, is there systematic measurement error in hyperactivity related to sex or salary size in either of the measurements?

9. Employees of Consolidated Widgets Limited are eligible for some age-related programs, including early retirement. It is therefore important for the company to have accurate age records. A sample of applicants for jobs reported the ages listed below in the first column. The employer followed up the information given on the application form and found documents, such as birth certificates and school records, that fixed the date of birth and from this computed the applicants' ages. The measurement error column lists the difference between the self-reported and documented age. If the error is positive, applicants are reporting themselves older than they are; if negative, the applicants are reporting themselves as younger than they are. The salary column reports the average annual incomes of employees already in the jobs applied for.

Reported Age (1)	Age According to Documented Date of Birth (2)	Measurement Error (1)-(2)	Sex	Salary ($ 000)
21	20	1	F	13
21	19	2	M	15
22	22	0	F	15
26	25	1	F	18
25	26	−1	M	20
27	26	1	F	22
26	27	−1	M	19
28	30	−2	F	31

Reported Age (1)	Age According to Documented Date of Birth (2)	Measurement Error (1)-(2)	Sex	Salary ($ 000)
30	32	−2	F	18
31	32	−1	M	30
33	32	1	M	25
32	35	−3	F	20
35	36	−1	M	43
39	42	−3	M	23
44	44	0	F	32
42	48	−6	F	28
46	49	−3	M	48
52	53	−1	M	44
48	54	−6	M	40
50	55	−5	F	30

(a) On the basis of this sample, what percentage of applicants would you expect to report ages different from the ages shown on their records?

(b) On the basis of these measurements, what confidence would you have in the accuracy of self-reported age?

(c) Looking only at the difference between self-reported and documented ages, would you say the error is systematic or random?

(d) Does the sex or salary of the job applied for appear to have any connection to the measurement error? In other words, is there a sex or salary size bias in either of the measurements?

(e) To obtain the information for computing the documented age took an average time of twenty-three minutes per applicant. The salary of the employees who researched the documents is about $18 an hour. The cost to the company of putting its age related programs in place one year early is about $10 a year. Is it worth the employer's time and money to check for inaccuracies in employees' reported ages? If you wanted to reduce the costs of checking for inaccuracies, how would you do it? Would your answers to part (d) be useful here?

CHAPTER 9

Data Analysis Design

CHAPTER CONTENTS

9.1 WHAT IS DATA ANALYSIS?

Data analysis is the organizing and displaying of sets of measurements in order to make relationships between causes and effects observable. The process is guided by the hypotheses under investigation, which postulate what the relationships should look like. When the observed and postulated relationships are identical, we conclude that the hypotheses are accurate; otherwise we conclude that they are inaccurate.

Relationships between causes and effects are made observable in the form of *patterns* in organized displays of sets of measurements. Findings or conclusions are *summaries* of the correspondence between predicted and observed patterns.

EXAMPLE: The hypothesis that sex is a cause of unemployment and that women have higher unemployment than men was investigated by measuring the sex and employed/unemployed status of a sample of individual cases. The original data (Table 9.1) appeared as a list of the cases and their measured sex and employed/unemployed status.

Table 9.1

Case	Sex	Employed or Unemployed
1	M	E
2	M	U
3	F	E
4	F	E
. . . .		
79	F	U
80	M	U
81	M	E

Table 9.2
Sex by Unemployment

Unemployed	Sex Male	Female	Row totals
No	Many cases	Few cases	?
Yes	Few cases	Many cases	?
Column totals	?	?	81

If the hypothesis is accurate the pattern below will be observable when the measurements are displayed in a cross-tabulation (cross-classification, crosstab) as in Table 9.2.

When the data is organized and displayed in a cross-tabulation, Table 9.3 below is the result.

The pattern in the crosstab appears to correspond to the pattern predicted by the hypothesis. The finding is that the hypothesis is accurate.

This statement summarizes the correspondence between the hypothesis and the observed display with regard to *direction* of the relationship, that is, which sex has higher unemployment. The question of the strength of the relationship—how much higher female unemployment is than male—addresses a different aspect of the relationship. One conventional way of summarizing the strength of a relationship between two qualitative variables is by percentage differences, as in crosstab 9.4.

By subtracting 31.8 (the percentage of unemployed males) from 67.6 (the percentage of unemployed females), we find that 35.8% more women than men are unemployed. This statement summarizes the strength of the relationship between sex and unemployment.

EXAMPLE: The hypothesis that male white-collar workers will have higher wages than female white-collar workers was investigated on a

Table 9.3
Sex by Unemployment

Unemployed	Male	Female	Total
No	30	12	42
Yes	14	25	39
Total cases	44	37	81

Table 9.4
Sex by Unemployment

Unemployed	Male		Female		Total
	N	%	N	%	
No	30	68.2	12	32.4	42
Yes	14	31.8	25	67.6	39
Total %		100		100	
Total cases	44		37		81

sample of individuals. The original data appeared as a list of the case numbers and their measured sex and hourly wages (see Table 9.5).

If the hypothesis is accurate, a pattern like that in Figure 9.1 will be observable when the wage measurements are classified according to sex.

Another way of displaying the data is to *average* the wages for the sex groups. The hypothesis predicts that the male average will be higher than the female. When the data is displayed and summarized in this fashion the result is as shown in Table 9.6.

There are a variety of averages available for summarizing quantitative effect variables. The most commonly used is the familiar mean or arithmetic average. The mean income is obtained by summing the observed hourly incomes of all male cases and of all female cases and then dividing the sums by the number of cases in each group. The difference between the average wages summarizes the data in a way that is comparable to that predicted by the hypothesis. The finding would be that the hypothesis is correct.

This finding addresses only the direction of the relationship. If a policy for equal wages is to be implemented, this finding says that women's wages will have to be increased in relation to men's. But by how much? In other words, how much difference is there between male and female wages? A simple and common summary of the difference is obtained by subtracting

Table 9.5

Case	Sex	Wages
1	M	2.42
2	F	2.15
. . . .	. . . .	. . . .
23	F	3.11
24	M	3.45

Figure 9.1
Wages by Gender

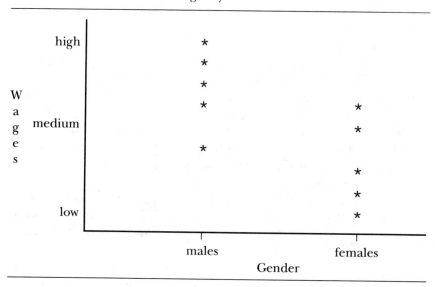

the smaller average from the larger: $3.092 − $2.196 = $0.896. To remove sex wage differences, women's wages will have to be raised about 90 cents.

Table 9.6
Hourly Wage Rates

	Men	Women
	3.18	2.14
	2.79	2.02
	2.42	1.85
	3.42	1.85
	3.15	2.15
	3.29	2.21
	3.45	2.14
	3.05	2.20
	3.14	2.32
	3.03	2.32
		3.11
		2.04
Sum	30.92	26.35
Number of cases	10	12
Mean	3.092	2.196

EXAMPLE: Suppose we are investigating the hypothesis that the greater the number of years of education, the higher the hourly income for a sample of individuals. The original data would appear as a list of the case numbers, a measure of the number of years of education, and a measure of annual income (see Table 9.7).

If respondents are grouped by high, medium, and low years of education, then the hypothesis predicts that the average hourly incomes of these groups will also be high, medium, and low. If the education groups include one year only, another reading is conventional: the overall pattern of points on a scatter plot can be summarized as having an upward or positive direction; as the value of years of education increases (or decreases), the value of the corresponding hourly wage is also likely to increase (or decrease).

If the years of education and annual income measurements are plotted as in Figure 9.2, the hypothesis predicts that the points on the plot should have an upward slope—as the years of education increase, the annual income also increases.

When the observations are actually plotted, the display appears as Figure 9.3 below. Though the plot is not exactly like the one above, it seems accurate to summarize the plot by concluding that as the cause (years of education) increases, the effect (annual income) also increases.

So the postulated direction of the relationship between education and income is correct. But how strong is the relationship? How much difference does education make to income? A simple summary is to compute the average change (increase) in income for each additional year of education. This change is equal to the slope of the line in the scatter plot above—about $4,500. On average, each additional year of education is worth about $4,500 in annual income.

Table 9.7

Case No.	Years of Education	Annual Income
1	11	$22,000
2	15	31,000
. . . .		
25	13	18,500
26	18	55,000

Figure 9.2
Income ($ 000's) by Years of Education

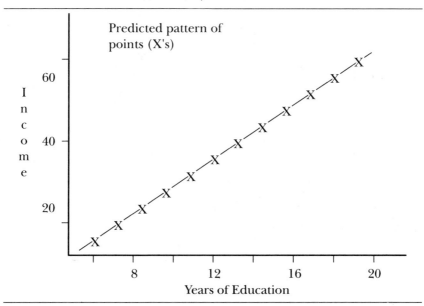

The examples above illustrate data analysis when the measurements are few and can be described exclusively as counts or quantitative measurements. Much data analysis also takes the form of narratives of events or episodes.

EXAMPLE: In Overton's (1988) study of public relief and social unrest in Newfoundland in the 1930s, the data display is a narrative of episodes of interaction between the government and the unemployed. The episodes are cases or time periods chosen to test the Piven and Cloward hypothesis that "relief, particularly in the form of work, is provided by elites in response to the unrest that results from the breakdown of social control, which is associated with unemployment. Relief work, then, acts as a surrogate form of control. And once it has served its function of 'regulating the poor,' it is then cut back and the quiescent unemployed are forced into the low wage labour market."

Overton's findings are a *summary* of what all the episodes indicate. "There is no evidence that it was a breakdown of social control caused by loss of work which led to social unrest in Newfoundland in the 1930s. For

Figure 9.3
Income ($ 000's) by Years of Education

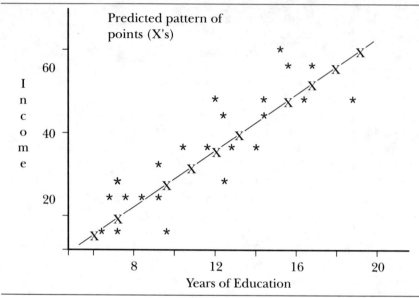

the most part poverty weakened people and rendered them submissive."
(Overton, 1988:165) Later Overton asks, "Does the framework provided
by Piven and Cloward provide a basis for understanding relief policy,
popular protest, and public unrest in Newfoundland in the 1930s?" and
answers, "I would suggest that. . .it does not capture well the processes at
work." (Overton, 1988: 166)

Overton does not specify the strength of the causal relationship. Why
not?

In the examples above, the hypotheses under investigation are theoretical—the kind of hypotheses that an entire project would have been
designed to investigate. Data analysis is also used to investigate "technical"
or "artifact" hypotheses—hypotheses about the presence or absence of an
artifact in the data or methods of data analysis.

EXAMPLE: A researcher postulated that the sample she drew using
random selection methods was not representative of the population from
which it was selected. This is a technical or artifact hypothesis. It postu-

Age Categories	Table 9.8 Percentage of Sample	Percentage of Population
-19	15	12
20-29	15	17
30-39	20	23
40-65	35	33
66+	15	15

lates that when the sample is compared to the population from which it was drawn, differences between the sample and the population will be large. Since the population is much larger than the sample, the appropriate display is the percentage sample and population characteristics. For age categories the data appeared as in Table 9.8.

The findings of this data analysis would probably be that the sample, though not a perfect miniature replica of the population, is close enough to be considered representative of the population. The hypothesis of sample bias is not accurate.

For virtually every technique used in each phase of a research project, technical hypotheses can be formed that state what artifact the technique may introduce. Each artifact potentially decreases confidence in the project findings. Technical hypotheses are merely a systematic way of thinking about and organizing the investigation of potential artifacts. Artifact or technical hypotheses postulate causal relationships in the same way that research hypotheses do.

Ordinary hypotheses:

$$\text{Causes} \rightarrow \text{influence} \rightarrow \text{Effects}$$

Technical or artifact hypotheses:

$$\text{Methods} \rightarrow \text{influence} \rightarrow \text{Data characteristics}$$

In the above example:

$$\text{Sample selection method} \rightarrow \text{influences} \rightarrow \text{sample characteristics}$$

9.2 WHY IS DATA ANALYSIS IMPORTANT?

In the data analysis phase, the empirical truth of the hypotheses under investigation is assessed in detail. The conclusions of every research project are statements about the results of the data analysis. When written up, descriptions of data analysis permit other readers and researchers to review the methods and the logic employed to arrive at conclusions. It is the phase where doubts about the accuracy of all the work in the project are given free reign. The work here forms a basis for *repetition* by other researchers.

9.3 WHAT ARE THE STEPS IN DATA ANALYSIS DESIGN?

The goal of a research project is to demonstrate the superiority of one theory over the alternatives. The relative superiority of alternative theories is not much of an issue until their accuracy is determined—the direction of every causal relationship postulated in each alternative theory should be correct.

EXAMPLE: In the investigation of the discrimination theory versus the education and experience theories of wage differences between men and women, the superiority of either cannot be determined until after it has been shown that it is true that (1) women receive lower wages than men, and (2) (a) the greater the education, the higher the wages and (b) the greater the experience, the higher the wages. If one or more of these hypotheses are not true, the correct direction of causal determination must be discovered.

So the first task in data analysis is to show that the postulated *direction* of causal influence in *each theoretical hypothesis* is correct.

The second main task is to show that all the causes in one theory are (collectively) stronger determinants of the effect than all the causes in an alternative theory.

EXAMPLE: In the debate between the discrimination theory of sex wage differences versus the education/experience theory, to show the superiority of the discrimination theory involves demonstrating that discrimination explains more of the differences between men's and women's wages than do the differences in education and experience. It has to be shown that a worker's wages are predicted better by the worker's sex than by his or her education and experience together.

What is needed then is a method that makes observable the direction of causal relationship between each cause and the effect, and a related

Table 9.9
Types of Indicators and Display Technique

Cause Indicator Treated as	Effect Indicator Treated as	Display Technique
Qualitative	Qualitative	Cross-tabulations, charts
Qualitative	*Quantitative*	Graphs, charts
Quantitative	*Quantitative*	Scatter plots, graphs, charts

technique that makes observable the relative strength of the influence on the effect of the causes, singly and collectively.

Recall from the examples at the beginning of this chapter that, if indicators are treated as qualitative, then different summary and display techniques are needed than when the indicators are treated as quantitative. Tables 9.9 and 9.10 present the most common options.

Summary technologies also vary according to whether the indicators are being treated as qualitative or quantitative.

a. Coefficients of determination

Coefficients of determination are used *only* to summarize the strength of causal relationships. They are single-purpose coefficients, unlike regression coefficients, which are useful both for expressing how causes influence effects as well as how much.

A general method for constructing coefficients to summarize the strength of a causal relationship is derived from the idea that a cause determines an effect. If a cause does determine an effect, then when you know how the cause varies, you will know how the effect varies. The stronger the determination, the larger the coefficient:

1. If variation in a cause completely determines the variation in an effect, the strength of relationship measure is made equal to 1.
2. If variation in a cause has no influence on the effect, the strength of relationship measure is set equal to 0.
3. If variation in a cause plays some role in determining the effect but does not completely determine it, then the strength of relationship measure should indicate the proportion of determination—somewhere between 0 and 1.

A measure of strength of causal determination as above can be constructed for any combination of qualitative or quantitative cause and

Table 9.10
Indicator types and summary techniques

Cause/effect indicators treated as	Direction of Causal Relationship	Strength of Causal Relationship
Qual/qual	Direction of percentage differences	Size of percentage differences Strength coefficients: "Lambda" "Uncertainty"
Qual/QUANT	Direction of average[a] differences	Size of average[a] differences Strength coefficients: Eta-square/R-square
QUANT/QUANT	Sign of regression coefficient[b]	Size of regression coefficient[b] Strength coefficients: R-square

a Averages: mean, median, mid-means
b Can be supplemented with Pearson's correlation coefficient and other special purpose coefficients such as Spearman's rho, Kendall's tau, and gamma.

effect indicators. The calculation will be different for each situation, but the general procedure is as follows:

1. The total amount of observed variation in an effect variable is measured.
2. This is separated into variation that *is* explained by the cause, and variation that *is not*.
3. The explained portion of the variation is divided by the total variation.

$$\text{Coefficient} = \frac{\text{Variation explained by cause}}{\text{Total variation in effect}}$$

Coefficients constructed in this fashion summarize the strength of causal determination of a cause on an effect. When two or more causes are employed to explain variation in an effect, it becomes a coefficient of multiple determination.

Table 9.11
Sex by Unemployment
Sex

Unemployed	Male N	%	Female N	%	Total
No	30	68.2	12	32.4	42
Yes	14	31.8		67.6	39
Total %		100		100	
Total cases	44				81

b. Percentaging Cross-tabulations

It may have occurred to the reader that the cross-tabulations can be percentaged for analysis in a variety of ways.
1. Column totals can be treated as 100, and then each number in the column is expressed as a portion of the total, as in Table 9.11.
2. Row totals can be treated as 100, and then each number in the row is expressed as a portion of the total, as in Table 9.12 below.
3. The overall table total can be treated as 100, and then each number in each cell in the table is expressed as a portion of the total, as in Table 9.13.

Each of these ways of percentaging has its uses. For purposes of causal analysis, however, provided that the cause values appear in columns and effect values in the rows, the percentaging rule is: treat the column totals as 100 and express each number in the column as a proportion of 100 (see 1. above).

The general idea here is that this form of percentaging treats the data as

Table 9.12
Sex by Unemployment

Unemployed	Sex Male	Female	Total N	%
No %	71.4	28.6	42	100
Yes %	35.9	64.1	39	100
Total cases	44	37	81	

Table 9.13
Sex by Unemployment

Unemployed	Male	Female	Total %	Cases
No	37.0	14.8	51.8	42
Yes	17.3	30.9	48.2	39
Total %	54.3	45.7	100.0	
Total cases	44	37		81

if equal numbers of cases had been observed for each value of the cause. The influence of the cause on the effect (if it has any) will show up as different row percentages (which correspond to different values of the effect).

What happens if this rule is not followed? Sometimes nothing: it is possible, for some sets of data, to percentage in the wrong direction and arrive at the conclusions more or less identical to those arrived at by percentaging in the right direction. For example, roughly the same conclusions would result from each of the tables above, although each is percentaged differently.

However, in general, percentaging in the wrong direction is likely to result in incorrect conclusions. The data in Table 9.14 would produce findings much like the original data. But note that there are now far fewer female cases than male cases.

When this table is percentaged in the wrong direction, as in Table 9.15, the findings become nonsensical. If this table is read as if it were percentaged correctly, the first row suggests that more males are not unemployed

Table 9.14
Sex by Unemployment

Unemployed	Sex		Total
	Male %	Female %	
No	68.7	35.3	50
Yes	31.3	64.7	31
Total %		100	
Total cases	64	17	81

Table 9.15
Sex by Unemployment

Unemployed	Sex Male	Female	Total %	Cases
No %	88.0	12.0	100	42
Yes %	64.5	35.5	100	29
Total cases	64	17		81

than females. But the second row suggests that relatively more males are unemployed than females. Given the logic of the design and measurement, only one of these conclusions can be accurate. Percentaging in the wrong direction is likely to lead to incorrect conclusions.

9.4 HOW ARE DATA ANALYSIS DESIGNS CHOSEN?

The most important criteria of data analysis design are discussed below. Since different criteria may point in opposite directions, they should be regarded as guides rather than rules. Design decisions are matters of judgement. The final guide is the researcher's responsibility to show clearly how his or her conclusions about the accuracy and relative merits of alternative theories were arrived at. Readers ought to be able to understand the results, analyse them critically, and replicate, triangulate, or extend the work.

a. Quantity of data (# cases x # measurements)

One basis for data analysis design is the sheer quantity of data. If the data set consists of a few cases/time periods and a few measurements, the quantitative method of display and summary is often superfluous. Verbal narrative display and summary methods are the most suitable choice here.

EXAMPLE: Overton (1988) investigated changes in social unrest as causes of changes in public relief in Newfoundland. His sample consisted of all such episodes in the decade of the 1930s. The narrative account of the episodes required many measurements, but there were only a few such episodes in the decade, so that quantitative display of the data added nothing to the narrative display.

The used of quantitative technology for small data sets may occasionally be misleading as well.

EXAMPLE: Percentage differences are a quantitative weighting device used primarily to make comparisons between groups easy to comprehend. The use of percentage for every small data sets seems to inflate the importance of minor differences. The finding that 33% more women than men had high wages seems important. But if in fact three women were compared to three men, the 33% difference actually means that two females had high wages compared to one male.

EXAMPLE: Scatter plots are quantitative display devices useful for quantitative causes and effects. The plotted points are used to estimate the straight line that summarizes the direction and strength of the relationship between the cause and effect. If all the plotted points are on the line, this indicates a strong relationship, and such a finding would appear to be important. But if the sample consists of only two cases or time periods, the finding is of no significance whatsoever. Two points define a straight line, so then *any* two points will always be on line, no matter what their values.

b. Numerical/non-numerical character of measurements

Another basis for design decisions is the character of the measurements. If the measurement is exclusively numerical or can easily be converted to numbers, then numerical methods should be used. And the reverse is also true: if the measurements are non-numerical and cannot be easily converted to numbers, then use verbal and narrative methods.

EXAMPLE: Indicators of a person's age, income, years of education, years married, number of children, number of brothers and sisters, monthly expenditures, and rent are usually all numerical and would ordinarily be treated as quantitative.

Indicators of a person's sex (male/female), marital status (single, married, separated, widowed, or divorced), ethnic or national origin, religious background, and simple party preferences and opinions (agree or disagree), are usually non-numerical. However, since the number of categories in each indicator is relatively small, they are often converted to numbers and treated numerically.

EXAMPLE: Jabbra (1984) investigates how ethnic community politics affects ethnic community boundaries, cleavages, and identities. She examines five disputes, which she describes as the "Lebanese-Syrian question," the "regional dispute," the "Maronite Bishop affair," the "Kataib-Marada split," and the "bringing of the priest." All her indicators of causes and effects are inherently non-numerical, and she uses ordinary narrative technique—sequential reports of events—in her data analysis.

c. Qualitative/quantitative character of data

1. When indicators are inherently qualitative, the researcher is obliged to treat them as qualitative in the data analysis. Qualitative indicators cannot be treated as if the different values were ordered quantitatively.

EXAMPLE: Males cannot be said to "have more sex" than females; the Scots cannot be said to have more national or ethnic origin than the Irish, the English, the Ukrainians, or the Latvians; the divorced cannot be said to have more marital status than the married, the single, the separated or the widowed. Sex, national origin, marital status, and many other indicators are inherently qualitative.

Indicators that are inherently qualitative cannot be treated as if they were ordered quantitatively. For the purposes of display and summary methods, when both cause and effect are inherently qualitative, the choices are restricted to cross-tabulations and percentage differences. When the cause is qualitative and the effect quantitative, the choices are charts and mean differences. It is best to avoid display and summary methods that require the cause indicators to be treated as quantitatively ordered.

2. When indicators are quantitative, the quantities may be used to create categories that are treated as if they were qualitative in numerical data analysis. The grounds on which the qual/quant treatment decision may be made are common sense, communicability, and probable application of the findings.

EXAMPLE: The Maxwells (1984) investigated the educational and occupational aspirations of private school girls in Toronto. They were interested in measuring the change from the 1960s to the 1970s, and so they treat year as a qualitative category rather than a quantitative one. They do a regression analysis for the 1966 data separately from the 1977 data instead of including both sets in a single analysis with year as a quantitative cause of change.

The Maxwells surveyed only grade nine and grade twelve students. In some of their analyses they treated grade as a qualitative category rather than a numerical index of amount of time spent in school.

In both cases above, the quantitative aspects of year or time were ignored in order to highlight the qualitative differences they represented.

EXAMPLE: Hiscott (1987) compared returning and non-returning migration as a cause of employment differences in residents of the Maritime provinces. His index of age is quantitative—number of years. In his data analysis, however, he treats age as a qualitative index by grouping it into three categories: 15-24, 25-34, and 35 and older.

One ground for this treatment is that an age difference of one year is ordinarily not enough to influence employment prospects but there are well-known differences in the employment experience of younger and older workers. In one sense the yearly age indicator is more precise than necessary. By combining the yearly age measurements into decade categories, the excess precision is ignored.

From the point of view of policy application, the broad groupings of ages are as precise as most governments would attempt. A government might have one special program for youth and another for mature workers. Programs for smaller age groups are quite rare.

Notice in the tables of display and summary options (Tables 9.9 and 9.10) that no lists appear for quantitative causes and qualitative effects. Though such options exist, they are in less common use than those listed. The problem is similar to the example above. Suppose yearly age is investigated as a cause of employment or unemployment. Any differences found in adjacent years is likely to be seen as random. For example, suppose that 35% of 18-year-olds, 15% of 19-year-olds, and 37% of 20-year-olds are unemployed. The peculiar low percentage for 19-year-olds is more likely to be a random anomaly than anything else. For these kinds of reasons, the quantitative cause is likely to be collapsed or grouped into a few categories. When this is done, the options become the same as for qualitative/qualitative or qualitative/quantitative indicators.

d. Measurement precision of data

Many indicators can provide very precise values, but that precision may be suspect.

EXAMPLE: Age can be measured in months and weeks or even days, hours, and minutes. Possessions can be given values accurate to the cent. Maps can show neighbourhood boundaries accurate to the millimetre.

Wage increases or declines may be quoted to one-thousandth of a decimal point.

EXAMPLE: Students are usually suspicious (and rightly so) of small differences in examination marks, especially when the marks are based on essay-type questions. The precision is suspect because it is thought to be spurious—it is not that fine distinctions cannot be made but that past a certain point they are likely to be arbitrary or random, and therefore meaningless and unfair.

In terms of measurement, the suspicion is that the small differences contain an unknown but unacceptably high degree of random error. By ignoring the fine distinctions, at least some of the random error in the measurements is discarded, and more accurate measurement is the result.

Where the high precision of an indicator is suspected to be more apparent than real, one possibility is to group or collapse quantitative categories into a few or even two qualitative categories.

EXAMPLE: Hollingshead and Redlich (1953) investigated the relationship between psychiatric disorders and social stratification, which is measured as a set of qualitative categories. A six-category scale for place of residence, a seven-category scale for occupation, and a seven-category scale for education were weighted and combined to produce a five-category social stratification indicator.

By grouping the values of the indicator Hollingshead and Redlich can then use cross-tabulations to examine the relationship of the indicator to the effect (psychiatric disorders).

9.5 WHAT CAN GO WRONG IN DATA ANALYSIS?

Research findings are descriptions of
1. how each cause changes the effect (direction),
2. how much each cause changes the effect (strength), and
3. to what degree the effect is determined by all the causes in each theory.

What can go wrong in data analysis is misanalysis, and any or all of the findings may misreport the actual causal relationships in the data. Misanalysis refers only to inaccurate findings that are the results of displaying or summarizing the data incorrectly. It does not refer to inaccurate findings that derive from inadequate variation, sample bias, or measurement error. These problems will lead to inaccurate findings quite independently of anything done in the data analysis phase. Data analysis alone cannot correct these problems, although the investigation of artifact hypotheses can give some indication of their presence. By itself, data analysis can produce accurate summary descriptions of whatever causal relationship information the data contains. Or it can produce misdescriptions—data analysis artifacts.

Some of the more common and likely sources of data analysis artifacts are discussed below.

a. Premature truncation of data analysis

If the researcher terminates the data analysis after examining the relations between each cause and the effect (while ignoring other causes), the result may be incorrect summaries of how and how much an effect is changed by a cause.

EXAMPLE: In a study of sex as a cause of wage differences, if education, experience, and age are not controlled, then the summary of the sex differences may be under- or overestimated. Similarly, if sex and the other causes are not controlled, the influence of education may be estimated incorrectly.

b. Combination of measurement categories

The combining of categories changes the amount of observable variation for an indicator. Direction and strength of causal relationship summaries are descriptions of how the variation in an effect is related to the variation in a cause. Combinations of categories, then, may influence the summaries.

1. If the indicator categories are combined only to reduce suspected random error in the measurements, the influence of the combination will be minimal.
2. When the combining is done for other reasons, the influence on the summaries may be large changes in the strength of causal relationships, and even changes in the direction.
3. Indicators may produce more variation than can be usefully analysed by a researcher, say because there are not enough cases with a particular value. (For example, only one respondent in a survey reports "widowed" as marital status, or only two respondents out of a hundred report ages less than eighteen). Or there may be too much variation because the indicators were designed to permit various combinations

of categories. Collapsing or combining categories or grouping quantitative values may affect the direction or strength relationships of the causes or effects involved, or both. This occurs because the variation is reduced by the act of combining, grouping, or collapsing.

c. Form of relationship errors

Ordinary regression analysis is designed to work on quantitative causes and effects when the relationships between them are linear—more or less straight lines. When the relationships are curves or anything other than a straight line, regression results will produce inaccurate summaries of direction and strength.

EXAMPLE: Regression analysis fits a straight line to a scatter plot, no matter what the pattern of points. When there is no pattern in the points, the regression line should have no slope—on average there is no change in the effect given a change in the cause (see Figure 9.4). But where the pattern of point is a symmetric curve (as in Figure 9.5), regression analysis again sees no change in the effect given a change in the cause. While this is true on average, it is a misleading description of the pattern in the points.

d. Summary weighting artifacts

The methods used to describe direction and strength of relationships are summaries of the patterns in the data. We cannot get the descriptions without summarizing, but the procedures (formulas) we use in summarizing may not always work the way we would like. It is possible that our summaries are as much a description of the techniques used to summarize as descriptions of the patterns in the data displays.

EXAMPLE: If the mean is used to summarize the difference between men's and women's wages in Table 9.16 below, the average wage difference is 66 cents.

Table 9.16
Female and Male Hourly Wages ($)

					Total	Mean	Median
Females	5.20	6.80	5.65	7.05	20.20	8.98	6.80
Males	6.40	8.50	9.30	10.50	6.90	8.32	8.50

Figure 9.4
Plot A

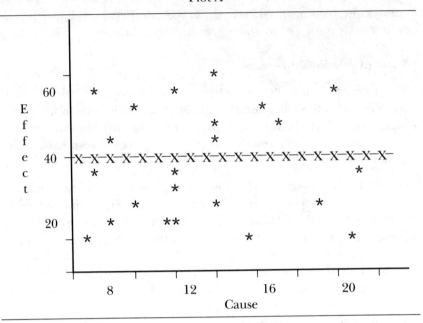

However, when the median is used as the average, the sex differences become $1.70. The sex difference shown by the mean is about 2 1/2 times larger than the same difference shown by the median. Since the same set of observations is used in both averages, the difference of appearances is obviously due only to the different formulas involved in their computation. When the mean is used, observations are weighted according to their magnitude: the more extreme they are, the greater the weight. This means that the one female high wage is given great weight and pulls the female average up close to the male average. The median weights observations as only above or below the median point. The distance of any point from the median is given no weight at all. Consequently, the one high female wage influences the median very little.

e. Outlier observations

Occasionally, one or a few observations have indicator values that are extremely high or low compared to the other observations. These

Figure 9.5
Plot B

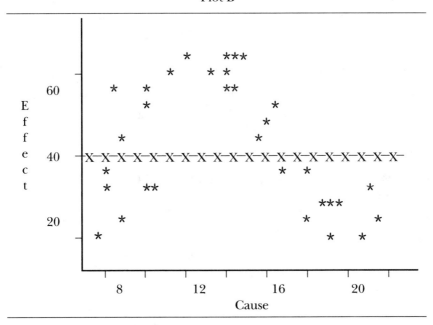

extreme values are called outliers, and they can create real problems as in the male/female wage example above. Regression analysis results can also be changed by the addition or deletion of one or two extreme outliers.

f. Interactive causes

In many theories, causes are said to operate on effects independently of other causes. In these theories the influence of a second cause *adds* its influence to the first. When causes do not operate on effects independently of each other, they are said to *interact* in determining the effect. If causes interact, their influences *multiply* instead of adding.

Interactions show up as peculiar and confusing patterns in the percentage differences or mean differences when one of the interacting causes is controlled.

EXAMPLE: Later in this chapter there is a detailed analysis of data on sexual discrimination vs the experience and productivity theories of wages. Sex, experience, and productivity accounted for 89, 19, and 4 cents respectively. When the other causes were controlled, these three causes accounted for 90, 25, and 10 cents. Ordinarily, the influence of each cause would be *diminished* by controlling; here it is *augmented*. This suggests that there is interaction among the causes—the three together explain more about wages than each separately.

If causes are interacting strongly, descriptions of their separate influence on the effect are inaccurate. In the example above, the interactions are relatively small and can be ignored for most practical policy purposes.

9.6 HOW CAN DATA ANALYSIS ARTIFACTS BE ASSESSED?

a. Premature truncation of analysis

Artifacts from premature truncation of data analysis can be prevented, of course, by completing the data analysis.

1. Researchers must be able to describe *how each cause changes the effect*. This ordinarily means how each cause changes the effect *after the influence of other causes has been controlled*. This requires what I refer to below as "multicausal" analysis, as opposed to "single-cause" analysis. The data analysis is ordinarily not complete until the multicausal analysis is finished.

   Single-cause analysis is suitable only when the project design justifies it. For example, when all causes except one have been controlled through experimental manipulations or sample selections, single-cause analysis is adequate. Since this is quite rare in social science projects, researchers ought to count on having to carry out multicausal analysis.

2. The researcher must be able to describe *how all the causes in each theory collectively determine the effect*. Wherever possible, a coefficient of determination should be computed for each theory under investigation. Comparing the coefficients provides an answer to the question of which theory is the better one. When the data is such that a coefficient cannot be computed, a narrative, qualitative description should be attempted.

3. It is often useful to be able to describe *how much each cause changes the effect*. Again, other causes should usually be controlled while one examines the strength of the effect of each cause on the effect. That is, we usually want to know how much influence a cause will have on an

effect without the influences of other causes. As in point (1) above, however, other causes should be controlled only when it makes theoretical sense to do so.

Until all of the above questions are answered, the data analysis is incomplete.

b. Combination of measurement categories

If there is any doubt about the influence that combinations of measurement categories might have on the data analysis results, the entire data analysis should be carried out on the uncombined measurements as well as the combined measurements and the results compared. The influence of the combination will appear as differences in the summaries of strength and direction of causal influence. When the results are remarkably different, careful consideration must be given to the justification of the category combinations.

c. Form of relationship errors

When the form of a relationship between a quantitative cause and a quantitative effect is not a straight line, there are two simple remedies.

1. When the plot appears to show two lines with different slopes as in Figure 9.5 above, the data set may be divided in two at the point where the direction of the slope changes. Each data subset can then be analysed separately. Obviously this remedy is only practical where the number of cases or time periods is large enough to justify separate analyses—all data analysis questions have to be answered on each subset.

2. Another simple procedure would be to treat the cause variable as qualitative rather than quantitative. Similar values of the cause measurements would be grouped together as in Figure 9.6 below.

The regression coefficient on the ungrouped cause values is −0.0003, suggesting the cause has almost no influence on the effect. If the values are grouped and treated as categories, we obtain a mean of 27.6 for group A, 61.6 for group B, and 30.5 for group C. The mean differences between group B and the other two shows that different values of the cause have strong influences on the effect.

There is a less simple remedy that should be mentioned. Occasionally a non-linear pattern fits a known mathematical equation for describing a curve. In that case, the data can be transformed so as to make a linear

Figure 9.6
Plot C

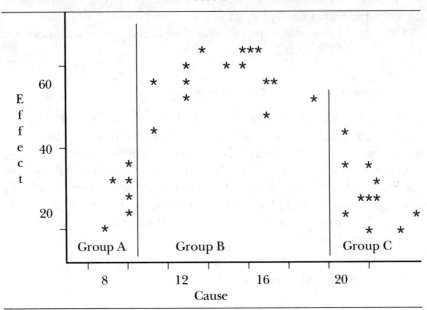

relationship between the cause and the effect. The analysis is carried out on the transformed data; then the results are transformed back into the observed data for interpretation and application.

d. Summary weighting artifacts

The usual method for controlling summary weighting artifacts is to triangulate the results of one technique with alternative summarizing devices. If the conclusions from several triangulating summaries are more or less the same, we can then say that the findings are free of summary weighting artifacts. Otherwise some or all of the findings must be seen as artifacts.

The devices for producing summary descriptions depend upon whether the indicators are treated as qualitative or quantitative. The table of display and summary options in section 9.3 gives the most common alternatives. Where the indicators involved are not inherently qualitative, more alternatives become available if the researcher is willing to treat qualitative indicators as quantitative and vice versa.

e. Outlier observations

The first thing to do to an observation with extreme values is to check for measurement error. Often extreme values may be the product of a very common recording error, such as reversing the order of two numbers and entering $4.90, for example, instead of $9.40.

If no measurement or recording errors are discovered, the data can be analysed with and without the outlier cases to see how much difference the outliers make. If the results are fairly similar, ignore the outliers. If the results are remarkably different and the researcher does not want to report results that are so heavily influenced by a few cases, two sets of results could be reported.

f. Interactive causes

The investigation of interactive causes requires only that the researcher be aware of the possibility of interaction and test each possibility. Computer programs have made this testing relatively easy.

9.7 CONVENTIONAL STATISTICAL SIGNIFICANCE TESTS IN SOCIAL SCIENCE RESEARCH

Statistical significance tests are ways of stating the probability that a project has estimated the direction of a causal relationship incorrectly. The most important finding of social science research projects is the description of *how* the causes influence the effect. When the direction of causal relationships is wrong, the policy and practice applications of the findings will be counterproductive. This being the case, it is useful to be able to describe the probability that the findings are wrong. Statistical significance tests are a means of doing this.

EXAMPLE: Suppose the findings of a research project are that cholesterol consumption increases the risk of heart disease. This finding could be right or wrong. It could be wrong in two important ways: there may be no relationship between cholesterol consumption and heart disease, or cholesterol consumption may decrease the risk of heart disease. The researchers report that the probability that there is no relationship between cholesterol consumption and risk of heart disease is 0.02. Since the probability that their findings are wrong is one chance out of fifty, the researchers report the connection between cholesterol consumption and heart disease with confidence.

EXAMPLE: A sample survey of voting intentions before an election found that a higher percentage of union members intended to vote for New Democratic Party candidates than for other (Liberal or Conservative) candidates. This finding could be wrong in either of two ways. The percentage of union members intending to vote NDP might be the same as those intending to vote for other candidates; the percentage of union members intending to vote NDP might be smaller than those intending to vote for other candidates. The researchers report that the likelihood that equal percentages of union members will vote for NDP and non-NDP candidates is 0.01. Since the probability of being wrong is so small, the researchers report their finding with confidence.

Statistical significance tests report a probability that certain events could have occurred by chance in a random process. Usually, this means that statistical significance tests should be used *only* on (1) samples that have been selected *randomly* or (2) cases that have been assigned *randomly* to different experimental treatments. The use of statistical significance tests on data sets in which a formally random selection or assignment process was not used reports the probability that events happened by chance when chance wasn't involved; it's like reporting how the future influenced the past.

In the examples above, the reports of probabilities would be meaningless if the respondents had not been chosen by formally random methods.

While any finding about the direction of a causal relationship may be wrong in two ways, statistical significance tests only report the probability of being wrong in one way. But there is a difficulty here. If you are interested in the probability of being wrong, and there is more than one way of being wrong, which way do you worry about? You worry about the way that, while being wrong, is most threatening—this is, the error that is closest to your conclusions, but still wrong.

EXAMPLE: Consider the cholesterol–heart disease study again. The first way the finding could be wrong is that there might be no relationship between cholesterol consumption and heart disease. What we referred to as the second way the finding could be wrong consists of an infinite number of possibilities. There could be, from cholesterol consumption, a very slight, slight, small, moderate, strong, or very strong benefit, through to the total prevention or cure of all heart disease.

Now if the finding is that cholesterol increases the risk of heart disease, which of these ways of being wrong is the most worrisome? The answer is the first way: the possibility that, in spite of the research finding, cholesterol consumption has no influence on heart disease. If it can be shown that this likelihood is very small, it follows that the likelihood that the other ways are wrong is even smaller. If it is reported that the probability that there is no connection between cholesterol and heart disease in the population sampled is .02, then the probability of there being, say, a slight benefit from cholesterol is a little smaller than .02; a moderate benefit somewhat smaller than .02; a strong benefit much smaller than .02, and so on. All of this is implied by the reporting of the .02 probability that there is no connection between cholesterol consumption and heart disease risk.

Now suppose that the finding was opposite—that cholesterol *reduces* the risk of heart disease. In order to describe the probability of being wrong, the researchers now have to consider that their results could have been produced by random sampling error from a population where (1) there is *no connection* between cholesterol and heart disease, or where (2) cholesterol consumption *increases* the risk of heart disease. Again, the probability that there is no connection between cholesterol consumption and heart disease is the most threatening way of being wrong. Again, the reporting of the probability that there is no connection between cholesterol consumption and heart disease also implies that the probability that cholesterol *increases* risk is smaller still.

Because the "no relationship" way of being wrong is critical to the strategy of reporting the probabilities of being wrong, it has been called the "null hypothesis." It should not be confused with the theoretical hypotheses that have been discussed earlier. The null hypothesis has only strategic meaning, and no theoretical or substantive meaning. (It is difficult, in fact, to imagine any important social causes and effects that are totally unrelated, as the null hypothesis postulates.) The null hypothesis is tested as part of the strategy of arguing that research findings are correct, because there is so little probability that they are wrong, not because anybody thinks that there is no relationship between a cause and an effect.

The "no relationship between cause and effect" way of being wrong is important in another way. In order to report a .05 probability of an event, it is necessary to calculate a "sampling distribution." Probability values like .9, .6, .5, .3, .10, .05, .01, .001, and so on, are read from these sampling distributions. Sampling distributions are descriptions of the probabilities of all possible samples that could be drawn from a population with known characteristics. As long as the characteristics of a population are known, a sampling distribution can be calculated. It is possible, then, to calculate sampling distributions for every possible value that a causal relationship might take. This truly daunting amount of work is avoided by using the null hypothesis and calculating only one sampling distribution—the one for the population where there is no relationship between the cause and the effect.

A statistical significance test is ultimately a comment on the sample size employed in a study—the amount of evidence on which conclusions are based. A finding that an observed relationship *is* statistically significant is a way of saying that the sample is large enough. A finding that an observed relationship is *not* statistically significant is merely a statement that the sample is not large enough. It can be shown that, given a sufficiently large sample, *all observed causal influence relationships* different from "no influence" will be seen as statistically significant.

This means two things. First, it means that researchers need never be discouraged if their results are not statistically significant: a sufficiently enlarged sample will produce statistically significant results. Of course, this may require such large samples that no funding agency would even consider supporting the project.

Second, it means that researchers can calculate how large their random samples will have to be in order to obtain statistically significant results. Using other research reports, the researcher can obtain estimates of the likely strength of a causal relationship. Going to the sampling distributions with this estimate of strength, the researcher can calculate the necessary sample size.

If the source of the estimate of the strength of the causal relationship is a study in which the results were not statistically significant, and the data was analysed by computer, there is another option. Most statistical packages routinely grind out statistical significance tests. Most also permit the researcher to have the computer treat each observation as if it were 2, 3, 10 or any other number of observations. By a process of trial and error it is usually easy to play with different imaginary sample sizes until one is found that will see the results as statistically significant.

It is hard to disagree with those researchers who argue that since statistical significance tests are mostly a comment on sample size, such tests should have only a small place in social science research. If statistical significance is desired, a little extra planning will provide it. Failure to achieve statistical significance is not an argument for discarding the results, but an indicator that more evidence is desirable. Certainly, no important policy or practice decisions should be based on the outcome of statistical significance tests alone. A social science study should be more than an extended commentary on the size of samples employed in its investigations. It should be an extended commentary on the relative accuracy of alternative theories of human social interaction.

9.8 EXAMPLES OF DATA ANALYSIS

Three examples of data analyses are presented below. In the study of student performance, both causes and effect are treated as qualitative. In the study of wage discrimination, the effect is quantitative while the causes are treated as qualitative. In the birth rate study, all causes and the effect are treated as quantitative.

The approach is to do a single-cause analysis, a multicause analysis, and finally an artifact analysis. Single-cause analysis refers to the investigation of relationships between each cause and the effect while other causes are ignored. Multicausal analysis refers to the investigation of the relationships between causes and effects when other effects are controlled rather than ignored. This approach is taken to illustrate the procedures. In many investigations where multiple causes are investigated, the single-cause analysis might not be reported at all.

Following the multicause analysis is a section on artifact analysis. The approach in the examples is to ask if any of the possible artifacts are large enough to require changes in the conclusions reached in the single or multicausal analysis. The reader should realize again that this approach is taken for illustrative purposes. Ordinarily the analysis of artifacts would not follow the conclusions but be an integral part of the data analysis.

It should be understood that the analysis of artifacts requires a strategic approach. The simplest project may produce many artifacts, and less simple projects may produce hundreds. The number of possible artifacts can be roughly estimated by multiplying the number of causes by the number of effects by the sample size (cases or time periods) by the number of measurement indicators by the number of data analysis operations. This formula is for errors of commission and does not necessarily include artifacts produced by errors of omission.

It would be possible to spend as much or more time checking for artifacts as doing the work that produces facts (or what are hoped to be facts). And of course the work involved in the checking for artifact may itself contain artifacts. It is possible for research to deteriorate into a neurotic search for error. Clearly some strategy guided by common sense is needed to manage the work.

The amount of artifact checking that goes into a single project is limited by an unwritten convention to the effect that serious possible errors must be checked out but that less serious possible errors need not be. *Serious errors are those that could reverse or otherwise dramatically change the conclusions of the project.* The convention is a common-sense strategy. It recognizes that the need for information is at least as important as the need for accuracy, and perhaps slightly more important; that even somewhat imperfect information is better than none at all. In other words, the desire for accuracy ought not overwhelm the need for policy and practice information.

The unwritten convention not only recognizes repetition, but relies on it: no single study represents the final word on anything. Subsequent projects can address the less serious of the possible errors as well as the more serious. This being the case, the responsibility of researchers is to do the best they can with the potentially serious errors, and leave the rest to other projects and other researchers.

a. Student performance: program quality vs IQ theories

Two alternative theories of the performance of students in school are the program quality theory and the IQ (intelligence quotient) theory. The program quality theory postulates that the quality of the educational program (teachers, learning materials, and experiences) is the principal determinant of student performance. The better the program, the greater the proportion of satisfactory grades. In this theory IQ is considered largely unimportant, but social class is considered to be important: high-quality programs will make a greater difference to students from the working class than from the middle class.

The IQ theory of student performance postulates that the higher the IQ of a student, the higher his or her marks will be. The quality of the program and the skill of the teachers are considered mostly irrelevant to their performance. Social class background of the students is seen to be irrelevant also, except that more students with a high IQ are likely to come from middle-class than working-class backgrounds.

Project Design

In a city in the Midwest, the school board had introduced a trial high-quality program in selected grade seven classes in selected schools. The high quality involved some extra teacher training and some equipment costs—books, video and audio tapes, lab equipment, field trips, and the like. After two years of operation, the school board wanted an evaluation of the effectiveness of the program in terms of students' marks.

Variation design: Variation was designed into the program quality variable by selecting students from both high-quality and ordinary program classrooms.

Sampling design: All 244 grade seven students currently in high-quality classrooms were selected. In schools with high-quality program classrooms, a random sample of 206 grade seven students in classrooms with ordinary programs were also selected.

Measurement design: All information was obtained from existing school records. The indicator for student performance was their marks, in percentages. The indicator for program was attendance at a high-quality program classroom. The indicator for IQ was score on the most recently written test. The indicator for social class was the status of parental occupations.

Data analysis design: the sample size of 450 students justifies using numerical technology, as does the numerical character of the indicators. Except for high-quality or ordinary program, the other indicators are quantitative.

Every cause was treated as qualitative because it was suspected there was a great deal of random error in the IQ scores and in the detailed occupations listed by students' parents. Marks were treated as qualitative because they were also thought to contain much random error. Finally, this treatment would produce results that were simple to translate into policy.

Marks were made into a two-category performance indicator: a student's marks were measured as satisfactory when 60% or above was obtained in every course, and all marks were as good as those of the previous year, or better. IQ was measured as high if a student scored 110 or above and as average if below. Students were measured as working class if both parents listed industrial types of occupations and middle class otherwise.

For teaching purposes, we shall look first at single-cause analysis—how each cause influences the effect, ignoring the other causes. Then we will

Table 9.17
Marks by Program Quality

Marks	Program Quality		Total
	High	Ordinary	
Satisfactory	67.2 %	32.0 %	51.1 %
Unsatisfactory	32.8	68.0	48.9
Total %	100.0	100.0	100.0
Total cases	244	206	450

look at multiple-cause analysis—how each cause influences the effect when other causes are controlled.

Single-cause analysis

The first task is to select and employ a suitable display and summary technology. Because all the indicators are treated as qualitative, the appropriate method is percentaged cross-tabulation. Shown in Tables 9.17 and 9.18 below are high-quality program and IQ (causes) cross-tabulated with the effect, students' marks.

These cross-classifications show that the hypotheses that predict how the cause will influence the effect are accurate. In the table showing grades by program quality, the percentage of unsatisfactory marks is smaller in the high-quality than in the ordinary program. In the grades by IQ table, the percentage of unsatisfactory marks is smaller for the high IQ students, as predicted.

How much do program and IQ influence marks? Note that the theories specify only that one cause will have more influence on the effect than

Table 9.18
Marks by IQ
IQ

Marks	% High	% Average	Total
Satisfactory	61.7	37.1	51.1
Unsatisfactory	38.3	62.9	48.9
Total %	100.0	100.0	100.0
Total cases	256	194	450

Table 9.19
IQ by Class

IQ	Class		
	Middle	Working	Total Cases
Aver.	57.1 %	56.6	256
High	42.9	43.4	194
Total cases	212	238	450

another, but not by how much more. In the last row of the table showing marks by program quality, high-quality program students have 32.8% unsatisfactory marks while ordinary-program students have 68.0% unsatisfactory. Difference in quality of program produces a 68.0 − 32.8 = 35.2% difference in marks. Similar calculations for the IQ crosstab show that different IQs produce 62.9 − 38.3 = 24.6% differences in marks.

Program quality produces about 11% (35.2 − 24.6) more satisfactory marks than IQ. This leads to the conclusion that the high-quality program is more important to students' marks than IQ.

The IQ theory has a sub-hypothesis that more high-IQ children come from the middle than the working class. Table 9.19 below tests this suggestion and shows that it is correct, but the differences are very small. The percentage of high-IQ students from the working class is slightly under 43%, and from the middle class slightly over 43%.

Multicausal analysis

The findings above may be incorrect. The displays of the relationship between one cause and the effect ignored the other cause. The two causes may be correlated or related to each other. If this is the case, it may be misleading to ignore one cause while examining the other. In crosstabulation analysis, other causes can be controlled by including them in the tables. In Table 9.20 below, two causes are included.

In the high-quality program theory, it is suggested that working-class children will benefit more than middle-class children. This can be determined by looking at program and class cross-tabulated against marks, as in Table 9.20. The hypothesis suggests that the difference between middle- and working-class students should be larger in the regular programs than in the higher-quality ones.

The table suggests that the hypothesis is correct. In ordinary programs

Table 9.20

Marks by Program Quality and Class

Marks	High Quality Program		Ordinary Quality Program		Total Cases
	Middle class	Working class	Middle class	Working class	
Satisfactory	69.4 %	64.0 %	48.9 %	17.9 %	230
Unsatisfactory	30.6	36.0	51.1	82.1	220
Total Cases	144	100	94	112	450

middle-class students get 31% (48.9 − 17.9) more satisfactory marks than working-class students. In high-quality programs middle-class students get only 5.4% (69.4 − 64.0) more satisfactory marks than working-class students.

The table permits another comparison. When the working-class students in ordinary and high-quality programs are compared, the improvement in satisfactory grades is 46.1% (64.0 − 17.9%). The comparable improvement for middle-class students is only 20.5% (69.4 − 48.9).

In the analysis so far, the causes from each theory have been investigated while the causes from the other theory have been ignored. Now we have to determine if the single-cause analysis is misleading. In the tables below all three causes are included in the cross-tabulation against grades.

The IQ theory controlling for program quality and social class

In Table 9.21 class and program quality are controlled so as to examine the accuracy of the IQ theory of performance without their influence. If the first two columns of figures are compared, the hypothesis is accurate: for middle-class children in high-quality programs, the high-IQ students obtain 12.5% (75 − 62.5) more satisfactory marks than average-IQ students. When columns 3 and 4 are compared, the high-IQ students obtain 55.6% (71.4 − 15.8) more satisfactory marks than average-IQ students.

For working-class students in high-quality programs, the IQ hypothesis is inaccurate. High-IQ students get 4.2% less satisfactory marks than their average-IQ counterparts. For working-class students in ordinary programs, however, the IQ hypothesis is again accurate: 28.5% (32.1 − 3.6)

Table 9.21
Marks by Class, Program Quality and IQ

| Grades | Middle Class | | | | Working Class | | | | |
| | High Quality | | Ordinary | | High Quality | | Ordinary | | Total |
	High IQ	Aver. IQ	High IQ	Aver. IQ	High IQ	Aver. IQ	High IQ	Aver. IQ	Cases
Satis.	60	40	40	6	40	24	18	2	230
	75.0%	62.5%	71.4%	15.8%	62.5%	66.7%	32.1%	3.6%	
Unsatis.	20	24	16	32	24	12	38	54	220
	25.0	37.5	28.5	84.2	37.5	33.3	67.9	96.4	
Total cases	80	64	56	38	64	36	56	56	450

more satisfactory marks are obtained by high-IQ students than average-IQ students.

Overall, the IQ theory appears to be only partly correct. When program quality and social class are controlled, the IQ theory is correct in only three out of the four possible comparisons.

The quality program theory controlling for IQ

The cross-tabulation below (Table 9.22) looks at the relationship between program and grade performance, controlling for IQ and social class background of the students. If the high- and ordinary-quality programs in each set are compared, it can be seen that in every case the students in high-quality programs have higher percentages of satisfactory grades than the ordinary-program students. This leads to the conclusion that the quality-program theory is accurate, even when the effects of IQ and class are removed.

The hypothesis that high-quality programs will make a greater difference to working- than middle-class students can also be examined in this table. In the high-IQ group, the working-class students in the high-quality program get 30.4% (62.5 − 32.1) more satisfactory marks than ordinary-program students, whereas middle-class students in the high-quality program get only 3.6% more than ordinary-program students. A similar finding holds for the average-IQ group as well.

Overall, it appears that the program theory is supported more consistently than the IQ theory: no matter what the values of IQ and social class, students in high-quality programs do better than students in ordinary

Table 9.22

Marks by IQ, Class and Program Quality

| | High IQ | | | | Average IQ | | | | |
| | Middle Class | | Working Class | | Middle Class | | Working Class | | |
Grades	High Quality	Ordin. Quality	High Quality	Ordin. Quality	High Quality	Ordin. Quality	High Quality	Ordin. Quality	Total Cases
Satis.	60	40	40	18	40	6	24	2	230
	75.0%	71.4%	62.5%	32.1%	62.5%	15.8%	66.7%	3.6%	
Unsatis.	20	16	24	38	24	32	12	54	220
	25.0	28.5	37.5	67.9	37.5	84.2	33.3	96.4	
Total cases	80	56	64	56	64	38	36	56	450

programs. The IQ theory, on the other hand, is accurate for only some values of social class and quality of program.

Preliminary Policy Recommendations

On the basis of these findings, it would be safe to recommend the continuation of the high-quality-program experiment. Beyond this recommendation, another aspect of the above table reveals important details about how the program should be expanded. Notice that the 63.1% (66.7 − 3.6) improvement brought about by the high-quality program in satisfactory marks for working-class children with average IQ is highest of all groups. The next-best improvement (46.7%) is for middle-class children with average IQ. This is followed by high-IQ working-class children (30.4%). The least improvement is found for high-IQ middle-class students (3.6%). This analysis provides clear priorities for expansion: expand the high-quality program in schools in working-class neighbourhoods, and choose average-IQ students rather than high-IQ students.

These recommendations are preliminary because we have not yet discounted the possibility that the findings are influenced by artifacts.

Measures of association

The percentage difference measure of how much a cause influences an effect becomes more difficult to use as the number of categories increases in either the cause or the effect variable. However, the general measures

Table 9.23
Measures of Association

Measure of Relationship	Strength of Relationship	Association of Grades with Program Quality	IQ
Lambda		.34	.23
Uncertainty		.20	.06

of association or strength of relationship discussed earlier will work, no matter how many categories are involved.

Two of these measures are the lambda coefficient and the uncertainty coefficient. When these are computed for the above crosstab displays of the data, the results are as below (Table 9.23). (Ordinarily, the computations are carried out on the unpercentaged figures.)

Although the absolute values of the coefficients are quite different, the relative values are similar: program is stronger than IQ. The lambda value for IQ is smaller than the lambda values for program. The larger strength coefficient for program suggests that it is a better theory of school performance than the IQ theory. This finding corresponds to the percentage difference findings discussed earlier.

Multiple strength of relationship coefficients are simple extensions of the procedures for bivariate strength coefficients. A coefficient of determination can be computed on the (unpercentaged) figures in any of the tables above in which all three causes are cross-classified against the effect. The multiple lambda coefficient is .35, which means that all the causes together explain about 1/3 of the variation in grades. The multiple uncertainty coefficient is .21, which means that all the causes together explain about 1/5 of the variation in grades. These values are different because the computing formulas for each coefficient weight the observations differently. Both suggest that important causes of variation in students' marks have been overlooked in this study.

Low coefficient of determination figures should restrain any over-enthusiastic hopes for the benefits that may be derived from expanding the high-quality program. With about 2/3 (lambda) or 4/5 (uncertainty) of variation in marks unexplained by all the causes examined, schools and administrations are forewarned that the influence of other factors in student performance may become manifest in further work with the program.

Checking for artifacts

The two most serious possible errors in the study—sampling bias and measurement error—are discussed below. Both variation and data analysis artifacts may be present, but they do not look serious. With regard to variation, given the use of the cause strategy, it is only essential that variation in high-quality or ordinary program be observable, and this was achieved. Any amount of variation in the mark indicator would serve the purposes of the research. Any collinearity would have become apparent when the full cross-classification was examined.

With regard to the data analysis, two methods of describing the relationships between cause and effect have been employed already (percentage differences and association coefficients), and both give essentially the same results.

CHECKING FOR SAMPLE BIAS

In this study, all students in high-quality programs were included in the sample. However, because there were many more students in ordinary programs than in high-quality programs, the ordinary-program students were randomly sampled. If this sample is unrepresentative of students in ordinary programs, the results may be misleading. To determine sample representativeness in terms of sex, age, and IQ, the ordinary-program sample students were compared to the ordinary program population—all ordinary-program students in the entire school district. Table 9.24 shows the results.

The sex and IQ distribution of the sample are very similar to that of the population and may therefore be regarded as representative for those variables. The age distribution differences, however, appear to be too large to ignore.

If age has an effect on how students respond to being in a quality program, then the over-representation of twelve-year-olds may influence the relationships between the causes—program, IQ, social class, and the effect, marks. This possibility can be initially investigated by comparing the marks of the eleven- and twelve-year-olds (see Table 9.25). If they are similar, we can have some confidence that the unrepresentativeness of the ordinary-program sample will have little effect on the conclusions of the study.

Table 9.25 makes clear that, for the ordinary-program sample, there is little difference between the elevens and twelves with regard to grade

Table 9.24
Population and Sample Comparisons
for Ordinary-Program Students

	Population (N=844) %	Sample (N=206) %
Sex		
Male	47	50
Female	53	50
Age		
11 years	68	58
12 years	32	42
IQ		
High	55	54
Low	45	46

performance. The unrepresentative distribution on the age variable can probably be ignored. It should be noted that this is not a complete investigation of the problem: it could be argued that even though there is no relationship between age and marks for the ordinary program sample, age may be related to the causes that could influence the results of the study. In addition, the age distribution of the high-quality program students is relevant to the question as well: if, for example, younger students respond better to the high-quality program, then the over-representation of the 12s in the ordinary program sample may give an overly positive view of the superiority of the high-quality program over the regular program.

Table 9.25
Ordinary Program Students: Grades by Age

Grades	11 years	12 years	Total
Satisfactory	32.3%	31.6%	32.0%
Unsatisfactory	67.7	68.4	68.0
Total %	100.0	100.0	100.0
Total cases	119	87	206

CHECKING FOR MEASUREMENT ERROR

The indicators for two of the causes measured—program quality and social class—are unlikely to contain much error. Social class was based on

Table 9.26
Number of Students with High and Average IQ scores
on two Different Measures

	High IQ	Average IQ	Total
Previous year's scores	256	194	450
Average of two years	242	208	450

the parents' occupations as reported in school records. Records of the high-quality program show that fewer than 5% of students admitted are dropped, and then usually because their parents are moving. The number of students admitted to the program after the beginning of the school year is less than 5%. It is unlikely then that the determination of whether a student was in the high-quality or ordinary program is seriously in error.

The measurement of the third cause—IQ—is a different matter. The indicator for IQ was the score on standardized IQ tests administered by the school district to all students in the previous school year. These tests, like all tests, are notoriously subject to much random error. The collapsing of the original scores into high (scores 110 and above) and average (scores below 110) would reduce the random error. We need be concerned only with those scores close to the cutting point of 110. Still, since this is where most of the scores will be, the random error could produce fairly serious mismeasurements of IQ. To check on this possible artifact, data from a new set of IQ tests was employed. The two IQ scores for each student were averaged and then classified again as high or low. The original and average scores are compared in Table 9.26.

The differences here are large enough to justify a re-analysis of the data using the NEWIQ scores, which have less random error than the original scores. The relationship between NEWIQ and grades is shown in Tables 9.27 and 9.28.

The direction of the relationship between NEWIQ and marks is the same as that between IQ and marks. Note that this is usual: random error in measurements will ordinarily not have any influence on *how* a cause influences an effect. The change in *how much* IQ influences performance is small. In the original analysis, different IQs produced a 24.6% difference in marks; with the NEWIQ indicator the difference is reduced to 22.6%. This difference is too small to cause any serious change in the conclusions.

The indicator for the effect—satisfactory marks—is unlikely to contain much random error. The satisfactory or unsatisfactory designations for

Table 9.27
Grades by NEWIQ

NEWIQ

Marks	High	Low	Total
Satisfactory	149	81	230
Unsatisfactory	93	127	220
Total	242	208	450

each student are averages of all the course work for an entire year, and so much random error will have already been averaged out. Furthermore, the marks used in the study are the same marks assigned by the school administrators and sent home with the students to their parents.

Systematic error in the measurement of performance is a different matter. If the quality-program teachers mark in a systematically different way from ordinary-program teachers, the conclusions of the study may be seriously in error. Any teacher may have a tendency to easy or hard grading, and the training for the high-quality program may have introduced or strengthened such tendencies. To determine if the training for the high-quality program had changed the way teachers mark, the average marks they assigned while in the high-quality program were compared to the ones they had assigned earlier. Small differences were found which suggested that their marking was slightly more severe than before.

To determine if the teachers of students sampled from ordinary programs were easier or harder markers than other ordinary-program teachers, the two groups were compared. Both groups had almost identical averages.

Finally, to test whether the high-quality-program teachers were easier or harder markers than ordinary-program teachers, each teacher marked two sets of student assignments. Both sets of teachers marked the assign-

Table 9.28
Grades by NEWIQ

NEWIQ

Marks	High	Low	Total
Satisfactory	61.5%	38.9%	230
Unsatisfactory	38.5	61.1	220
Total	242	208	450

ments roughly the same on average. The quality-program teachers assigned somewhat lower marks than ordinary-program students.

The above information is strong evidence against serious systematic error in the evaluation of students' performance by teachers. Since high-quality-program teachers mark slightly harder than ordinary-program teachers, the conclusion of the study—that the high-quality program improves the marks of students—probably understates the beneficial influence of the program.

Final Policy Implications

The original policy implications were twofold. First: it is safe to recommend the continuation of the high-quality program. Second: if the high-quality program is to be expanded, schools in working-class neighbourhoods should be chosen, and students of average IQ should be chosen over students of high IQ. There do not seem to be any artifacts that would require that the implications be strongly qualified. Ordinary everyday caution regarding the results should be sufficient for most practical purposes.

b. Wages: Sex discrimination vs experience/productivity theories

The experience and productivity theory of wage differences between men and women is a simple alternative to the sexual discrimination theory. The sexual discrimination theory postulates that women are paid less than men because employers discriminate against female employees. In this theory, experience and productivity are seen as minor determinants of wage differences between men and women.

The experience and productivity theory postulates that differences in the wages of male and female workers are due to differences in their work experience and job productivity. In other words, wage differences are due to management policies of paying higher wages to workers with greater experience and greater productivity. In this theory, sexual discrimination plays a minor or non-existent role in producing wage differences between men and women.

Project design

The two theories were investigated in a large financial company that was interested in pursuing an equitable wage policy because some disgruntled previous employees had threatened to take their case to the human rights commission. One of the few company job classifications that had roughly equal numbers of male and female members was clerk-typist. Twenty-two cases were randomly sampled from all company workplaces.

Wages were measured in terms of an hourly rate. Benefits were excluded, but year-end bonuses and the like were added into the hourly wage rate.

Sex was measured in terms of the usual categories.

Productivity was measured according to the supervisors' assessment of the employees. Each employee was placed on a scale with the following categories: below average, average, above average, well above average, and superior in getting tasks finished.

Experience was measured in terms of the number of months' experience in the same type of job claimed by the employee at the time of hiring.

Note that sexual discrimination was not measured directly. It was treated as a kind of residual: if wage differences between men and women could not be explained by experience and productivity, it must be caused by discrimination.

Data analysis: on the grounds that the bias of supervisors might lead to random error in the productivity ratings, the number of categories was reduced to two: average (average and below average) and strong (above average, well above average and superior).

Since the employees' reports of their previous experience had not been checked, and consequently there might be errors in the reports, those who reported two months' experience or less were categorized as having none, and those with more were categorized as having some.

With this collapsing of categories, all the causes could be treated as qualitative. Since the wage measurements were quite accurate, they were treated as quantitative. The appropriate display and summary technology are graphs and charts and average differences.

Single-cause analysis

The hypotheses specify which of the sex, experience, and productivity categories will receive the higher wages. Table 9.29 below shows the hourly wage paid to the sample of clerk-typist employees.

The list of wages display the sample of hourly wages, but in a fashion that makes it difficult to tell whether the hypotheses are supported or not. We need to summarize the differences between the categories of the cause variables. The mean—the arithmetic average—is appropriate for this

Table 9.29
Hourly $ Wage of 22 Clerk-typists

| Sex | | Productivity | | Experience | |
Men	Women	Average	Strong	Some	None
3.18	2.14	3.18	3.29	1.85	1.85
2.79	2.02	2.79	3.45	2.04	2.02
2.42	1.85	2.42	3.05	2.14	2.14
3.42	1.85	3.42	3.14	2.15	2.32
3.15	2.15	3.15	3.03	2.20	2.32
3.29	2.21	2.14	2.21	2.21	2.42
3.45	2.14	2.02	2.20	3.03	2.79
3.05	2.20	1.85	2.32	3.05	3.18
3.14	2.32	1.85	2.32	3.11	3.29
3.03	2.32	2.15	3.11	3.14	3.45
	3.11		2.04	3.15	
	2.04		2.14	3.42	

purpose. Mean wages are found by summing all the observations for each group and then dividing this sum by the number of observations in the group, as in Table 9.30.

The differences between the means show that the causes influence wages. Men have higher average wages than women; strong performers have higher average wages than average performers, and experienced workers are paid more on average than inexperienced workers. These are the kind of differences predicted by the hypotheses, and they show that the hypotheses are correct.

How much does each cause influence the effect? We compare the average wages of each category of the cause. Sex produces a $3.09 – $2.20 = $0.89 average hourly wage difference; productivity produces a $2.69 – $2.50 = $0.19 difference, and experience produces a $2.62 – $2.58 =

Table 9.30
Average (Mean) Hourly $ Wages of 22 Clerk-typists

| | Sex | | Productivity | | Experience | |
	Men	Women	Average	Strong	Some	None
Sum	30.92	26.352	24.97	32.292	31.488	25.78
Cases	10	12	10	12	12	10
Average	3.09	2.20	2.50	2.69	2.62	2.58
Difference		.89		.19		.04

Table 9.31
Average Wages by Experience, Controlling for Sex and Productivity

Sex	Productivity	Experience	No. of Cases	Average Wage	Difference
Female	Strong	None	3	2.26	
		Some	4	2.39	.13
Female	Average	None	2	1.94	
		Some	3	2.05	.11
Male	Strong	None	2	3.37	
		Some	3	3.07	−.30
Male	Average	None	3	2.80	
		Some	2	3.29	.49

$0.04 difference. These figures seem to show that sex has the strongest influence; productivity and experience are considerably weaker.

Multicausal analysis

There are two different ways of doing a multicausal analysis of a data set with qualitative causes of a quantitative effect. Both are techniques for controlling or removing the effects of one cause while examining the influence of another. One can be called the "add and subtract" method and the other the "grouping" method. The grouping method is the simplest and we will look at it first.

CONTROL BY GROUPING:

If we take only women with strong productivity and then look at the wage difference according to experience, for example, we can say that since everyone in the group is female and has strong productivity, any wage differences among them can only be the influence of experience. In Tables 9.31-9.33 below, two causes are controlled, while wage differences according to the third cause are examined.

Table 9.31 displays the average wage differences for workers with none and some experience after grouping according to sex and productivity. In the single-cause analysis it was observed that those with some experience had higher average wages than those with none. In the above table we see that this is the case except for men with strong productivity: those with no experience make on average about 30 cents more than those with some experience.

The single-cause analysis of productivity showed that strong perform-

Table 9.32
Average Wages by Productivity, Controlling for Sex and Experience

Sex	Experience	Productivity	No. of Cases	Average Wage	Difference
Female	None	Strong	3	2.26	·
		Average	2	1.94	.32
Female	Some	Strong	4	2.39	
		Average	3	2.05	.34
Male	None	Strong	2	3.37	
		Average	3	2.80	.57
Male	Some	Strong	3	3.07	
		Average	2	3.29	−.21

ers had larger average wages than weak performers. In Table 9.32, where sex and experience are controlled, the same finding is observable, except for men with some experience.

In Table 9.33 the single-cause results are repeated: men have higher average wages than women when productivity and experience are controlled.

The strengths of relationships discovered in the single-cause analysis are also found in the multivariate. Sex was the cause of the largest average wage difference when the other causes are ignored, and this result is repeated when other causes are controlled. In Tables 9.31, 9.32 and 9.33, compare the size of the average differences in wages. The male/female differences are larger than the productivity differences, which, in turn, are larger than the experience differences.

Table 9.33
Average Wages by Sex, Controlling for Productivity and Experience

Productivity	Experience	Sex	Cases	Average Wage	Difference
Strong	None	Female	3	2.26	
		Male	2	3.37	1.11
Strong	Some	Female	4	2.39	
		Male	3	3.07	.68
Average	None	Female	2	1.94	
		Male	3	2.80	.86
Average	Some	Female	3	2.05	
		Male	2	3.29	1.24

In sum, if we carry out the multivariate analysis as above, (1) the direction of the relationships between the causes and the effect are similar to those of the single-cause analysis, with the exceptions noted; and (2) the strengths of relationship found are identical to those found in the single-cause.

One of the most serious problems with the control-by-grouping technique is that many cases are required. Note in the above tables that all of the conclusions are based on comparing two or three cases to two or three other cases. If it became necessary to add another cause, it is likely that some conclusions would be based on comparisons of two cases, and it is possible that some of the groups we want to compare might have no cases at all. Now conclusions are not necessarily incorrect just because they are based on a small number of cases. But it is difficult to have much confidence in such conclusions because we suspect that the addition of only one more case might change the results entirely. The alternative method of control does not suffer from this kind of difficulty.

CONTROL BY ADDING AND SUBTRACTING

This method uses the quantitative nature of the effect variable to remove the influences of other causes. For example, it is shown above that the average wage is $2.62 for those with some experience and $2.58 for those with none. The mean wage for the entire sample is $2.60. This means that the some-experience group is $0.02 above the overall mean and the no-experience group is $.0.03 below. If we subtract $0.02 from the wage of everyone in the some-experience group and add $0.03 to every wage in the no-experience group, we will have removed the effect of experience from the wages: after adding and subtracting, the mean wage of both groups will be $2.60. Whatever variation remains in the wages must then be caused by sex and productivity. We can next remove the influence of productivity in a similar fashion, and then any variation in wages must be caused by sex, the only cause whose influence has not been subtracted. If we change the sequence in which the effects of the different causes are removed, we can obtain the mean wages for each cause with the effects of the other removed. The results are presented in Table 9.34.

Rows 1 and 2 show the average difference between male and female wages when the average wage for the productivity and experience categories have been set to the overall average wage of $2.60. Rows 3 and 4 show the mean wage differences between strong and average performers when sex and experience group average wages have been set to $2.60.

Table 9.34
Average (Mean) Hourly Wages($)

Row		Sex		Productivity		Experience	
		Men	Women	Average	Strong	Some	None
1	Average	3.08	2.18	2.60	2.60	2.60	2.60
2	Difference		.90		0.0		0.0
3	Average	2.60	2.60	2.75	2.50	2.60	2.60
4	Difference		0.0		.25		0.0
5	Average	2.60	2.60	2.60	2.60	2.68	2.58
6	Difference		0.0		0.0		.10
7	Average	3.09	2.20	2.50	2.69	2.62	2.58
8	Difference		.89		.19		.04
9	Cases	10	12	10	12	12	10

The differences is rows 1–6 can be compared to rows 7 and 8, which show the (single-cause) average wage differences when no attempt is made to control the influences of the other causes. Though the influence of productivity and experience are a little stronger when the other causes are controlled, our conclusions would remain the same: the postulated directions of relationships are supported, and sex is the most important cause of wage differences, with productivity a weak second, and experience an even weaker third.

The above figures make clear that the sexual discrimination theory is the better one. This is true whether productivity and experience are ignored (single-cause analysis) or controlled (multicause analysis): men make about 90 cents an hour more than women.

The application of these findings seems straightforward. Women's wages will first have to be brought up to the level of men's wages, given comparable experience and productivity. Further investigation will be needed to discover how the discrepancies came into being. Were there differences at the point of hiring? Did women start at the same wages as men and then receive smaller and less frequent raises? Are all supervisors guilty of discrimination or are some much worse than others?

Using coefficients to measure strength of causal relationships

Each of the causes is treated as if it had only *two values*. When more than two values are involved, the average-difference measure of strength, like

Table 9.35
Strength of Relationship of Wage with

	Sex (ignoring experience and productivity)	Experience (ignoring sex and productivity)	Productivity (ignoring sex and experience)
R-square	.67	.002	.32

the percentage-difference measure used in the first example, will not always be easy to use and will not always give clear answers to the question of how much each cause influences the effect. The percentage-of-variation-explained method is more general: it will work no matter how many categories the cause has. The strength-of-relationship coefficient appropriate to this kind of data is called R-square (and sometimes Eta-square).

For a single-cause analysis, R-square has the values shown in Table 9.35.

The relative size of these coefficients is identical to the relative size of average wage differences: sex is again seen to be more strongly related to wage income than are experience and productivity.

For multicause analysis, the results are similar.

Single-cause analysis ignores the possibility that some of the apparent influence of sex may have been due to the hidden influence of productivity and experience and vice versa. In multicause analysis, the influence of other causes on wages can be removed rather than ignored. We can remove the effects of sex and look at how much wage variation is explained by productivity and experience, and vice versa. The results in Table 9.36 are similar to those of single-cause analysis.

A final question of interest is whether all the causes together account for the variation in wages. R-square for all the variables together is .757. This means that 24% of wage variation among these workers is not accounted for. It suggests that other causes ought to be investigated. What

Table 9.36
Strength of Relationship of Wage Income with

	Sex (with productivity and experience controlled)	Productivity and Experience (with sex controlled)
R-square	.649	.091

common-sense causes of wage differences have been ignored that might be included?

Checking for artifacts

The most serious possible problems in the wages study involve the measurement phase. Observable variation in each of the causes and the effect appears to be sufficient, and no collinearity showed up in the multicausal data analysis. This suggests that little attention need be given to variation artifacts.

Nor need much attention be given to one aspect of sample bias. Since the sample includes all employees of the company in clerk-typist positions, it may be considered as the entire population of clerk-typists. Whether or not female clerk-typists are a biased sample of all female employees might require further investigation. However, the findings of this study are quite similar to several other studies, all of which conclude that women are discriminated against. These studies investigate women at the highest, middle, and lowest job levels.

CHECKING FOR MEASUREMENT ERROR

Two possibly serious errors are found in the measurement phase. The first is that a 4-cent or 10-cent difference in wages deriving from experience differences seems somewhat small. This result could be the result of mismeasurement of experience. Recall that experience (as a clerk-typist) was measured only in months of experience before the current job. The amount of time the employees have logged in their current positions would have been excluded by this indicator. Going back through the sample employee records, the researchers discovered that about half of them had more than two years' seniority with the company. A new cause indicator called "new experience" was created by combining the experience indicator and the seniority indicator. If an employee had both experience and more than two years' seniority, they were categorized as having "some" job experience; otherwise their experience was classified as "none."

Table 9.37 shows the results of the analysis with the new experience indicator as a cause in place of the experience indicator used earlier.

Rows 7 and 8 show that those employees with some new experience make about 54 cents more than those without when the other causes are ignored.

Rows 5 and 6 show that when the influence of the other causes is removed,

Table 9.37
Average (Mean) Hourly Wage ($)

Row		Sex		Productivity		New Experience	
		Men	Women	Average	Strong	Some	None
1	Average	3.11	2.25	2.60	2.60	2.60	2.60
2	Difference		.86		0.0		0.0
3	Average	2.60	2.60	2.57	2.80	2.60	2.60
4	Difference		0.0		.23		0.0
5	Average	2.60	2.60	2.60	2.60	2.81	2.56
6	Difference		0.0		0.0		.25
7	Average	3.09	2.20	2.50	2.69	3.00	2.46
8	Difference		.89		.19		.54
9	Cases	10	12	10	12	12	10

those with some new experience make about 25 cents more than those without. Rows 3 and 4 show that when the influence of new experience and sex are removed, strong producers make about 23 cents more than average producers. With the influence of new experience and productivity removed, rows 1 and 2 show that men make 86 cents more than women.

Note that the more accurate measurement of experience shows that experience is a much stronger determinant of wages than the less accurate measure. Since this change would not lead to the modification of any of the original conclusions, it might seem that the concern for accuracy is misplaced. However, by removing the measurement error that might lead to scepticism about the original results, the project also removes one of the reasons for doubting those results and failing to adopt remedial measures. In this case more accurate measurement has strengthened the credibility of the conclusions.

The second serious possible error in the measurement work is systematic error in the productivity ratings. Any sexual bias in judging productivity could have strongly influenced the conclusions. Further investigation showed that the twenty-two employees had three male and two female supervisors. The supervisors' average rating of their employees was about the same. However, when the sex of the supervisor and the employee was the same, the productivity ratings were on average one category lower than when the sex of supervisor and employee was different. This result suggested the operation of a kind of reverse discrimination—supervisors may have been extra hard on employees of their own sex to avoid the charge of discrimination.

To determine the accuracy of the supervisors' ratings, employee records used for the initial ratings were given to a group of non-supervisors for an independent rating, but the sex of the employees was hidden. The results of the independent rating were virtually identical to the supervisors' ratings. On these grounds it was concluded that supervisors' productivity ratings were accurate enough for the purposes of the project.

CHECKING FOR DATA ANALYSIS ARTIFACTS

In the data analysis phase there appears to be no major sources of error. In the original analysis one small aspect of the results was puzzling: the causes appeared to have stronger influences on the effect when the other causes were controlled than when they were not. This suggests that the causes were interacting or multiplying together rather than adding together to determine wages. In the analysis using the new experience indicator, the interaction effect disappears. The influence of productivity ratings on wages increases, but the influence of sex and experience diminishes when the other causes are controlled.

Finally, there is the possibility that if some average other than the mean were used to summarize the influence of the causes, the picture of the relative influence of the causes might change.

Table 9.38 compares findings based on the mean and the median. The median is an average like the mean, but it identifies the point that divides all of the observations into two equal-sized groups, half above the median point and half below. How each cause influences the effect is unchanged, and though the influence of each cause when measured by median

Table 9.38
Average (Mean) Hourly Wages ($)

Row		Sex		Productivity		Experience	
		Men	Women	Average	Strong	Some	None
7	Average	3.09	2.20	2.50	2.69	2.62	2.58
8	Difference		.89		.19		.04
	Median	3.15	2.15	2.29	2.68	2.62	2.37
	Difference		1.00		.39		.25
9	Cases	10	12	10	12	12	10

differences appears larger than when measured by mean differences, sex remains the most influential, and experience the least.

The differences between mean and median in the single-cause analysis are large enough to justify a multicausal analysis (using control by grouping) with medians rather than means. When this is done, the original conclusions are unchanged: the differences between the medians and the means are relatively small, and sex remains by far the most important cause of wages.

c. Birth rates: women's status vs employment/immigration theories

One simple theory of birth rates can be called the "more effective contraception" theory. In this theory, the invention of a new method of preventing conception will result in lower birth rates because it is assumed that some significant proportion of conceptions are not desired by the parents. The invention of the highly effective oral contraceptive, for example, is seen as a determinant of declining birth rates.

A second theory of birth rates is the "demographic transition" theory in which the birth rates are believed to be a response to death rates generally, and infant death rates in particular. The chief cause of the long-run decline in birth rates in Western societies is thought to be industrialization and urbanization, which are believed to have (1) brought improvements in nutrition, health, cleanliness, and disease control, which (2) bring reductions in the infant and general death rates, which (3) bring declines in the birth rate.

A third theory of changes in the birth rates sees changes in women's status as the basic cause. In this theory, the more equal the relationships between men and women, the lower the birth rate will be. The recent history of Europe and North America is seen as one where women have struggled for equality with men. One of the responses of women to their gains in this struggle is to have fewer children as they take advantage of livelihoods other than housewife. One response to losses in equality is an increase in the number of children as women's control over reproduction is reduced.

A final alternative to be considered is the employment and immigration theory of birth rates. The basic idea is that high unemployment rates cause couples to postpone or give up their plans for parenthood. Immigration operates as a determinant in this theory because one of the influences on unemployment rates is the rate of immigration. When immigration is high, unemployment rates will remain high or stable, and birth rates will respond appropriately. Both unemployment and immigration are affected by government policy as well as by the international situation.

One proponent of this theory, Easterlin, argues that the baby boom was the product of the unprecedented low unemployment rates brought about by the Second World War and the restrictions on immigration. As the economic prosperity of the war and post-war years evaporated and the immigration barriers were taken down, the high birth rates of the baby boom years declined. Easterlin argues that the baby boom was similar to earlier rises and falls of birth rates in the United States. The boom was unique in magnitude but only because of a remarkable conjunction of very low unemployment and immigration rates brought about by the events surrounding the war.

The first theory above, the improved-contraception theory, cannot be considered as a serious alternative because it only predicts declines in birth rates. While overall decline is the major pattern, the baby boom and other similar rises in birth rates have occurred in the twentieth century in both Canada and the United States, and there has been no decline in birth control technology that corresponds to them. So we will not consider this theory further.

The demographic-transition theory is similarly flawed as a serious alternative. We will see below that the rates of infant mortality and general mortality have, with infrequent exceptions, proceeded steadily downward. The increases are not large enough to explain the baby boom, for example, nor do they precede the baby boom in such a way that they can be seen as plausible causes.

For these reasons, only the employment and immigration and the women's status theory were used in the design of the study of changes in the Canadian birth rate.

Project Design

Variation design: Since birth rates have declined overall during the twentieth century, care has to be exercised in finding increases as well as decreases in birth rates. The theories we want to test predict increases as well as decreases in certain circumstances. If case or time periods are selected with only one kind of change, the determination of which theory is superior will be difficult.

From Figure 9.7 below, of changes in the crude birth rates (CBR) in Canada from 1921-1982, it can be seen that the important changes in the direction of the rates occur in the late 1930s and in the late 1950s. In order to include these changes in direction, the period chosen was 1930-1980.

Sampling design: Canada was chosen as the single case primarily on the basis of availability of data. The selection of 1930-1980 represents a sample of the process of reproduction in Canada.

Measurement design: The effect indicator chosen as a measure for birth rates was the crude birth rate—the number of registered live births recorded per 1,000 women aged 15-45 resident in Canada for a particular year.

The indicator for women's status selected was women's labour force participation—the percentage of women aged 15-65 that are either working or looking for work.

Figure 9.7
Plot of Crude Birth Rate (CBR) by Year, Canada, 1920-1980

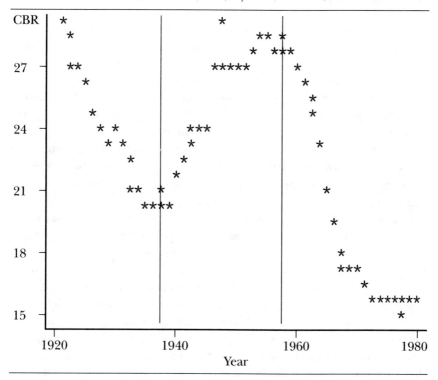

The indicator for unemployment was the yearly average percentage of labour force participants who were unemployed and looking for jobs.

The indicator for immigration was the total number of immigrants who arrived in Canada in a particular year.

Although we will make only limited use of them, indicators for urbanization and infant deaths were also chosen. Urbanization: the number of Canadians living in population centres of 2,500 or larger as a percentage of all Canadian residents for that year. Infant death rate is the percentage of all live births that do not survive past the first month.

Data analysis design: the number of cases or time periods is large enough to justify numerical analysis of data. All of the indicators for the causes as well as the effect are quantitative and are such that little would be gained by collapsing the values into a smaller number of categories. The appropriate display method is scatter plots; the appropriate summary method is regression analysis.

Single-cause analysis

Let us first show why the demographic transition theory needs very little attention as an explanation for the baby boom and bust. Vertical markers have been drawn on the plot (see Figure 9.7) at 1937, the year of the lowest birth rate, and at 1957, the year after which no increases are observable. If a cause is to be considered seriously, its pattern of change must have some observable relationship to the pattern of upward and downward fluctuations observable in the birth rate.

The second scatter plot (see Figure 9.8) shows infant death rates with the vertical markers at 1937 and 1957. With the exception of a small increase in 1936, the rate is uniformly downward. It is clear that a cause that only falls is not a good candidate to explain an effect that falls, then rises, and then falls again. The next plot (see Figure 9.9) shows the rate of urbanization, to which the same argument applies. Urbanization in Canada is uniformly upward, while the birth rates falls, then rises, and then falls again. On the basis of these observations we will give no more attention to causes derived from the demographic transition theory.

It can be seen that the plot of womens' labour force participation (WLFP) (see Figure 9.10) should be considered further as a cause of birth rate changes. The rate slowly rises till the mid-1940s, and then falls just when the birth rates hit their peak. The WLFP rate starts climbing just as the birth rate starts to decline and continues to rise as the birth rate continues to fall.

Figure 9.8
Plot of Infant Death Rate (INFD) by Year, Canada 1931-1980

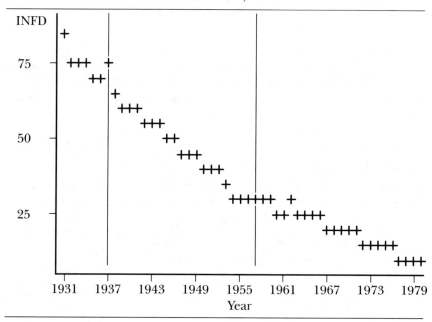

Figure 9.9
Plot of % Urbanization (URB) by Year, Canada, 1931-1980

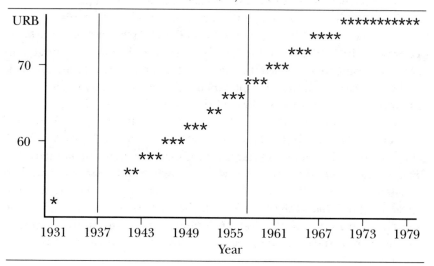

Figure 9.10
Plot of % Womens' Labour Force Participation (WLFP) by Year,
Canada, 1931-1980

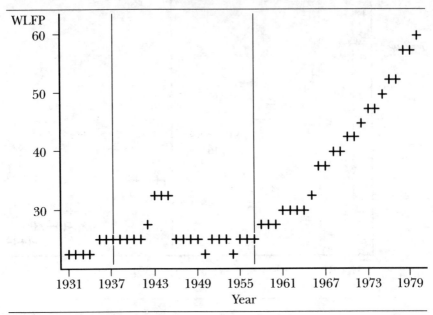

The plot of unemployment rates (see Figure 9.11) should be noted, but its relationship to changes in the birth rate is less clear than women's labour force participation. The unemployment rate hits a pre-war high in 1933 and then drops to very low rates during the war. In 1948 it starts upward, preceding the beginning of the fall in birth rates, perhaps. However, after 1958 while the birth rate is declining steeply, the unemployment rate also drops until the mid-1960s, and then turns upward. Thus the changes in the unemployment rate sometimes look like a cause of birth rate changes and sometimes do not.

The plot of immigration (see Figure 9.12) is uniformly low in the pre-war and war years, but it starts upward in 1945. This trend peaks in 1957, the very year the birth rate starts to decline. However, the immigration rate then declines and fluctuates with no clear trend from then on. The constant immigration rates from 1931-45 are not a good bet for explaining the decline and rise of the birth rates in this period, but the peaking of the immigration rate in the late 1950s is suggestive of an influence on the decline of birth rates in this same year.

Figure 9.11
Plot of Unemployment Rate (UNEMP) by Year, Canada, 1931-1980

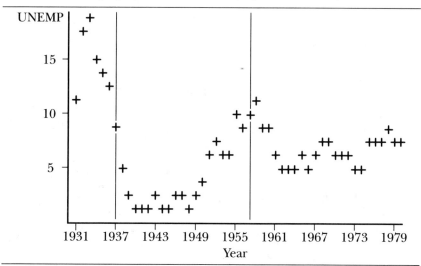

The plots above give a picture of how changes in the postulated causes apparently influence the birth rates. It looks as if participation by women in the labour force is the best of the three. We can compute regression coefficients to see if that impression is correct.

The regression coefficient of birth rates with women's labour force participation is −0.322. The negative sign supports what was observed in the plots: when the women participate more in the labour force, the birth rate declines. The value of the coefficient −0.322 means that, on average, for each increase of one percentage point in women's labour force participation, the crude birth rate declines by one-third of one birth. It is easier to think of this number as an average decline of one birth (per 1,000 women) for every increase of three percentage points in women's labour force participation.

The regression coefficient for birth rate on unemployment is −0.16. The negative sign here also agrees with our observation of the plots: as the unemployment rate rises, the birth rate falls. The value of −0.16 means that for each 1% increase in unemployment, the birth rate declines on average by about 1/6 of one birth per 1,000 women. For immigration the regression coefficient is −0.01: for every 1,000 increase in immigration, the birth rate declines by 1/100 of a child.

Figure 9.12
Plot of Total Immigration (TIMM) in 1000's by Year,
Canada,1931-1980

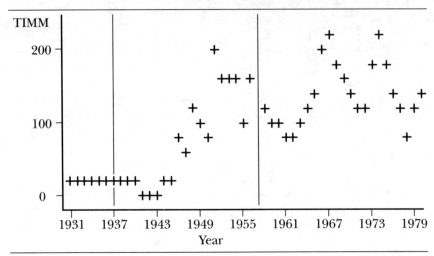

These findings are only tentative because we have not yet looked at how well either theory does when the causes from the other are controlled. Moreover, the unemployment and immigration theory postulates that these causes operate together. Let us turn to the multivariate analysis.

Multicausal analysis

The method of controlling the influence of one cause while examining the influence of another when all causes and the effect are quantitative is similar to the add and subtract method described in the previous example.

Recall that, when the causes are qualitative, the influence of an effect on a cause is removed by adding and subtracting so that the average value of the effect is identical for every cause category. The influence of sex is seen to be removed when the average wages of men and women are equal. Any variation in wages remaining must be the influence of other causes.

When the causes are quantitative, the influence of one cause is removed in a similar fashion. A regression coefficient predicts a value of the effect for each value of the cause. The predicted values can be represented as a line (P's in Figure 9.13 below). If the observed values of birth (the o's) are larger than the predicted value, the difference is subtracted; if smaller, the difference is added. The new values of birth rate (with the influence of women's labour force participation removed) are called residuals.

That the influence of WLFP is indeed removed can be shown by plotting the birth rate residuals (r's in scatter plot Figure 9.14 below) against women's labour force participation: for a unit change in participation there is, on average, no change in birth rate

Regression coefficients computed on residuals from which the influence of other causes have been removed are called "partial regression coefficients." If we remove the influence of all but one cause of changes in

Figure 9.13
Plot of Crude Birth Rate (CBR) by % Womens' Labour Force
Participation (WLFP)

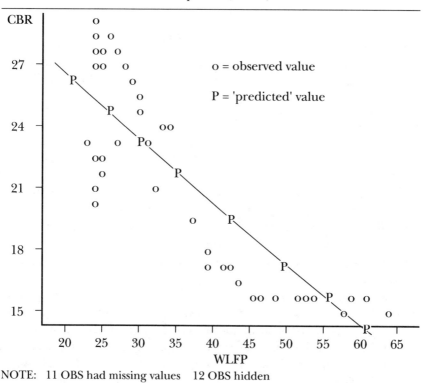

NOTE: 11 OBS had missing values   12 OBS hidden

Figure 9.14
Plot of Crude Birth Rate Residuals by % Womens' Labour
Force Participation

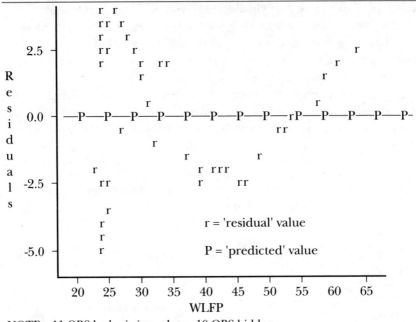

NOTE: 11 OBS had missing values   10 OBS hidden

the birth rate and then examine the influence of the remaining cause, we get the partial regression coefficients shown in Table 9.39.

The signs of the partial regression coefficients for women's labour force participation and unemployment are the same as for the single-cause analysis. For immigration the sign has changed. This means that when the other two causes are controlled, the influence of immigration on birth rate is reversed: instead of increases in immigration causing decreases in birth rates, it appears to increase it.

Note that each partial regression coefficient is slightly larger than its non-partial counterpart. The differences are quite small and can probably be ignored. They are likely the product of a slight interaction among the causes—together their influences are multiplying rather than just adding.

Which theory is the best? This has not been clear so far, because, while the regression coefficients tell how, and how much, each cause influences the effect, the coefficients are not easily compared. Each one tells how much the effect changes for a change of one unit of the cause. Since each cause is measured with a different indicator, the sizes of the regression coefficients are not easily compared. For example, how much bigger or

Table 9.39
Regression Coefficient

	Single cause analysis Original regression coefficients	Multicause analysis Partial regression coefficients
WLFP	−0.322	−0.36237174
UNEMP	−0.158	−0.21284036
TIMM	−0.007	0.01540799

smaller is one percentage change in women's labour force participation compared to a change of 1,000 immigrants?

There are a couple of ways to determine which theory is better. The simplest is the R-square coefficient. It measures what proportion of the variation in the effect (crude birth rate) is explained by variation in a cause.

The R-square for women's labour force participation when the other causes are ignored is .64. This means that about 2/3 of the variation in birth rates is explained by WLFP. By comparison, unemployment and immigration together have an R-square of .03. About 3% of the variation in birth rates is explained by these two causes together when WLFP is ignored.

When unemployment and immigration are controlled, women's labour force participation has an R-square of .689. This is slightly larger than when unemployment and immigration are ignored. When WLFP is controlled, unemployment and immigration together explain about 8% of the variation in crude birth rate. Again this is larger than when WLFP is ignored, but the much stronger influence of WLFP on crude birth rate is clear, whether unemployment and immigration are ignored or not.

Together these findings appear to point to women's labour force participation as the major determinant of birth rates. Increasing WLFP lowers the birth rate; when WLFP is lowered, the birth rate rises. To influence women's labour force participation would require medium and long-run policies: the upward trend in participation has been in existence for fifty years or so and is not likely to be changed easily.

Checking for artifacts

Variation artifacts do not appear to be serious. The time period was chosen to guarantee observable variation in the birth rate. An examination of the time plots of each cause shows ample variation in the values of each process as well as changes in the trend of each process.

Sample bias is possible in two respects. First, the data analysed encompass only the last 50 years more or less. The processes have been operating for much longer than that, and if the 50 years preceding 1931 were included, the conclusions might be different. Second, Canada is only one case, and its experience may be quite unlike that of other nations. Checking whether these possible sample biases exist is left as an exercise.

Systematic measurement error is unlikely to be a serious problem for the birth rate data. Physicians and hospitals in Canada are required by law to record and report every birth. Very few births are to likely to have gone unrecorded in the years in the sample period. The small amount of random error here and in estimating the number of women between fifteen and forty-five resident in Canada can probably be safely ignored.

There is likely to be some systematic measurement error in women's labour force participation and the unemployment indicator. Other studies have shown that the higher the unemployment rate, the more people stop reporting themselves as "looking for work." If this is the case, it means that the higher the unemployment rate, the greater the error in the women's labour force participation and in the unemployment rate. This error is unlikely to change the results very much because the influence of women's labour force participation is so strong in relation to the other causes.

As everyone knows, however, there is likely to be systematic undercounting of immigrants in Canada. Throughout the seventies, for example, the number of illegal immigrants in Canada was so large that the federal government declared amnesty periods in which illegal or undeclared immigrants could gain landed status merely by reporting to immigration offices. Though thousands of immigrants were legalized in this manner, some people have estimated that as many again did not identify themselves. So while there is error here, there is no way to determine how much or what influence it might have on the findings.

Finally, there do not appear to be any major data analysis artifacts—such as form of relationship or strongly interactive causes.

In short, there is the possibility of serious error in sampling and measurement but it is mostly of the variety that is difficult to estimate. For that reason these findings should be used with caution.

9.9 SUMMARY

Data analysis consists of organizing and displaying sets of measurements in order to make the relationships between causes and effect observable. Hypotheses predict what patterns the set of observed measurements should exhibit. Findings report the correspondence between the predicted and observed patterns.

Data analysis design consists of choosing a suitable method for displaying and summarizing how and how much causes influence effects, and planning for the control of data analysis artifacts. The main decisions are whether to treat measurements as qualitative or quantitative.

Data analysis artifacts can be produced by stopping the analysis too soon, combining or collapsing measurement categories, assuming incorrect form of relationships, using summary weighting artifacts, or assuming incorrect relationships among causes or by the existence of outlier cases. Each of these causes can be controlled or guarded against by appropriate procedures.

When project data is from a sample chosen by random methods, conventional statistical significance tests can be employed to describe the probability that an error was made in determining how a cause influences an effect (the direction of a causal relationship). Failure to achieve statistical significance indicates the desirability of more evidence.

9.10 EXERCISES

1. The following displays were produced from data to evaluate the following hypotheses. Do the patterns in the display suggest that the hypotheses are accurate, inaccurate, or ambiguous?
   (a) Hypothesis: The larger the family, the more likely the child is to become delinquent.

Number of Delinquent Acts Reported for Previous Year	Number of Brothers and Sisters	
	0-2	3 or more
None	62%	50%
Some	38	50
Total	100	100

(b) Hypothesis: The larger the family, the more likely the child is to become delinquent.

Number of Delinquent Acts Reported for Previous Year	Number of Brothers and Sisters			
	0-2	3-4	5-6	6 or more
0	60%	60%	57%	50%
1-2	35	34	30	28
3 or more	5	6	13	22
Total	100	100	100	100

(c) Hypothesis: Countries that chose to remain a colony of a European country in the early twentieth century are likely to be dominated by foreign enterprise in the late twentieth century.

Percentage Foreign Ownership 1985	Countries Remaining as Colonies until 1930	Countries Not Remaining as Colonies as of 1930
50 or more	67%	9%
30-49	25	44
0-29	8	47
Total	100	100

(d) Hypothesis: Persons who have discontinuous work histories are more likely to work part-time and are less likely to have adequate pensions than their counterparts.

Pension	Discontinuity in Work History		
	Low %	Moderate %	High %
More than adequate	35	45	25
Adequate	58	55	30
Less than adequate	7	0	45
Total	100	100	100

Figure 9.15
Plot of Complaints by Status Score

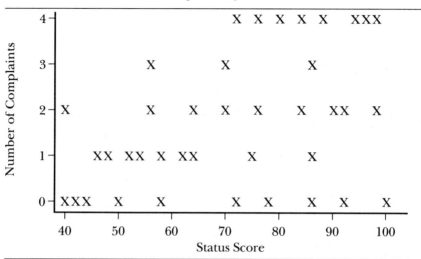

(e) Hypothesis: The higher the status of individuals within minority groups, the greater the number of discrimination complaints they bring (see Figure 9.15).

(f) Hypothesis: The amount of time pseudo-patients get per visit to doctors' offices depends upon the doctors' sexist, racist, class, and age biases. To control for class biases, all pseudo-patients dressed in standard business wear, and all reported the same "persistent, upper back and neck aches."

Name	Sex	Ethnicity	Age	Time Waiting	Time with Doctor
John	male	Anglo	27	17	14.5 minutes
Mary	female	Anglo	27	5	12.0
Tim	male	Chinese	27	20	13.3
Julia	female	Chinese	27	19	8.8
Jack	male	Black	27	24	10.8

Figure 9.16
Plot of % Women Candidates by % Women Winning

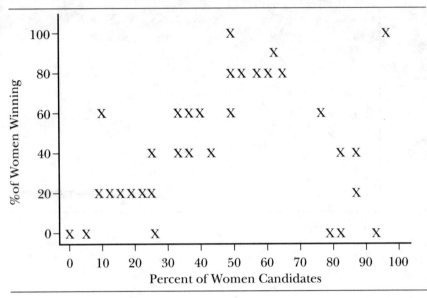

(g) Hypothesis: Colonies experience their greatest capitalist development when their ties to the colonial power are weakest.

Ties to the Colonial Power

Foreign army present	yes	no	no	no
Foreign head of state	yes	yes	no	no
Foreign bureaucrats	yes	yes	yes	no
Over 50% of trade	yes	yes	yes	yes
Colonies' average % increase in gross national product	−1.5	2	5.4	3.2

(h) Hypothesis: The larger the number of women running in an
election, the higher the rate of women winning (see Figure 9.16).

2. The data displays for question 1 have patterns that would show the
hypothesis to be accurate, inaccurate, or ambiguous. For each display,
show what the display would have to look like to support the two
conclusions other than the one you arrived at.

3. Construct the data display that could be employed to investigate the following hypotheses. You will have to do some measurement design to come up with values or categories for some of the indicators.
   (a) The more insecure the status of a minority ethnic or racial group, the lower its fertility rate.
   (b) The stronger the ideology of individualism in a society, the higher its rate of suicide.
   (c) The greater the support for "amateur" sports, the greater the number of Olympic medals obtained.
   (d) The more sophisticated the technology used by a firm, the greater the profits.
   (e) The stronger the women's movement, the higher the rate of charges brought for childhood sexual abuse.
   (f) Periods when physicians are on strike have lower rates of death than periods where they are working full-time.
   (g) The greater the separation of production from consumption, the greater the degree of political corruption.
   (h) The higher the relative price for current technology, the greater the amount of research for alternative technologies.
4. Many patterns of data could appear in each of your data analysis design answers to question 3 above. Show what the data would look like if the direction of causal influence on the effect was (a) the opposite to the hypothesis,(b) the same as the hypothesis, and (c) the direction of causal influence was unclear.
5. For your answers to questions 3 and 4 above, describe your indicators as qualitative or quantitative and then name the appropriate *summary* technology for describing (a) *how* the cause influences the effect (the direction of the causal relationship) and (b) *how much* the cause influences the effect.
6. For the hypotheses and percentage tables below,
   (a) Read the table percentages to determine if the hypothesis is accurate or not.
   (b) Determine if the tables are percentaged in the right direction for reading *how* the cause influences the effect.
   (c) If the percentaging is incorrect, redo them and then decide if the hypothesis is true or not.
      i) The lower the rate of smoking, the lower the risk of heart disease.

No. of Cigarettes per Day	Risk of Heart Disease		
	High %	Moderate %	Low %
0	5	24	15
1-5	20	13	20
6-10	35	20	25
11-20	20	33	35
20 or more	20	10	15
Total %	100	100	100
Total cases	88	76	92

ii) The faster the rate of change, the greater the experience of stress.

No. of Recent Important Personal Changes

Experience of Stress	High	Moderate	Low	Total %
High	5%	24%	15%	100%
Moderate	35	20	25	100
Low	20	10	15	100
Total cases	150	125	225	

iii) The higher the population growth rate, the lower the average per capita calorie consumption.

Population Growth Rate

Average Calorie Consumption	High %	Moderate %	Low %
High	25	32	38
Moderate	35	28	25
Low	40	40	37
Total %	100	100	100
Total cases	30	22	24

iv) The stronger the belief in fundamental Christianity, the stronger the anti-choice attitude toward abortion.

Strength of Christian Fundamentalist Belief

Attitude toward Choice on Abortion		Low	Moderate	High	%	Total Cases
Pro-choice	%	50	35	15	100	350
Undecided	%	35	35	30	100	180
Anti-choice	%	40	20	40	100	70
Total cases		330	210	60		600

v) The greater a country's volume of international trade, the more prosperous the economy of the country.

Prosperity of the Economy

Volume of International Trade		Low	Moderate	High	%	Total Cases
Lowest 25%	%	31	44	25	100	16
Middle 50%	%	28	44	28	100	18
Highest 25%	%	31	44	425	100	16
Total cases		15	22	13		

7. (a) For any of the data analysis displays involved in the above exercises, determine the minimum sample size that the design and display requires.

  (b) For any of the data analysis designs involved in the above question, determine the minimum sample size required by your design.

8. For the following hypotheses, create a data analysis design.

  (a) Government agencies set up to regulate a market in the interests of consumers will initially regulate against sellers. After a period of time the agency will end up regulating against consumers.

  (b) The stratification order, the cultural beliefs, and inter-racial conflict influenced the content of Canadian narcotics legislation. (Cook, 1969:45).

  (c) The higher the socio-economic status background of the students in a school, the greater their readiness to learn. The more easily teachers obtain compliance from their students, the more satisfied teachers will be with their professional status. (Murphy, 1977:49)

   (d) Revolutions lead to wars and wars lead to revolutions. (Sorokin, 1956:346)
   (e) Right-wing political groups that create a crime wave scare may do so in order to deflect attention from class inequality.
   (f) Alternative 1: Canada's foreign policy toward Third World countries represents a consensus among major interest groups and the electorate.
   Alternative 2: Canada's foreign policy toward Third World countries always represents the interests of the capitalist class; it may or may not represent a consensus or the interests of other groups.

9. Specify in detail the variation, sample, and measurement designs that are implied by your data analysis designs for question 8. Specify the minimum sample size the data analysis design requires.

10. In chapter 8, questions 6, 7, and 8 each contained an indicator or measurement error as well as several other indicators. Design a data analysis plan to determine if (a) measurement error is present and (b) whether it is systematically related to other indicators.

11. (This exercise is based on data collected as part of a course project by former students, Jackie Bedard and Margaret Wiebe, in the early 1980s.)

What factors influence the outcome of child custody decisions after married couples separate? In an effort to discover some part of the answer to this question, custody cases that went to court between 1970 and 1982 were sampled. Interest centered on four causes of custody awards: (a) whether the mother or father had interim custody (control and care of the children until the case was brought to court), (b) the age of the child, or of the youngest child when more than one was involved, (c) whether the mother or the father had a better lifestyle in conventional terms, and (d) whether the mother or the father provided the better home environment for child rearing.

The crosstabs below show the relationship between each of these causes and the effect, final custody awarded by the court.

   (a) What do the following four tables show regarding the relationship between the cause and the effect?
   (b) If you were advising someone on the best way to proceed in order to gain final custody of the children, what would you advise?

Interim Custody

Final Custody	Father	Mother	Total
Father	54.2%	28.1%	35
Mother	45.8	71.9	45
Total	48	32	80

Age of Youngest Child

Final Custody	Over 8	Under 8	Total
Father	66.7%	39.7%	35
Mother	33.3	60.2	45
Total cases	12	68	80

Lifestyle

Final Custody	Equal	Father Best	Mother Best	Total
Father	50.8%	50.0%	7.7%	35
Mother	49.2	50.0	92.3	45
Total cases	63	4	13	80

Home Environment

Final Custody	Equal	Father Better	Mother Better	Total
Father	65.5%	27.3%	38.9%	35
Mother	34.5%	72.7%	61.1%	45
Total cases	29	33	18	80

(c) What would be a good reason for temporarily ignoring the influence of quality of home environment as a factor influencing final custody?

(d) Multicausal analysis was carried out with interim custody, age of youngest child, and quality of lifestyle as causes of final custody. Since interim custody was fixed at the time the case came to court, only the following two tables were examined in the first stage of the multicausal analysis.

What advice would you give to a parent trying to obtain final custody on the basis of the information in the tables below, and would this advice be different than that based on the single-cause analysis?

Final Custody by Age of Youngest Child, Controlling for Interim Custody

Age of Youngest Child[a]

Final Custody	over 8	under 8	Total
Father	75.0%	50.0%	
Mother	25.0	50.0	
Total	8	40	48

[a]Father has interim custody.

Age of Youngest Child[a]

Final Custody	over 8	under 8	Total
Father	50.0%	25.0%	
Mother	50.0	75.0	
Total	4	28	32

[a]Mother has interim custody.

Final Custody of Lifestyle, Controlling for Interim Custody[a]

Quality of Lifestyle

Final Custody	Equal	Father Better	Mother Better	Total
Father	63.2%	33.3%	14.3%	
Mother	36.8	66.7	85.7	
Total	38	3	7	48

[a]Father has Interim custody.

	Quality of Lifestyle[a]			
Final		Father	Mother	
Custody	Equal	Better	Better	Total
Father	32.0%	100.0%	0.0%	
Mother	68.0	0.0	100.0	
Total	25	1	6	32

[a]Mother has interim custody.

(e) The final step in the multicausal analysis is presented below. What do you think these tables show about the relationship between the causes and the effect? On the basis of the information in these tables, what advice would you give to parents attempting to gain final custody of their children?

Final Custody By Quality of Lifestyle,
Controlling for Interim Custody and Age of Youngest Child[a]

	Quality of Lifestyle			
Final		Father	Mother	
Custody	Equal	Better	Better	Total
Father	85.7%	0.0%	.	
Mother	14.3	100.0	.	
Total	7	1	0	8

[a]Father has Interim Custody.
Age of youngest child is over 8.

	Quality of Lifestyle[a]			
Final		Father	Mother	
Custody	Equal	Better	Better	Total
Father	58.1%	50.0%	14.3%	
Mother	41.9	50.0	85.7	
Total	31	2	7	40

[a]Father has interim custody.
Age of youngest child is under 8.

Quality of Lifestyle[a]

Final Custody	Equal	Father Better	Mother Better	Total
Father	50.0%	.	.	
Mother	50.0%	.	.	
Total	4	0	0	4

[a]Mother has interim custody.
Age of youngest child is over 8.

Quality of Lifestyle[a]

Final Custody	Equal	Father Better	Mother Better	Total
Father	28.6%	100.0%	0.0%	
Mother	71.4	0.0	100.0	
Total	21	1	6	28

[a]Mother has interim custody.
Age of youngest child is under 8.

(f) What arguments could be made for controlling the causes in a different order? For instance, would it make sense to control for quality of lifestyle and age of youngest child, and then look at the relationship between interim custody and final custody? Why or why not?

(g) Can you think of any reasons why the relationships between home environment and final custody and lifestyle and final custody are more puzzling than the other causes?

(h) In addition to the above causes, a good lawyer, and a sympathetic judge, what other factors would you advise a parent wanting final custody to consider?

(i) To what degree do these data give support to the old adage that "possession is 99% of the law"?

12. The Canadian Food Store Workers Union in one of the Maritime provinces struck their employer, Multinational Foods, although the strike vote was not unanimous. While the majority of the workers (picketers) turned out on the picket line, some of the union members (scabs) crossed the picket lines and worked during the strike. Four years after the strike, it appeared to the union that management was surreptitiously but systematically reducing the working hours of the picketers relative to the scabs. This seemed like a means of getting rid of picketers: as their time was reduced, some workers would seek other jobs and quit if they found a new one. Since any prejudicial

assignment of hours was a violation of the collective agreement, the union began investigating.

The union obtained data on each employee's hours for the year before the strike, the year that the strike occurred, and the first complete year after the strike, for each store involved. If the union's suspicions were correct, differences between scabs and picketers that did not exist in the year prior to the strike would appear in the year after the strike. In preliminary negotiations, it became clear that management would argue that whatever differences were found between scabs and picketers after the strike would be merely the result of random differences in requests for time off, sickness, family crises, differences in seniority, and so on.

Average differences in hours worked according to strike status (picketers/scabs), year (before strike/after strike), store (A, B, C, and D) are presented below.

(a) Compute the differences between the 1983 and 1985 average weekly hours.

(b) Do the single cause mean differences between scabs and picketers support the union or the management position?

(c) What advice would you give to the union on the basis of this data? Do they have a chance of winning a grievance?

(d) Are the average weekly hours between stores large enough to suggest that the union should investigate differences between scabs and picketers in each store separately?

	Number of Employees	Average Weekly Hours 1983	Average Weekly Hours 1985
Store A	21	29.3	25.1
Store B	13	26.8	20.7
Store C	25	25.6	19.9
Store D	12	25.4	20.6
Scabs	30	24.9	20.8
Picketers	41	28.3	22.3

The averages below for scabs and picketers are computed after controlling for differences among stores. The averages for store are computed after controlling for the influence of scab/picketer status.

(e) Compute the differences between the 1985 and 1983 average weekly hours.

(f) Do the mean differences between scabs and picketers (controlling for store) support the union or the management position?

(g) What advice would you give to the union on the basis of this analysis of the data? Does it have a better chance of winning a grievance than it would have on the basis of the single cause analysis?

(h) Are the average weekly hours between stores large enough to suggest that the union should investigate differences between scabs and picketers in each store separately?

	Average Weekly Hours	
	1983	1985
Store A	28.3	25.5
Store B	26.9	20.5
Store C	26.1	19.6
Store D	24.7	20.8
Scabs	25.1	22.1
Picketers	27.9	21.1

(i) Management argued that the decrease in the hours of the picketers had nothing to do with the fact that they picketed but with the fact that business had declined after the strike and every employee was affected equally. What do you think of this argument?

(j) What other factors might cause the differences in scab/picketer hours other than the ones already discussed?

(k) What other products of data analysis (such as coefficients of strength and statistical significance tests) might be useful to either the union or the management's case? How would they be useful?

13. What are the determinants of ordinary immigration rates in industrialized countries? One theory points to labour needs as a major determinant. When an economy is growing rapidly the need for labour is increased, but if growth slows the need for labour is reduced. There are two obvious sources of labour—young people (born in the country) coming into the market for the first time, and immigrants. The less young people new to the job market are able to satisfy labour needs of the economy, the greater should be the reliance on immigrant labour.

One alternative theory postulated that immigrant arrivals are determined more by "push" factors—wars, famines, depression, and other crises—in countries and regions that send immigrants to industrialized countries. The stronger these factors, the more likely that persons with advanced training and qualifications would want to emigrate. This training and qualification would increase the chances that they would be admitted as immigrants in industrialized countries.

The data below can be used to investigate, in a preliminary fashion, the labour needs theory for Canada. The indicator for young people entering the labour market is the crude birth rate (births per 1,000 people) twenty years earlier. The indicator for growth of the economy is the gross national product (GNP) in billions of 1981 dollars. The indicator for immigration is the number of immigrants in 1000s. Data for these rates were obtained for the years 1952 to 1982 (birth rates are for 1932–1952). All rates are quantitative so plots and regression methods are appropriate.

Plots of the values of the effect, immigration, and the two causes, lagged birth rates and GNP, are presented below.

(a) Inspecting the time plots (Figures 9.17-9.21), what do you think is the likelihood that birth rate and GNP will explain much of the variation in immigration? Which of the points in the following plots bear double checking for accuracy?

(b) The plots below show the pattern between the causes and the effect. Describe the pattern apparent in the plots. What do these patterns suggest about the relationship between the causes and the effect?

(c) The single cause regression coefficients for immigration and crude birth rate is +.020; for immigration and GNP, −.035. Are the signs of these coefficients correct? If not, is it useful to proceed to the multicausal analysis of the data?

(d) Describe what the coefficients mean in terms of how much change in the effect comes from a change in the cause. You should first review the units used in the scales described above.

(e) A study of the time plots makes clear that the immigration rate fluctuates up and down, while the causes show strong upward trends. When this is the case it is often useful to "detrend" the processes—remove the trend from the data to make it easier to see if the changes from year to year in the causes influence the year to year changes in the effect. When this is done, the regression coefficients are as follows: immigration and crude birth rate +.097; immigration and GNP +.39. Do these signs correspond to the hypotheses? Interpret what these coefficients mean in terms of how much change in the effect comes from a change in the cause.

Figure 9.17
Plot of Immigration (IMM) (1000s) by Year

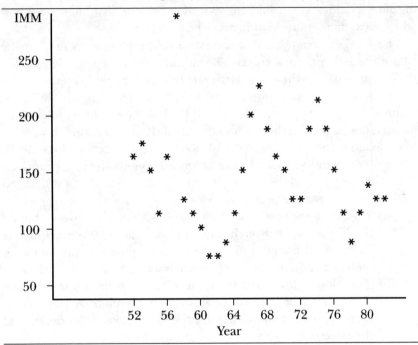

(f) If a multiple regression analysis is carried out with a detrending factor included, the partial regression coefficient for immigration and crude birth rate is +.121; for immigration and GNP, +.89. Interpret what these coefficients mean in terms of how much change in the effect comes from a change in the cause (controlling for trend and the other cause).

(g) The multiple cause R-square is .20. How much of the variation in immigration remains unexplained by birth rate and GNP (and a detrending factor)? What does this suggest about the effectiveness of the labour supply theory of immigration?

(h) Review Section 9.5. What data analysis artifacts might be influencing the above results, in addition to those already mentioned?

(i) Outline the policy/practice application of the above findings. Do they make sense? Why or why not?

Figure 9.18
Plot of (lagged) Crude Birth Rate (BR) by Year

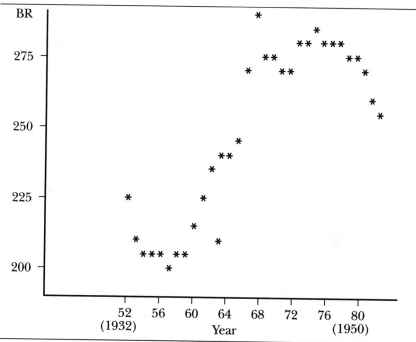

(j) What other factors would you add to make the labour needs theory more effective as an explanation for immigration? Why is it impossible to tell from this analysis whether the labour needs theory is better than alternative "push" theories?

(k) How would you construct indicators for the "push" theories of immigration?

Figure 9.19
Plot of GNP ($ Billion) by Year

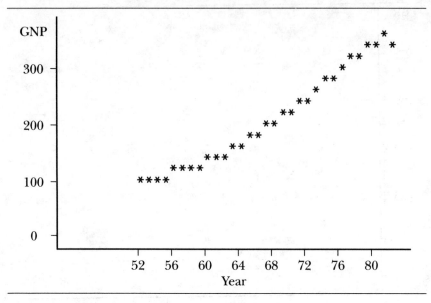

Figure 9.20
Plot of Immigration (IMM) and Crude Birth Rate

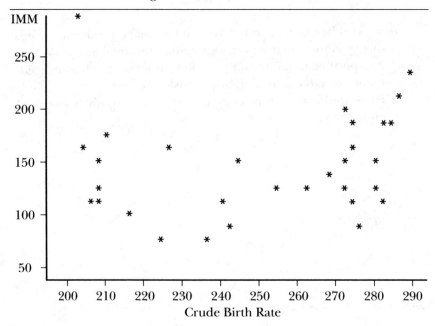

Figure 9.21
Plot of Immigration (IMM) by GNP

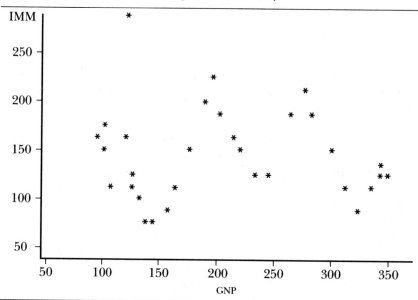

REFERENCES

Abrams, Lisa. 1982. "Resistance behavior and teaching media for children in day surgery." *American Operating Room Nurses* 35(2):244-58

Babbie, E. 1986. *Observing ourselves*. Belmont, California: Wadsworth

Baxter, Helen. 1988. "Mandatory retirement tops Council's agenda" *CAUT Bulletin* 35(3):1,19

Berelson, B., and G.A. Steiner. 1964. *Human behavior: an inventory of scientific findings*. New York: Harcourt Brace and World

Berger, John. 1972. *Ways of seeing* New York: Viking

Binder, Arnold, and G. Geis. 1983. *Methods of research in criminology and criminal justice*. New York: McGraw-Hill

Bonacich, Edna. 1987. "The limited social philosophy of affirmative action." *The insurgent sociologist* 14(1):99-119

Brinton, Crane. 1965. *The anatomy of revolution*. New York: Vintage

Brodie, M. Janine, and J. Jenson. 1981. "The party system," in Whittington, M.S., and G. Williams (eds.), *Canadian politics in the 1980s*. Toronto: Methuen, 198-205

Campbell, Norman. 1952. *What is science?* London: Dover

• Carchedi, G. 1983. "Class analysis and the study of forms," in Morgan (1983)

Chalmers, Lee, and Pamela Smith. 1987. "Wife battering: psychological, social, and physical isolation and counteracting strategies," in McLaren, A.T. (ed.), *Gender and Society*. Toronto: Copp Clark Pitman, 1983

Chesler, Phyllis. 1972. *Women and madness*. New York: Avon

Clark, Terry N. 1968. *Community structure and decision-making: comparative analyses*. San Francisco: Chandler

Colletti, Lucio. 1973. *From Rousseau to Lenin*. London: New Left Books

● Cook, Shirley J. 1969. "Canadian narcotics legislation 1908-1923: a conflict model interpretation." *Canadian Review of Sociology and Anthropology* 6(1)36-46

Cousineau, D.F., and J.E. Veevers. 1972. "Incarceration as a response to crime: the utilization of Canadian prisons." *Canadian Journal of Criminology and Corrections* 14(1) 19-31

Coward, Ros. 1989. "Kicking the habit." *New Internationalist* no. 191(January): 8-9

deCatanzaro, Denys. 1981. *Suicide and self-damaging behavior: a sociobiological perspective*. New York: Academic

Durkheim, E. 1951. *Suicide*. New York: Free Press

Evans, John L., D. Hepworth, A, Himelfarb, and H. Johnson. 1982. *Reported and unreported crimes*. Ottawa: Solicitor General of Canada

Fitzgerald, M., C. Guberman and M. Wolfe (eds.). 1981. *Still ain't satisfied!: Canadian feminism today*. Toronto: Women's Press

Friedman, S.B., P. Chodoff, J.W. Mason, and D.A. Hamburg. 1963. "Behavioral observations on parent anticipating the death of a child." *Pediatrics* 32(4) part 1:610-25

Gerber, L.M. 1984. "Community characteristics and out-migration from Canadian Indian reserves: path analyses." *Canadian Review of Sociology and Anthropology* 21(2): 145-65

Glaser, Daniel, and Kent Rice. 1959. "Crime, age, and unemployment." *American Review of Sociology* 24: 679-86

Glueck, S., and E. Glueck. 1950. *Unraveling juvenile delinquency*. New York: Commonwealth Fund

● Grayson, J.P. 1983. "Male hegemony and the English Canadian novel." *Canadian Review of Sociology and Anthropology* 20(1):1-21

Hackler, J.C., and C.T.L. Janssen. 1985. "Police killings in perspective." *Canadian Journal of Criminology* 27 (2):227-232

Hartmann, George W. 1936. "A field experiment on the comparative effectiveness of 'emotional' and 'rational' political leaflets in determining election results." *Journal of Abnormal and Social Psychology* 31:99-114

Harvey, E.B., and R. Kalwa. 1983. "Occupational status attainments of university graduates: individual attributes and labour market effects compared." *Canadian Review of Sociology and Anthropology* 20(4):435-53

Harvey, E.B. 1984. "The changing relationship between university education and intergenerational social mobility." *Canadian Review of Sociology and Anthropology* 21(3):275-286

Haywood, R.M. 1958. *The myth of Rome's fall*. New York: Thomas Y. Crowell

Hertler, C.A. 1983. "Social class membership and incidence of Schneiderian hallucinations and delusions among schizophrenic patients." M.A. thesis, University of Manitoba

Hetherington, R.W. 1982. "Response to innovation: the problem-oriented system in a mental health setting." *Canadian Review of Sociology and Anthropology* 21(2):202-30

Hirschi, T., and H. Selvin. 1967. *Delinquency Research*. New York: Basic

Hiscott, R.D. 1987. "Recent migration from Ontario to Atlantic Canada: a comparison of returning and non-returning migrants." *Canadian Review of Sociology and Anthropology* 24(4):586-699

Hollingshead, A.B., and F.C. Redlich. 1953. "Social stratification and psychiatric disorders." *American Review of Sociology* 18:163-9

● Homans, George C. 1967. *The nature of social science*. New York: Harcourt, Brace & World

Hopkins, T.K., and I. Wallerstein. 1987. "Capitalism and the incorporation of new zones into the world economy." *Review* 10(5/6):763-9

Illich, Ivan. 1975. *Medical nemesis: the expropriation of health*. London: Calder and Boyars

Jabbra, N.W. 1984. "Community politics and ethnicity among Lebanese in Nova Scotia." *Canadian Review of Sociology and Anthropology* 21(4):449-65

Kaplan, Abraham. 1964. *The conduct of inquiry: methodology for behavioral science*. San Francisco: Chandler

Karlins, Marvin, and H.I. Abelson. 1970. *Persuasion: how opinions and attitudes are changed*. New York: Springer

Kopinak, K.M. 1985. "Women in Canadian municipal politics: two steps forward, one step back." *Canadian Review of Sociology and Anthropology* 22(3):394-410

Kuhn, T.S. 1970. *The structure of scientific revolutions*. Chicago: University of Chicago Press

Ladner, Joyce, A. (ed.). 1973. *The death of white sociology*. New York: Vintage

Lexchin, Joel. 1984. *The real pushers: a critical analysis of the Canadian drug industry*. Vancouver: New Star Books

Liberman, Robert. 1964. "An experimental study of the placebo response under three different situations of pain." *Journal of Psychiatric Research* 2:233-46

● Lofland, John. 1971. *Analyzing social settings*. Belmont, California: Wadsworth

Macintoch, Rob. 1989. Growing up peaceful. *Briarpatch* 18 Number 2:18-22

Macleod, R.C. 1978. "The shaping of the Canadian criminal law, 1982-1902." Canadian Historical Association. *Historical papers*: 64-75

Marchak, M. Patricia. 1973. "The Canadian labour farce: jobs for women," in M. Stephenson (ed.), *Women in Canada*. Don Mills: General

Masson, J.M. 1985. *The assault on truth: Freud's suppression of the seduction theory.* London: Penguin

Maxwell, M.P., and Maxwell, J.D. 1984. "Women and the elite: educational and occupational aspirations of private school females 1966/76." *Canadian Review of Sociology and Anthropology* 21(4):371-94

McCrorie, J. 1971. "Change and paradox in agrarian social movements: the case of Saskatchewan," in Ossenberg R.J. (ed.), *Canadian society: pluralism, change and conflict.* Scarborough, Ontario: Prentice-Hall

McKay, Ian. 1988. "The crisis of dependent development: class conflict in the Nova Scotia coalfields, 1872-1876." *Canadian Journal of Sociology* 13(1-2):9-48

McKie, D.C., B. Prentice, P. Reed. 1983. *Divorce: Law and the family in Canada.* Ottawa: Statistics Canada

Mendelsohn, R.S. 1979. *Confessions of a medical heretic.* Chicago: Contemporary

Middleton, Russel. 1960. "Ethnic prejudice and susceptibility to persuasion." *American Review of Sociology* 25(5):679-86

Millett, Kate. 1970. *Sexual politics.* New York: Ballantine

Morgan, G. 1983. *Beyond method.* London: Sage

Murphy, R. 1977. "Academic stratification and education plans: a reassessment." *Canadian Review of Sociology and Anthropology* 14:48-57

• Nachmias, C. and D. Nachmias. 1981. *Research methods in the social sciences.* New York: St. Martin's

Nutrition news. 1988. *Prevention* 40 (April)

Ossenberg, R.J. (ed.) 1971. *Canadian society: pluralism, change and conflict.* Scarborough, Ontario: Prentice-Hall

Overton, Jim. 1988. "Public relief and social unrest in Newfoundland in the 1930's: An evaluation of the ideas of Piven and Cloward." *Canadian Journal of Sociology* 13(1-2):143-69

Pammett, Jon. 1987. "Class Voting and class consciousness in Canada." *Canadian Review of Sociology and Anthropology* 24(2):269-90

Pearce, Frank. 1978. *Crimes of the powerful.* London: Pluto

• Phillips, D. 1971. *Knowledge from what? Theories and methods in social research.* Chicago: Rand McNally

Portes, A., and John Walton. 1981. *Labor, class, and the international system.* New York: Academic

Pugh, Terry. 1989a. "Putting the squeeze on refugees." *Briarpatch* 18 (2):12

Pugh, Terry. 1989b. "Agriculture and the corporate agenda." *Briarpatch* 18 (3):7-11

Querido, A. 1959. "Forecast and follow-up: an investigation into the clinical, social, and mental factors determining the results of hospital treatment." *British Journal of Preventative Medicine* 13:33-49

Ramu, G.N., and S.D. Johnson. 1976. *Introduction to Canadian society: sociological analysis.* Toronto: Macmillan

Ramu, G.N. 1984. "Family background and perceived marital happiness: a comparison of voluntary childless couples and parents." *Canadian Journal of Sociology* 9(1):47-68

Rosenhan, D.L. 1973. "On being sane in insane places." *Science* 179:250-8

Rotstein, A., and Gary Lax. 1974. *Getting it back: a program for Canadian independence.* Toronto: Clark, Irwin

Russell, D.E.H. 1984. *Sexual Exploitation: rape, child sexual abuse, and workplace harassment.* London: Sage

● Russett, Bruce M. 1979. "Forward" in Singer, J.D. (ed.), *Explaining war: selected papers from the correlates of war project.* London: Sage, 7-10

Satzewich, V., and Peter S. Li. 1987. Immigrant labour in Canada: the cost and benefit of ethnic origin in the job market." *Canadian Journal of Sociology* 12(3):229-242

Schorr, A.L. 1975. "Public policy and private interest," in Horowitz, I.L.(ed), *The use and abuse of social science: behavioral research and policy making.* New Brunswick, New Jersey: Transaction Books, 24-38.

Schreier, Avis, and D. Kaplan. 1983. "The effectiveness of a preoperation preparation program in reducing anxiety in Children." *Children's Health Care* 11(4):142-7

Schultz, Richard. 1981. "Regulatory agencies," in Whittington, M.S., and G. Williams (eds.), *Canadian Politics in the 1980s.* Toronto: Methuen, 313-24

Scott, Robert, and Andrew Scull. 1978. "Penal reform and the surplus army of labor." In Greenaway, W.K., and S. Brickey (eds.), *Law and Social Control in Canada.* Toronto: Prentice-Hall.

● Seeley, J.R., R.A. Sim, and E.W. Loosley. 1956. *Crestwood Heights.* Toronto: University of Toronto Press

Selltiz, C., T. Wrightsman, and S.W. Cook. 1959. *Research methods in social relations.* Chicago: Holt, Rinehart and Winston.

Smandych, R.C., C.J. Mathews, and S.J. Cox. 1987. *Canadian criminal justice history: an annotated bibliography.* Toronto: University of Toronto Press

Smelser, N.J. 1976. *Comparative methods in the social sciences.* Englewood Cliffs: Prentice-Hall

Smye, M.D., J.D. Wine and B. Moses. 1980. "Sex differences in assertiveness: implications for research and treatment," in Stark-Adamec (1980)

Sorokin, P. 1957. *Social and cultural dynamics.* Boston: Porter Sargent.

Stark-Adamec, C. (ed.). 1980. *Sex roles: origins, influences and implications for women.* Montreal: Eden Press Women's Publications, 164-75.

Status of Women Canada. 1988. *The Canada-U.S. Free Trade Agreement and Women.* Ottawa.

Sutherland, E.H. 1947. *Principles of criminology.* New York: Lippincott

Teevan, James J. Jr. 1972. "Deterrent effect of punishment: the Canadian case." *Canadian Journal of Criminology and Corrections* 14(1):35-48

Terry, K.C., and R. Schultz. 1973. "Canadian electoral behavior: a propositional inventory," in Kruhlak, O.M., R. Shultz, and S.I. Pobihushchy (eds.), *Canadian political processes: a reader*. Rev. ed. Toronto: Holt, Rinehart and Winston

Tesh, Sylvia N. 1988. *Hidden arguments: political ideology and disease prevention policy*. London: Rutgers University Press

Torrance, Judy M. 1986. *Public violence in Canada, 1867-1982*. Montreal: McGill-Queen's University Press

Tudiver, Sari, 1981. "More radical with age: women and education." In Fitzgerald, M., C. Guberman, and M. Wolfe (eds.), *Still aint' satisfied!: Canadian feminism today*. Toronto: Women's Press

University of Toronto Magazine. 1989 "Connell greets funding news with call for bold reforms," *University of Toronto Magazine* XVI(3) Spring:31-2

● Van Maanen, John, (ed.). 1983. *Qualitative Methodology*. London: Sage

Vogel, Richard D. 1983. "Capitalism and incarceration." *Monthly Review* 34(10):30-41

Vold, G.B. 1958. *Theoretical criminology*. New York: Oxford University Press

Wallace, M.D. 1979. "Arms races and escalation: some new evidence." *Journal of Conflict Resolution* 23(1)

Walters, Vivienne. 1983. "Occupational health and safety legislation in Ontario: an analysis of its origins and content," *Canadian Review of Sociology and Anthropology* 20(4):413-434

Wynne, D.F., and T.F. Hartnagel. 1975. "Race and plea negotiation." *Canadian Journal of Sociology* 1(2):147-56

● Zeller, R.A., and E.G. Carmines. 1980. *Measurement in the social sciences: the link between theory and data*. London: Cambridge University Press

Author Index

Subject Index

Index of Examples

All of the material identified as an EXAMPLE in the text are indexed below. A number in a bracket after an entry such as the (2) for the blood pressure and calcium entry means there are 2 examples on that page.